54.178

THE COMPLETE OPERAS OF
RICHARD STRAUSS

THE COMPLETE OPERAS OF VERDI
LETTERS OF GIUSEPPE VERDI
THE CONCERT SONG COMPANION
THE COMPLETE OPERAS OF MOZART
W.H. AUDEN: THE LIFE OF A POET
THE COMPLETE OPERAS OF PUCCINI
THE WORLD THEATRE OF WAGNER
THE DICTIONARY OF OPERA
SCHUBERT AND HIS VIENNA
VERDI: A LIFE IN THE THEATRE

THE COMPLETE OPERAS OF
RICHARD STRAUSS

CHARLES OSBORNE

MICHAEL O'MARA BOOKS LIMITED

First published in Great Britain by
Michael O'Mara Books Limited
20 Queen Anne Street,
London W1N 9FB

British Library Cataloguing in Publication Data

Osborne, Charles, *1927–*
　The complete works of Richard Strauss.
　1. Opera in German. Strauss, Richard, 1864–1949.
　Critical studies.
　I. Title
　782.1′092′4

ISBN 0 948397 51 9

Editor: Richard Wigmore
Picture research: Mia Stewart-Wilson
Design: Simon Bell
Index: Alex Corrin

Music examples are reproduced by kind permission of
Boosey & Hawkes Music Publishers Limited
for details see p. 242

Typeset by Florencetype Limited, Kewstoke, Avon
Printed and bound by Printer Portuguesa,
Mem Martins, Portugal

Contents

Introduction

Of the five greatest composers of opera, Verdi, Mozart, Puccini, Strauss and Wagner, Richard Strauss is, I suppose, the most problematical. The contemporary of Puccini, he lived on until the middle of the twentieth century, producing fifteen operas some of which are among the finest works of their time. For many years he was known primarily as the composer of the enchanting *Der Rosenkavalier*, the decadent *Salome* and the violent *Elektra*, and it was generally assumed that his later operas revealed a falling-off of his creative powers.

In the years since Strauss's death in 1949, however, his operas have undergone a re-appraisal, as stage productions have become more frequent. Some of his less familiar operas, among them *Arabella* and *Die Frau ohne Schatten*, have been found to work remarkably well on the stage, and have come to rival the popularity of those earlier masterpieces. Others, such as *Friedenstag* and *Die Aegyptische Helena*, remain comparatively unknown.

This volume, the fourth in a series whose earlier volumes are devoted to the operas of Verdi, Mozart and Puccini, sets out to provide an introduction to all of Strauss's operas, placing each in the context of the composer's life, and discussing the music and the provenance of the libretto. Though this is not a full-scale life of Strauss, discussion of the operas is embedded into a biographical narrative.

C.O.

To NICOLAI GEDDA

Superb artist and
dear friend

ONE

Guntram

Opera in Three Acts
opus 25

Dramatis personae
The Old Duke   (bass)
Freihild, his Daughter   (soprano)
Duke Robert, her Husband   (baritone)
Guntram, a Singer   (tenor)
Friedhold, a Singer   (bass)
The Duke's Jester   (tenor)
An Old Woman   (alto)
An Old Man   (tenor)
Two Young Men   (basses)
Three Vassals   (basses)
A Messenger   (baritone)
Four Minnesingers   (two tenors, two basses)

LIBRETTO by Richard Strauss

TIME: mid-thirteenth century

PLACE: Germany

FIRST PERFORMED at the Grossherzogliches Hoftheater, Weimar, 10 May 1894, with Heinrich Zeller (Guntram), Pauline de Ahna (Freihild), Franz Schwarz (Duke Robert), Ferdinand Wiedey (Friedhold) and Karl Bucha (The Old Duke), conducted by the composer.

I

WHEN one thinks of the great composers of opera, the names of five come to mind: in chronological order they are Mozart, Wagner, Verdi, Puccini and Richard Strauss. Mozart, Wagner and Verdi are undoubtedly composers of the first rank, but perhaps where Puccini and Strauss are concerned the case remains to be proven. Strauss actually said of himself, on one occasion, 'I may not be a first-rate composer, but I am a first-class second-rate composer.' One knows what he meant, and for much of his non-vocal music the description is not all that unfair. As a composer of music for the theatre, however, Richard Strauss, like Puccini, was a genius.

Richard Strauss. His first name is used more often than the given names of Wolfgang Mozart, Giuseppe Verdi, Richard Wagner or Giacomo Puccini, in order to distinguish him from the great Austrian family of composers whose most famous member was Johann Strauss II, the 'Waltz King'. The family of Richard Strauss was not Austrian, nor is it related at all to the Austrian Strausses, though Richard's grandfather was a Johann Strauss. These Strausses were Bavarians, and Johann Strauss, born in 1800, was the son of a civil servant. At the age of twenty-one, he got a local girl, Maria Walter, pregnant: her child, baptized Franz Joseph Strauss, was born in 1822 and was brought up by the girl's uncle, Johann Georg Walter, a musician in the Bavarian town of Regensburg. It was not surprising, therefore, that Franz Strauss revealed an interest in music at an early age, mastering several instruments, among them the guitar, the French horn and the viola.

By the time he reached adult age, Franz had decided to concentrate on the French horn. In his early twenties he became a horn player in the Munich Court Orchestra, and before long he had become the orchestra's first horn. At the age of twenty-nine, he married Elise Sieff, the daughter of an army bandmaster, and they produced two children. But a cholera epidemic in Munich in 1854, three years after their marriage, killed Elise and both the children. In the years that followed, Franz Strauss rose to the top of his profession as an orchestral player. He became a Professor at the Music Academy in Munich, and was generally regarded as the finest horn player in Germany. Between 1865 and 1870 he played in the premières of four Wagner operas in Munich: *Tristan und Isolde*, *Die Meistersinger von Nürnberg*, *Das Rheingold* and *Die Walküre*. In 1863, nine years after the death of his first wife, Franz Strauss married Josephine Pschorr, one of the daughters of a well-known Munich brewing family; ten months later, on 11 June 1864, a son, Richard Georg, was born to them. In 1867 another child, Johanna, was born.

Life for the Strauss children was comfortable, for Franz Strauss earned

2

reasonable salaries from his positions with the Court Orchestra and the Music Academy, while Josephine Strauss's family, the Pschorrs, were extremely wealthy. At the instigation of his father, young Richard began his musical studies at the age of four-and-a-half, beginning with the piano and later going on to the violin. His first piano teacher was his mother, a gifted musical amateur, but after a few months the child was considered sufficiently advanced to study with a member of the Court Orchestra. By the time he was eleven he was being given tuition by Carl Niest, one of Munich's leading teachers of the piano, and Benno Walter, his father's cousin and leader of the Court Orchestra.

At the age of eleven young Richard also began to study musical theory, for, like Mozart's father, Franz Strauss was convinced that his son would become a great composer. The child had already begun to write music when he was six: according to his sister Johanna, his very first composition was a polka which his father wrote down from Richard's performance at the piano. The first composition which the child himself wrote unaided was a Christmas carol. By his mid-teens he had composed more than thirty pieces—chamber music, piano music and songs. His teacher of composition was Friedrich Wilhelm Meyer, a leading Munich musician and conductor of the Court Orchestra, from whom Richard learned, as he said in later years, all that he needed to know about musical theory and form. His father also ensured that he was taken regularly to concerts and operas, especially to performances of works by Mozart, whom the elder Strauss worshipped.

Richard was only twelve when he composed his first piece for full symphony orchestra, a Festival March whose publication five years later was paid for by his uncle, Georg Pschorr. Soon after that, the March was performed by an amateur orchestra which the senior Strauss had formed in 1875 and which he occasionally conducted. Though not startlingly original, the Festival March is a confidently and professionally written piece. It was shortly afterwards followed by other orchestral works and, three years later, by a string quartet which was accepted for publication, this time without subsidy, as Strauss's opus 2.

Richard had entered a High School, the Ludwigsgymnasium, at the age of ten. Eight years later he was admitted to Munich University where he read philosophy, aesthetics, the history of art, and literature. In his first year he somehow found time to compose a Violin Concerto, a Horn Concerto and a Cello Sonata. His father, who had known Richard Wagner well, having often played under him, hated Wagner's music and would not have a note of it played in his house. One evening, Richard took home a piano score of *Tristan und Isolde* and began to play it. When his father, practising the horn in an adjacent room, heard it, he rushed into Richard's

3

room in a fury. Father and son argued fiercely that evening; neither of them convinced the other, but Franz made no further serious attempts to dissuade his son from listening to Wagner.

After two years Richard left the University, and his father paid for him to go to Leipzig, Dresden and Berlin to listen to music and to make himself known in the musical circles of those cities. While travelling, the young composer began work on a symphony which he completed in January 1884 in Berlin. His father showed Richard's score to Theodor Thomas, an American conductor who was visiting Europe, with the result that Thomas gave the first performance of the work on his return to New York. In 1885 the famous conductor and Wagner disciple Hans von Bülow was so impressed with Strauss's symphony that he offered him a position as his Assistant Conductor with the Meiningen Orchestra, allowing the young musician to make his début conducting his symphony and also playing at the same concert, under Bülow's baton, a Mozart piano concerto. Brahms was present at that concert, and congratulated Richard on his symphony with the words '*Ganz hübsch, junger Mann*' (Quite pretty, young man). The twenty-one-year-old student had now become a professional musician.

Shortly after Richard Strauss joined the Meiningen Orchestra, Bülow resigned his post as conductor, and Strauss took over from him. However, he remained the orchestra's conductor for no more than a few months. When the Duke of Saxe-Meiningen decided to reduce the size of his orchestra to thirty-nine, Strauss resigned and accepted a three-year contract as third conductor at the Munich Court Opera, where his father was still the first horn player.

In Meiningen Strauss had made the acquaintance, which soon blossomed into close friendship, of Alexander Ritter, a violinist in the orchestra. Ritter, thirty years Strauss's senior, was also a minor composer, a fervent Wagnerian who had married Wagner's niece Franziska. Ritter encouraged the young Strauss in his appreciation of Wagner's music, introduced him to Wagner's philosophical theories, and generally presided over the younger man's conversion to 'the music of the future', which meant music in the style of Wagner. Ritter also aroused Strauss's interest in Liszt, and this in turn led to Strauss composing tone poems for orchestra, the earliest of them being *Aus Italien*, which Strauss wrote after a visit to Italy in the summer of 1886 before taking up his new post in Munich.

The principal conductors at the Munich Court Opera were Hermann Levi and Franz Fischer: it was they who conducted the more interesting or prestigious works in the repertoire, leaving the third conductor, Strauss, to deal with routine revivals and to direct piano rehearsals of new productions. Strauss made his Munich début with Boieldieu's *Jean de Paris*, conducted *Un ballo in maschera*, a Verdi opera with which he was completely unfamiliar, after only one rehearsal, and was also assigned to *Così fan tutte*, at that time in Germany considered one of Mozart's lesser operas, with a libretto in rather poor taste.

During his three years in Munich, Strauss was able to accept occasional engagements to conduct elsewhere, often including one of his own compositions in the programme. The first performance of his *Aus Italien* in Munich was greeted with cat-calls, which merely amused the now serenely confident young composer-conductor. In 1887 he conducted his symphony in Milan with great success. The first new production with which he was entrusted at the Munich Opera was *Die Feen*, Wagner's earliest opera, which had waited forty years to be performed. However, after Strauss had been rehearsing the work for some weeks, Franz Fischer was allowed to conduct the première on the grounds that he was senior to Strauss.

When the opportunity came to leave Munich in 1889, Strauss grasped it firmly. He went first to Bayreuth where he was engaged, on the recommendation of Hans von Bülow, as assistant to Hermann Levi who was conducting Wagner's *Parsifal* at the summer festival. Strauss was joined in Bayreuth by Pauline de Ahna, a young singer whom he had met during his summer holiday in 1887 at Feldafing on the Starnbergersee, near Munich.

Pauline de Ahna, the daughter of a retired general, was a beautiful young woman, somewhat haughty and very conscious of her social superiority to Strauss, by whom, however, she found herself strongly attracted. During the summer of their first meeting Strauss gave Pauline some musical coaching and also, according to a letter he wrote to his parents, worked on a 'unique, tragic and original' opera libretto in three acts. This was, in due course, to become *Guntram*. As a now fully fledged Wagnerian, Strauss expected to write his own libretti, as Wagner had done.

After his summer in Bayreuth, Strauss accepted an engagement as Third Grand Ducal Kapellmeister in Weimar, where one of his first tasks was to conduct Wagner's *Lohengrin*. 'I managed a very nice performance of it,' he informed his parents. The tenor Heinrich Zeller, who sang the title-role, and the baritone Franz Schwarz, who sang Telramund, were both later to appear in Strauss's first opera, *Guntram*. *Don Juan*, the earliest of the composer's tone poems to win popular acclaim, was given its first performance in Weimar, and it was here that Strauss completed an even more successful work in the same genre, *Tod und Verklärung* ('Death and Transfiguration').

By now the young Strauss was establishing a firm reputation both as composer and conductor. While still based in Weimar, he conducted concerts in a number of other German towns, and continued to perform his own compositions whenever possible. When his friend Pauline de Ahna joined the opera company in Weimar, Strauss conducted Wagner's *Tristan und Isolde* there in 1892, with Pauline as Isolde. He had not been in good health for some time, and more than once he had succumbed to influenza. He now went down with pneumonia, which developed into bronchitis and pleurisy. When his Uncle Georg paid for him to take a long convalescent holiday, Strauss set out for Greece and Egypt in the summer of 1892. He was away for eight months, and it was in Egypt that he composed the greater part of *Guntram*, whose libretto he had begun to draft five years earlier.

II

IT was Strauss's friend, the Wagnerite Alexander Ritter who encouraged him to attempt the composition of an opera, and who guided him towards his choice of subject. In the summer of 1887 Ritter had drawn Strauss's attention to an article in the Viennese newspaper, *Die Neue Freie Presse* (The New Free Press), about the various secret societies which had existed in Austria in the Middle Ages, some of them religious societies set up in opposition to the secular guilds. Strauss was immediately fired with the idea of inventing a plot involving such a secret society. He began to create characters to people his story, and on 6 September 1888 he wrote to his parents to inform them that he had completed a first draft of his libretto.

From its very beginnings the opera was modelled along Wagnerian lines. Its hero was to be called Guntram, his name a cross between Gunther in *Götterdämmerung* and Wolfram in *Tannhäuser*. The other characters' names were also amalgams from Wagner: Guntram's companion was to be Friedhold, and the leading female character was Freihild. The close and confusing similarity between these two names was apparently not noticed by the inexperienced librettist.

Having completed a first draft of his libretto, Strauss must then have set it aside, for it was not until a year later, on 28 November 1889, that he wrote, 'Today I again began work on my libretto.' A year after this, his father wrote to him about the libretto, which was now considered complete by its author, criticizing it in some detail. The senior Strauss's comments were tinged with his anti-Wagnerian bias, though they were also quite sensible. 'You must be very careful', he wrote, 'not to get too much into the atmosphere of *Parsifal* and *Tannhäuser* . . . I am sure the whole thing is rather too long, there are too many words in the monologues, and above all the allusions to the church and the priests must be entirely omitted; they are quite unnecessary and will only make you a great many enemies.' Strauss had also informed the conductor Hans von Bülow of his plans, and Bülow's response had been to try to interest him in setting an Ibsen play to music instead.

With his father's criticisms in mind, Strauss set to work to revise his text, but illness impeded him and it was not until the autumn of 1891 that he was able to devote his attention fully to *Guntram*. In March of the following year he informed his mother that he had finally completed the libretto to his satisfaction. Despite this, he substantially rewrote the text of the third and final act in Athens in November 1892. The warm sun and the splendours of the classical world proved excellent restoratives, and he began enthusiastically to compose the music of *Guntram* during his wanderings in Greece and Egypt. Most of the opera was written in Cairo (at Shepheard's Hotel) and Luxor in the winter of 1892–93. At Shepheard's he finished the work in short score, adding the inscription '*Dea Gratia! Und dem heiligen Wagner.*' (Thanks to God, and to the sacred Wagner.)

Methodically, and at a leisurely pace, he set about the orchestration of his score. Act 1 was completed in Egypt, and Act II the following June at the villa of Count Gravina and his wife Blondine (daughter of Hans von Bülow) at Ramacca in Sicily. (Strauss's room in the villa had a splendid view of Mount Etna.) Act II was orchestrated in August and early September while Strauss was holidaying with his parents at a small town, Maquartstein, in the Bavarian Alps. By 5 September *Guntram* was absolutely complete.

Now recovered from his various illnesses, and from the composition of *Guntram*, Strauss returned to Weimar where, on 23 December 1893, he conducted the première of Humperdinck's first opera, *Hänsel und Gretel*. On 10 May of the following year, *Guntram* was produced in Weimar. Four performances were given, conducted by the composer, with Heinrich Zeller as Guntram, and Strauss's friend Pauline de Ahna as Freihild. At the dress rehearsal, there was an argument on stage between Pauline and Strauss (described later in this chapter) which ended with Pauline rushing to her dressing-room, followed angrily by Strauss. Raised voices were heard, and then silence. When the leader of the orchestra knocked on the door, it was opened by Strauss. The orchestra leader told the composer that the players were appalled by the behaviour of Pauline de Ahna, and hastened to assure him that they would refuse to play in any opera in which she sang. 'That pains me very much', Strauss replied, 'for I have just this moment become engaged to Fräulein de Ahna.' Their engagement was publicly announced on the day of *Guntram's* première.

The performances, although given with an orchestra about half the size of that for which Strauss had scored his opera, were apparently passable, but the work failed to please its audiences, and critical reaction was discouraging. Many years later, Strauss erected a tombstone in the garden of his villa in Garmisch in the Bavarian Alps. It read:

Hier ruht	(Here rests
der ehr- und tugendsame Jüngling	the honourable and virtuous youth
Guntram	Guntram
Minnesänger	singer of love songs
der vom symphonischen	who by the symphonic
Orchester seines eigenen	orchestra of his own
Vaters grausam	father was cruelly
erschlagen wurde.	stricken down.
Geruhe in Frieden!	Rest in Peace.)

When *Guntram* was published in 1895, Strauss sent a copy of the score to the living composer whom he most admired, Giuseppe Verdi. 'Illustrious Master', he wrote in an accompanying letter,

From my own experience, I know how annoying dedications can be. Nevertheless, I dare to send you, the true master of Italian opera, a copy of my first work in this category, *Guntram*, as a token of my sincere admiration, and with the hope that you will kindly accept it.

I can find no words to describe the impression made on me by the extraordinary beauty of *Falstaff*. Consider my dedication as thanks for this reawakening of your genius.

The eighty-two-year-old Verdi replied courteously and promptly:

A few days ago I received a work which you so kindly sent me, and which enjoyed such a success. I am now on my way to Milan, where I shall spend a few days, and therefore I do not have time now to read your score. However, dipping into it here and there, I can tell that your *Guntram* is a work fashioned by a knowledgeable hand. It is a pity that I cannot understand the text, not because I wish to pass judgment (this I would not presume to do), but rather because I wish to admire and to share your pleasure.

Strauss treasured and preserved Verdi's letter all his life. (He might not have done so had he known that, before replying, Verdi had asked his publisher whether this Strauss was connected with the Viennese Strauss who wrote waltzes!).

IN 1942, at the age of seventy-eight, Strauss wrote an essay, 'Reminiscences of the First Performances of My Operas'. Here is what he had to say about *Guntram*:

The score of Act I was completed in Luxor in 1893, and the opera was accepted by Weimar for production in the spring of 1894. The Weimar orchestra at that time consisted of six first violins, five second violins, four violas, three cellos and three double basses! The third horns, which were recruited from the military band when needed, accorded ill with those of the Court orchestra, probably even in Liszt's days (cf. the three flutes in the third act of *Tannhäuser*). But *Guntram*, whose score was completely unsuited to conditions there, is an example of my incredible *naïveté* at the time. They rehearsed it, and my poor and courageous pupil Heinrich Zeller suffered torments with the ridiculously taxing main role: someone calculated that his part contained several bars more than that of Tristan. He became more hoarse with each rehearsal, and finished the first performance only with difficulty. My fiancée, as she then was, was completely on top of her role, and not only sang excellently but gave a fine dramatic performance. After the second act, she was enthusiastically applauded in Weimar, as she also was in a disastrous subsequent performance in Munich.

During one of the final rehearsals, when I had to interrupt Zeller time and time again, we finally came to Pauline's scene in Act III, which she clearly knew. Despite this, she did not feel sure of herself, and apparently envied Zeller because I had given him so many opportunities to repeat passages. Suddenly she stopped singing, and said to me, 'Why don't you interrupt me?' 'Because you know your part', I replied. 'But I want to be interrupted', she said, and with that she threw the piano score, which she happened to have in her hand, at my head. To the orchestra's delight it landed on the desk of the second violinist, Gutheil.

Guntram scored a *succès d'estime*, but after a few futile attempts to revive it in Prague [in 1901] and Frankfurt [in 1910] by making huge cuts, it disappeared completely from the stage, and with it there disappeared for the next six years my courage in writing for the theatre.

A single unfortunate performance was given in Munich. The leading singers there, Madame Ternina and Heinrich Vogel, had refused to sing their parts. The orchestra also, under the leadership of my own cousin and violin teacher, the concert master Benno Walter, had gone on strike, and a deputation had been sent to the *Generalintendant*, Perfall, to ask him to spare the orchestra this 'scourge of God'. The tenor Mikorey, whose memory had failed him in places, even during the first performance, declared afterwards that he would sing in further performances only if his pension was increased. There was, therefore, no further performance until my seventieth birthday [in 1934] when Berlin Radio broadcast a concert performance with extensive cuts under [Hans] Rosbaud, which showed that this work—in spite of the many new operas which had been premièred since 1894—contained so much beautiful music that *Guntram* well deserved a revival, if only because of its historic interest as the first work of a musical dramatist who was later to become successful. Thereupon, I published a new edition with cuts, which had a magnificent resurrection in Weimar in 1940 under [Paul] Sixt. The second half of the second act and the whole of the third act made a strong impression, and even I had to confess that, compared with all the operas which had been written (apart from mine) in the past forty years, the work was still viable. In the meantime *Guntram* has been accepted by the Berlin State Opera, where it is sure to make its full impression for the first time with the large orchestra there. In Weimar, the Freihild was excellent, and the Guntram was praiseworthy, if only because of his stamina, although intellectually he was not quite equal to his task. But even there the misfortune which had dogged the work from the beginning held: the singer was unable to go on singing the part because of a protracted illness.

The imminent Berlin production of the revised version of the opera to which Strauss refers took place in June, 1942, at the Staatsoper, under the baton of Robert Heger, with Franz Völker in the title role and Hilde Scheppan as Freihild. It did not, however, lead to any permanent increase in *Guntram's* popularity. In 1964, on the occasion of the hundredth anniversary of Strauss's birth, excerpts from the opera were broadcast by the BBC, with Robert Thomas (Guntram), Marie Collier (Freihild) and the BBC Scottish Orchestra conducted by Norman del Mar. In 1981 the BBC broadcast the entire opera, in its 1940 version, with William Johns (Guntram), Carole Farley (Freihild) and the BBC Symphony Orchestra under John Pritchard. Although the Preludes to Acts I and III had been heard in the USA as early as 1895, the opera was not performed in America until 1983 when the 1940 edition was given in concert performance at Carnegie Hall, New York, conducted by Eve Queler with Reiner Goldberg as Guntram and Ilona Tokody as Freihild. This 1940 revision must now, presumably, be regarded as the definitive version of *Guntram*.

IV

THE action of *Guntram* takes place in Germany in the middle of the thirteenth century. Guntram (tenor) and Friedhold (bass), members of a fraternal order of knights called the Champions of Love, are first seen in a woodland glade by a lake, sharing food with the starving subjects of Duke Robert, a tyrant who has recently put down a revolution caused by his oppressive rule. Guntram resolves to attempt to convert Duke Robert to his own noble ideals but, as he is about to depart on this mission, Freihild (soprano) rushes in, and is about to drown herself in the lake when Guntram prevents her. The wife of Duke Robert, she abhors her husband's cruel oppression of the peasants, and had thought to end an intolerable existence by suicide. Freihild's father, the Old Duke (bass) arrives, and Guntram is invited to the Ducal castle.

In Act II, during the festivities at the castle to celebrate Duke Robert's victory over the insurgents, Guntram sings a song in which he contrasts the delights of peace with the horrors of war. When Duke Robert orders his vassals to arrest Guntram, they hesitate, whereupon Robert himself attacks Guntram. In defending himself, Guntram kills Duke Robert, and the Old Duke has no option but to order the knight's arrest. Guntram offers no further resistance.

In a dungeon of the castle, in Act III, Guntram expresses his remorse. Freihild enters, confesses her love for him, and begs him to flee with her. Guntram's companion Friedhold, however, arrives and declares that Guntram should appear before a tribunal of the Champions of Love and atone for his crime. Guntram does not accept that he has committed any crime, since he acted in self-defence. Nevertheless he regrets that an element of jealousy was involved, for he now realizes that he was already in love with Freihild when he killed her husband. He explains to Freihild that he must now renounce her love and live his life in solitude and contemplation. He takes his leave of her, while she prepares to face her own solitude.

In his first draft of the libretto, Strauss had Guntram subject himself to the authority of the Champions of Love. When he revised the last act, making Guntram reject a moral authority which interposed itself between him and his God, Strauss's friend Alexander Ritter was profoundly shocked. In his view, which was that of a devout Catholic, Strauss's new ending was positively immoral. He objected with all his being to the attitude which Guntram now expressed in the lines:

Mein Leben bestimmt
meines Geistes Gesetz;
mein Gott spricht

11

durch mich selbst nur zu mir.
(The law of my spirit will govern my life;
my God speaks to me only through myself.)

Ritter's objection to Strauss's new ending to the libretto was twofold: not only, in his opinion, was Strauss challenging the authority of the Catholic church, but in having Guntram reject Freihild's love he was also turning against the Wagnerian concept of redemption through love. Ritter wrote to Strauss:

As a result of reading your new Act III, I have experienced the most profoundly painful emotions of the past ten years of my life. Through this latest version of your Act III you have fundamentally destroyed your work, because (i) the opera is now completely devoid of tragedy; (ii) it is robbed of the slightest trace of artistic unity which is so essential; (iii) the character of the hero has become psychologically quite impossible; (iv) the tendency of the work is now an immoral mockery of every ethical creed . . . Dear friend, come to your senses! Do not utterly waste the first two acts of so beautiful a work! Take this new Act III, even if you have already set it to music, and throw the whole of it into the fire! Then, for the sake of your inner enlightenment, read a chapter from the Gospels, or from the ethical writings of Schopenhauer, or Wagner's 'Art and Religion'. Then produce a new Act III following the earlier draft, and reinstating the passage in which Guntram completes his heroic deed of self-sacrifice by humbly placing himself under the authority of the Champions of Love.

One is tempted to identify the virtuous knight Guntram as Strauss himself, and his mentor Friedhold as Alexander Ritter; for, just as Guntram rejects Friedhold's call to submit to the judgement of the *'Streiter der Liebe'*, so Strauss rejected Ritter's plea that he discard his revised Act III. Ritter never forgave Strauss for this, and their friendship did not survive the creation of *Guntram*.

Strauss continued to think well of his libretto for the rest of his life, though it is really an ill-written, turgid piece of pre-Raphaelite romanticism. Writing after the 1942 Berlin production of the opera, he considered that, although the libretto was no masterpiece, 'and is by no means perfect in terms of language, this apprentice piece by a youthful Wagnerian, who was feeling his way towards independence, did lead to much fresher, more melodious, lusher-sounding music. All things considered, it is still no worse than the libretto of the famous *Trovatore*.'

V

EACH of *Guntram's* three acts begins with an orchestral Prelude. The Prelude to Act I falls into three sections: an opening one, calm, but containing within itself the seeds of deep feeling, a representation of spiritual love; a central section, which presents the themes later to be associated in the opera with the League of the Champions of Love; and a final section, representing the figure of Guntram himself. Labels can be attached to most of the themes heard in the Prelude, for Strauss, unquestioning Wagnerian that he was at this stage of his career, took over Wagner's system of leitmotifs, themes to be associated not only with specific characters but also with feelings and states of mind.

It is in no way helpful, however, to the opera-goer encountering Guntram for the first time to be instructed in which phrases in the Prelude represent 'pity', which 'unselfishness', or which 'Christ on the cross', for these associations are to be felt subconsciously in performance and not examined analytically. But if the newcomer to Guntram wonders where he has previously encountered the expansive phrase (Ex. 1) which he hears at the beginning of the Prelude, the answer is that he has heard it in the concert hall, for Strauss quotes it in *Ein Heldenleben* ('A Hero's Life'), the autobiographical tone-poem which he wrote four years after *Guntram*.

Ex.1

Although the Guilds which gave Strauss the initial idea for *Guntram* were Austrian, the composer chose to set his opera in thirteenth-century Germany. The curtain rises on a woodland glade, surrounded by forest, with a small lake in the background. In the foreground there is a well. It is a sunny morning in spring. The knight Guntram enters, leading a group of poor people consisting of an old man, two middle-aged men, and an old woman who leads a boy by the hand. Guntram encourages them to rest by the lake and to share with him his simple meal of fruit and bread. The poor people, weighed down by the bundles which they carry on their backs, stop to rest, and Guntram distributes food to them. Another knight, Friedhold, enters after the others, and sits by the lake somewhat apart from them.

When Guntram asks the people why they are fleeing from their homeland, he is told of the oppressive regime of their reigning Duke Robert, of villages burned, of daughters dishonoured. Only the fair Freihild, wife of the Duke, has listened to their cries of distress and done what she could to ameliorate their condition. But the Duke has now succeeded in segregating her from the people, and has brutally put down the rebellion of the peasants. Their leaders executed, the survivors have been forced to flee.

At this point Friedhold speaks. (The similarity of his name to that of the Duke's wife Freihild is an unnecessary confusion: one wonders why Strauss chose such names.) Friedhold enjoins Guntram to be faithful to his duty, and to remember the oath he has sworn. 'May the blessing of the League go with you', he says to Guntram as he departs. 'Farewell now, Champion of Love.' Guntram attempts to ask when they shall meet again, but Friedhold leaves without replying. The poor people gather up their bundles, offer their thanks to Guntram for his kindness and continue on their way.

The music of this first scene has been content to underline the words, following the mood of the various characters' utterances, the underlying atmosphere being one of gloom and despair until the Old Woman curses the Duke and all his race in an outburst worthy of, and indeed more than somewhat reminiscent of, Isolde's curse in Act I of *Tristan und Isolde*. Perhaps it was here that, during rehearsal, a cellist replied to Strauss who had corrected his playing. 'But Maestro, we never get this passage right in *Tristan*, either.'

'*Gott gebe dir ein glückliches Loos*' (God grant you a happy fate) is the salutation of an old peasant to Guntram as he and his comrades move off. '*Ein glückliches Loos?*', Guntram echoes as he begins an extended aria in which he first muses on the beauty of nature before recalling how the natural world is desecrated by the wickedness of such as Duke Robert. Clasping the cross which he wears around his neck, he calls on Christ to grant him the power to awaken the conscience and move the cruel heart of the Duke. Gaining sustenance from his prayer, he ends with a cry of '*Auf, an's Werk, Streiter der Liebe*' (On with the task, Champion of Love).

The earlier, meditative section of the aria, as Guntram contemplates 'the innocent smiles of awakening nature', quotes the childhood theme from the composer's tone-poem, *Tod und Verklärung* ('Death and Transfiguration'), and the theme is referred to again at the words '*flüstern die Blätter Lob ihrem Schöpfer*' (the leaves whisper praises to their creator). The music gathers momentum as Guntram sings of war and wickedness, swelling into an impassioned ecstasy in the prayer which leads to the climax of Guntram's monologue. (The 1940 abridged version of *Guntram*, which shortens the opera by half an hour, makes a cut of twelve bars in this aria.)

The authentic voice of Strauss is heard in this, the first of Guntram's extended utterances, especially in its first section. Once he had broken free from his Wagnerian bonds, which he was already beginning to do in *Guntram*, Strauss found his own mature voice very quickly. Like Verdi, he lived to a great age. Unlike the Italian composer, however, Strauss's musical language did not alter or develop greatly over the years. It is a far shorter journey from *Guntram* to *Die Liebe der Danae* than it is from *Nabucco* to *Otello*.

As Guntram turns to enter the forest, Freihild, the beautiful but unhappy wife of the Duke, rushes on to the scene in great agitation. Approaching the lake, she implores its clear waters to end her suffering, and is about to fling herself into its depths when Guntram suddenly steps forward and prevents her. She tries to free herself from him, but falls to the ground in a faint. When Guntram revives her with water from the well, the violas at this point introducing a rising figure which Strauss was to use again to more memorable effect in *Don Quixote*, Freihild is dismayed to find herself still alive, and attempts to rush back to the lake. She still yearns for death, and kneels at Guntram's feet, begging him to release her.

When Guntram announces that he is a Singer, and asks her to reveal the nature of her distress so that he might help her, Freihild is scornful, for to her a Singer is a mere minstrel. She tells him to hurry to the Duke's castle and claim his reward for having saved her. A voice offstage is heard calling 'Freihild!' Freihild admits that to be her name, and Guntram now throws himself at her feet, exclaiming that he has been sent by God to protect her from her cruel husband.

The orchestral passage which accompanies Guntram's ministrations to Freihild when he moistens her brow with water is pure Strauss: it would not sound out of place in *Der Rosenkavalier*. But elsewhere, particularly in the vocal parts, the influence of Wagner prevails. At times it is less a question of influence than of a conscious echoing of a phrase from *Die Walküre* or a harmony from *Tristan und Isolde*. A long section of 207 bars, in which Guntram reveals his profession and Freihild reacts contemptuously, was deleted by Strauss in 1940, which is a pity for it contains an excellent early example of Strauss's impassioned arioso style of writing for the soprano voice. Two other cuts were made in 1940 in this scene between Guntram and Freihild: one of twelve bars from Guntram's part, and another of twenty-four bars at the end of the scene.

Members of a hunting party now appear upon the scene. The first to arrive is the Old Duke, Freihild's father, followed by the Court Jester. The Old Duke is overjoyed to have found his daughter, whose flight from his protection had perplexed him. Guntram introduces himself as Freihild's rescuer, is again identified as a wandering minstrel, and is invited to the castle as a guest of the Old Duke. The voice of Duke Robert is now heard in the distance, angrily shouting at his followers. Freihild looks terrified at her husband's approach. Guntram asks her to have courage, and to trust him, murmuring that he is not what he appears to be but that he will reveal himself to her in due course.

Duke Robert now enters, with other members of the hunting party, hustling ahead of them with hunting lances the peasants who had earlier been attempting to escape. When Robert threatens them with imprisonment for having tried to flee from his domain, Guntram begs the Old Duke to grant the peasants their freedom, as a favour to him. This the Old Duke does, with the reluctant concurrence of Duke Robert. All are invited to a festive banquet at the castle, and in an ensemble the various characters express their feelings. Duke Robert is suspicious of his wife's interest in the minstrel; Guntram contemplates throwing off the character of minstrel to devote himself to his missionary task as a Champion of Love; the Old Duke is anxious to think that all is well; and the Jester, who is obviously devoted to Freihild, utters a few inanities. He is given to prefacing most of his comments with 'Hei-di-del-dum-di', which is not one of the happier inventions of Strauss the librettist. As they all move off, the vassals and retainers of the Duke's party sing in praise of Freihild, and the curtain falls quickly on Act I.

There is little in this final section of the first act that requires comment. The ensemble finale is brief and fairly conventional: its closing bars have reminded other writers on Strauss of later works of the composer, the tone poem *Till Eulenspiegel* and the opera *Arabella*. Guntram is given an optional and ineffectively placed high C in the ensemble. From a passage of dialogue in arioso, Strauss cut fifty-five bars in 1940, mostly from the Old Duke's part.

Act II is set in the Banqueting Hall at the Old Duke's castle. The walls are hung with tapestries, a huge chandelier hangs from the richly decorated ceiling, while on the floor there are carpets worked with gold. The Old Duke is seated on a platform with Robert and Freihild on either side of him. The women of the court, as well as the Duke's minstrels and vassals, are seated at tables between which pages move, pouring wine. Guntram stands slightly apart from the festive scene.

Before the curtain has risen on this scene, however, an orchestral prelude of suitable pomp and splendour has helped to create atmosphere. Originally, the act opened with a song by the Jester, but in the 1940 revision Strauss shortened the prelude and also deleted the Jester's song. Now, as the curtain rises, four minstrels sing in praise of Duke Robert in a rather dull chorus, while the Jester utters a sarcastic commentary. The Old Duke notices his daughter's sad countenance, which she explains by claiming that she is unaccustomed to all this festive splendour. Guntram is beginning to realize that he has fallen in love with Freihild when the Old Duke calls on him to give the assembled company an example of his art. Guntram takes up his lyre and begins to sing, somewhat in the manner of Tannhäuser at the Hall of Song. As he does so, Freihild recalls his earlier words to her, when he asked her to trust him until he was able to reveal his true calling.

Guntram's solo is the most extended aria in the opera, a long and rambling description of peace, followed by a considerably shorter account of the ravages of war: shorter because it was drastically cut by Strauss when he revised the opera. The composer also sanctioned an earlier cut in the aria, to be made if the singer's stamina should prove unequal to the full version. The aria is somewhat stiffly written for the voice, though the gently swelling sea of orchestral sound on which it rests is attractive. The most impressive section of the monologue, its conclusion, was unfortunately deleted in Strauss's revision. However, even in its shortened version, Freihild, her father and the vassals are moved by Guntram's vision of a world at peace, only Duke Robert professing to remain untouched.

A messenger now bursts in, announcing that the rebels whom Robert had thought defeated have reassembled and are about to attack. Guntram urges the vassals present in the Banqueting Hall to join him and oppose Duke Robert. There will, he tells them, never be peace in the land until the tyrant has been defeated. Robert draws his sword and rushes at Guntram who, in defending himself, mortally wounds his opponent. All, including Guntram, are horrified, and the Old Duke in his grief regrets bitterly that he had ever listened to Guntram or invited him to the castle. He calls on the vassals to follow him in battle against the insurgents, and orders Guntram to be thrown into prison to await torture and death. As he is seized and dragged away, Guntram offers no resistance. At the Old Duke's behest, four monks carry Duke Robert's body to the chapel.

When Duke Robert is killed, it is the theme of Guntram's love for Freihild which is heard in the orchestra, a Wagnerian touch which alerts us to the fact that Guntram's motives are, at this moment, subconsciously not entirely free of personal feelings. The march to which the Old Duke and his followers depart is rather banal, but Strauss redeems himself and the entire second act with the music he gives Freihild in her solo scene. Left alone, she begins to realize that the death she had formerly longed for is now abhorrent to her. She has been restored to a love of life by Guntram, and at the climax of her aria she bids the columns of the castle, the clouds, and the stars in the sky to hear her confession of love. '*Guntram, Guntram, ich liebe dich*', she cries ecstatically as she rushes out of the hall.

Freihild's solo, beginning *'Fass' ich sie bang, sehnsucht'gen Traumes traurige Erfüllung?'* (Is it the unhappy fulfilment of my yearning dreams that I now perceive sadly?), is the earliest of Strauss's characteristic monologues for the soprano voice, which he so obviously loved. This particular monologue was, of course, composed with the voice of his fiancée, Pauline de Ahna, in mind. Even though years later, after Pauline's retirement from the stage, he was to write for such sumptuous voices as those of Lotte Lehmann, Elisabeth Rethberg, Maria Jeritza and Viorica Ursuleac, it may be that he continued to hear, in his mind, the voice of his beloved Pauline. The long and passionate phrases of Freihild's solo culminate in her cry of love for Guntram, rising to the soprano's top B.

In the original version of the opera, after her declaration of love Freihild hears a military march in the distance, turns to go, and then notices that the Jester is still present. She enlists his aid to rescue Guntram, and the Jester promises to drug the guards and then depart, never to see Freihild again. Strauss was surely wise to delete all of this in his 1940 revision of the opera, and to have the curtain fall quickly after *'Guntram, Guntram, ich liebe dich!'*

Act III takes place in the dungeon in which Guntram is imprisoned. It is preceded by another orchestral prelude, brief and restless, which, when the curtain rises, gives way to the off-stage chanting of the monks praying for Duke Robert's soul. (The beginning of this scene was shortened in the revision.) Guntram has been haunted by a vision of Duke Robert, a spectre whom he attempts to dispel by insisting that he had acted in self-defence and that his hands are unstained. (In the longer version, he has first cursed the monks and their chanting.) The apparition presumably departs, but its place is taken in the doorway by a real figure, that of Freihild. As she stretches out her arms to him, he draws back, thinking she is merely another hallucination. (In the revised version there is a cut of twenty-eight bars in Guntram's part, when he sees and recoils from Freihild.) Their scene begins with her cry of 'Guntram' on a sustained high A.

Freihild is at first disconcerted by Guntram's reaction to her presence. When he is convinced that she is really present in his dungeon, he speaks tenderly to her before losing consciousness and sinking to the ground, overcome by his ecstasy of delight and love. She awakens him with kisses, and in a long, passionate aria, one of the finest in the opera, she sings of her love for him, her monologue punctuated by his increasingly anguished exclamations of 'Freihild!' This is the kind of extended solo for soprano which Strauss was to favour throughout his career as a composer of opera, until he ended it with the closing scene of *Capriccio*, for solo soprano, nearly half a century later.

'Come away, escape quickly, to eternal, wonderful bliss', Freihild sings at the climax of her aria, to which, having decided that he must renounce love, for he now realizes that love of Freihild was an element in his killing of her husband, Guntram replies, 'Yes, away in speedy escape, far from you, eternally alone!' Forbidding her to follow him, he starts to leave, but Freihild rushes after him and holds him in a passionate embrace, desperately struggling to hold him to her. 'If you love me, then stay with me, you cruel, ungrateful man', she exclaims, flinging 'ungrateful' (*'undankbarer'*) at him on a high B. Guntram tears himself from her arms and rushes to the door of the dungeon, at which Friedhold, his companion from Act I, suddenly appears.

Friedhold informs Guntram that the high assembly of the League of the Champions of Love is waiting to pronounce judgment on him. 'What league? What judgment?' asks Guntram in confusion. He seems to have forgotten about the Champions of Love, he is unwilling to acknowledge that he has committed a crime (as distinct from a sin), and he even seems not to remember his former companion. 'Who are you?' he asks. 'What do you want with me?'

After spending a few moments in silent prayer, Friedhold reminds Guntram of what one might call the League's articles of association, prominent among which are a high-minded piety and an unhealthy confusion of love with suffering. Guntram appears to respond positively to this, but when he is told of the severe laws of the Champions of Love, laws designed to prevent members from straying from the League's righteous path, he rejects these external restraints. 'No League will punish me', he exclaims, 'because the League can punish only the deed.' The deed of Robert's slaying, in his view, was not in itself a bad thing. Only Guntram's own will can atone for the sin he now acknowledges, the sin of having killed Robert for a not entirely pure reason. And only Guntram himself can expiate his guilt, not through submission to another authority but through self-inflicted punishment.

As she listens to his words, Freihild murmurs to herself her approval of them. Friedhold, however, is appalled at what he takes to be Guntram's arrogance. He asks the knight what he intends to do, and is told that this will be revealed only to Freihild. Guntram dismisses Friedhold with the words, 'Continue dreaming, you good people, of the salvation of humanity. You will never be able to understand what moves me.' Still conscious of his moral superiority, Friedhold departs sadly. 'May God forgive you', he says to Guntram, 'for that which my mind cannot comprehend.'

Friedhold's grave utterances are not of great musical interest, though they are necessary to the action, and Strauss was surely right to delete, in his revision of the opera, a good 240 bars from Friedhold's dialogue with

Guntram, including the passage in which, told that the League has the right to judge him because it had given Guntram his lyre and the gift of song, Guntram breaks his lyre, swearing that he will never play or sing again. The themes of love and pity from Example 1 are heard in the orchestra as Friedhold prays silently. It is with these phrases that the opera had begun, and their return in the same form at this point emphasizes that here is the true dramatic climax of the opera, a moment at which the authority of a religious body is pitted against the free spirit of man.

Guntram has won that battle. The more difficult battle has now to be won, and it is the subject of the final scene of the opera, in which Guntram has to make Freihild understand that he had rejected the authority of the Champions of Love, not in order to find freedom and happiness in her arms but, on the contrary, in order to renounce love and to seek redemption only in contemplation of the grace of God. Freihild weeps bitterly as she begins to comprehend the meaning of his words, but she takes heart when Guntram describes how she will return to her people, will continue to be their benefactress, and will win their love and gratitude. He asks her to release him, and in reply, incapable of speech at that moment, she kisses his hand. 'Farewell for ever, Freihild, purest of women', says Guntram as he slowly leaves. 'God be with you.' Freihild is seen to be summoning up her strength and resolution to live her life without Guntram, as the curtain slowly falls.

Although in his revision, Strauss cut 178 bars near its beginning, mostly from Guntram's part, it is Guntram who sustains this taxing final scene. After her initial ecstatic outburst when she thinks she has won Guntram away from his League, Freihild is silent for the remainder of the act. The relationship of Guntram and Freihild in this scene is reminiscent of that of Parsifal and Kundry in Wagner's final opera, and the grave beauty of the central slow section of Guntram's monologue is musically reminiscent of that work. Here, the motifs of love and pity make themselves heard again in the orchestra as Guntram sings of his need to expiate his guilt in solitude and contemplation. Towards the end of the scene the music conveys a warmth of feeling which one will, in time, come to recognize in the later operas as typical of Strauss. What one will not find typical of Strauss in the later operas is such sympathetic writing for the tenor voice. The role of Guntram is Strauss's first and virtually his last gift to tenors. It is also a most taxing role, though made somewhat less so by the cuts of 1940. The final cut made by Strauss in his revision was of 118 bars towards the end of the scene. In the original version, the Jester makes another appearance to announce that Freihild's father, the Old Duke, has been killed in battle with the insurgents who have, however, proclaimed their allegiance to Freihild, and are on their way to greet her. This is useful but not vitally necessary information, and the reappearance of that tiresome Jester is too high a price to pay for it. To cut him out of the final act was a good idea. Would that Strauss had gone further and deleted him entirely from the opera: it could have been done without damage either to the drama or to the musical structure.

Strauss clearly retained an affection for his first opera, and it is not difficult to understand why. In many ways *Guntram* is an apprentice work, looking back to *Parsifal* and other operas of the composer whom Strauss revered at the time. But in some respects it is a prophetic work as well, anticipating *Die Frau ohne Schatten* and other operas of Strauss's maturity. If it is a less original piece than any one of the tone-poems which Strauss was composing at the same period of his life, it is nevertheless also an enjoyable example of post-Wagnerian German opera, and one in which the individual voice of Richard Strauss is already to be heard, especially in the revised version in which, as well as reducing the opera's length, the composer lightened its orchestration. Strauss said in his old age that the whole of *Guntram* was a prelude. It was, indeed, a worthy prelude to a remarkable series of operas in which the influence of Wagner was quite early to weaken into virtual inaudibility.

TWO

Feuersnot

Poem for Singing in One Act
opus 50

Dramatis personae
Schweiker von Gundelfingen, the Bailiff   (tenor)
Ortolf Sentlinger, the Mayor   (bass)
Diemut, his Daughter   (soprano)
Elsbeth   (mezzo-soprano) ⎤
Wigelis   (alto)   ⎬ Friends of Diemut
Margret   (soprano)   ⎦
Kunrad, the Cabinet-maker   (baritone)
Jörg Pöschel, the Innkeeper (bass)
Hämerlein, the Haberdasher   (baritone)
Kofel, the Blacksmith   (bass)
Kunz Gilgenstock, the Baker and Brewer   (bass)
Ortlieb Tulbeck, the Cooper   (tenor)
Ursula, his Wife   (alto)
Ruger Aspeck, the Potter   (tenor)
Walpurg, his Wife   (soprano)

LIBRETTO by Ernst von Wolzogen, based on a Flemish legend, 'The Quenched Fires of Audenarde' in *Sagas of the Netherlands* edited by Johann Wilhelm Wolf

TIME: The legendary past

PLACE: Munich

FIRST PERFORMED at the Königliches Opernhaus, Dresden, 21 November 1901, with Annie Krull (Diemut) and Karl Scheidemantel (Kunrad), conducted by Ernst von Schuch.

I

AS Strauss wrote in his 1942 reminiscences of his opera premières, the failure of *Guntram* discouraged him from attempting to write for the stage again for six years. Three months after the first performance of *Guntram*, he conducted at the Bayreuth Wagner Festival for the first time. The opera was *Tannhäuser*, and Pauline de Ahna sang Elisabeth. In the following month, September, Strauss married Pauline in Weimar. It was to be a happy marriage, though it always seemed to their friends that Pauline bullied Strauss, and that her temperament became increasingly shrewish over the years. If this was so, it must have suited Strauss. Twenty-five years later, the soprano Lotte Lehmann spent a summer with Richard and Pauline Strauss at Garmisch, and described their relationship in her book *Singing with Richard Strauss.*

. . . I came to know yet another aspect of Strauss during those days: the hen-pecked and rather subdued husband. His wife, Pauline, nimble-witted and with a caustic tongue, derived an almost perverse pleasure from proving to her husband that no amount of fame could alter her personal opinion of him as essentially nothing but a peasant, a country yokel.

Strauss himself warded her off with an indulgent smile, not even bothering to listen while she explained in great detail how and why their marriage constituted, in fact, a shocking *mésalliance* as far as she was concerned; she could have married a dashing young hussar. Nor was his music, as she readily explained to all who would listen, anywhere near comparable to that of Massenet. She in fact behaved like a shrew, snapping and snarling at him whenever and wherever she could, but I suspect that actually he rather enjoyed it all. 'Believe me, Lotte,' he said to me the day I was leaving, 'the whole world's admiration interests me a great deal less than a single one of Pauline's fits of rage.'

On their wedding-day, Strauss presented his bride with the four songs of his opus 27, dedicated 'to my beloved Pauline'. These are four of his most beautiful *Lieder*: 'Ruhe, meine Seele', 'Cäcilie', 'Heimliche Aufforderung' and 'Morgen'. He composed many more songs in the years immediately following his marriage: the vast majority of his finest *Lieder* were written in his twenties and thirties. Even at those periods when he was not at work on an opera, he was continuing his love-affair with the voice, especially the soprano voice.

In the autumn of 1894, Strauss moved back to Munich from Weimar, taking up a more senior post than he had previously held. He enjoyed conducting the operas of Wagner and Mozart, toyed with the idea of writing a comic opera, but abandoned it, and in the winter of 1894–5, wrote what was soon to become one of his most popular tone poems, *Till Eulenspiegels lustige Streiche* ('Till Eulenspiegel's Merry Pranks'). This was followed in 1896 by *Also sprach Zarathustra* ('Thus spake Zarathustra') and in 1897 by *Don Quixote*. In 1896 Strauss had become chief conductor at the Munich Opera, at the comparatively young age of thirty-two. He continued to accept conducting engagements outside Munich, and visited London for the first time in 1897, when he conducted the first English performance of *Tod und Verklärung* at the Queen's Hall. In April 1897, a son, Franz, was born to the Strausses.

After three years, Munich was becoming rather irksome to Strauss as a city in which to work and live. When he was simultaneously offered the conductorship of the New York Philharmonic Orchestra and of the Court Opera in Berlin, he decided to go to Berlin for his first appearance at the prestigious Opera House on the Unter den Linden. On 1 November 1898 he chose to conduct *Tristan und Isolde*. Before the end of the year, he had completed the composition of another tone-poem, *Ein Heldenleben* ('A Hero's Life'), which was to be his last purely orchestral work for the next three years. He had for some time been thinking seriously of writing another opera, and had been actively searching for a suitable libretto. It was now that, serendipitously, he met Ernst von Wolzogen, a poet and satirist.

Wolzogen, nine years Strauss's senior, was, like the composer, a native of Munich with one or two scores to settle with his home town. He had founded the 'Überbrettl' (or 'Superplank') cabaret in Berlin, an intimate theatre where satires on contemporary German life were presented. (The Austrian Oscar Straus was one of the many composers who wrote music for the topical songs of the 'Überbrettl'.) Wolzogen and Strauss found each other congenial company, and Strauss asked the poet if he could suggest a subject suitable for operatic treatment. (Ernst von Wolzogen was confused by Alan Jefferson in his 1973 life of Strauss with Hans Wolzogen, his elder half-brother who had been a friend of Wagner, and editor of the *Bayreuther Blätter*.)

Attracted by the thought of collaborating with the most talked-of young composer of the day on an opera which could in some way satirize what both men thought of as Munich's philistinism, Wolzogen drew Strauss's attention to a Flemish legend, 'The Quenched Fires of Audenarde'. (The Flemish spelling of the town's name is Oudenaarde.) The action, Wolzogen suggested, could be moved to Munich, and the libretto written as a satire on the bourgeois mentality of the Bavarian capital. Strauss responded enthusiastically to the idea, and Wolzogen, it is said, completed

(left) The composer at the age of ten

(right) Hugo von
Hofmannsthal and Richard
Strauss at Hofmannsthal's
villa in Rodaun, 1912

(above) Richard and Pauline Strauss, their son Franz, and a friend at the Strauss villa in Garmisch, 1910

(left) Strauss in 1934 with his 6 year-old nephew Richard

his libretto during a holiday of one week in 1900 with a lady-friend on the island of Rügen in the Baltic Sea, just off the German (now East German) coast near Stralsund.

Strauss began to compose the opera, to which his librettist had given the title *Feuersnot* (Fire Famine), in October 1900, and by the end of the year had completed a rough sketch. Revision and orchestration occupied him until 22 May (Wagner's birthday) when he was able to write on the last page, 'Completed on the birthday and to the greater glory of the "Almighty".' He decided against presenting the opera in Berlin, considering that parts of the libretto might be thought too daring by the prudish Prussian court. Gustav Mahler in Vienna and Ernst von Schuch in Dresden both let it be known that they would be honoured to give the première performances of *Feuersnot*; Strauss, who admired both musicians, gave the première to Dresden, fearing that the Habsburg court in Vienna might raise objections to the libretto. As it happens, even Dresden insisted on some textual modifications, but the first performance of the opera there on 21 November 1901 was a great success. 'Schuch is a marvel,' Strauss wrote to his father. 'He has allowed me to see my work as it really is.'

The Vienna première of *Feuersnot* followed two months later, on 29 January 1902. An amusing glimpse of the Strausses in Vienna is given in Alma Mahler's *Gustav Mahler: Memories and Letters*, written nearly forty years later. (The Vienna *Feuersnot* première took place only some weeks before the marriage of Alma Schindler and Gustav Mahler):

At the end of January there was the première of Richard Strauss's *Feuersnot* and Pauline Strauss was in our box for the occasion. She raged the whole time. Nobody, she said, could possibly like that shoddy work. We were only pretending to; we knew as well as she did that there wasn't an original note in it. She stopped at nothing; and we could only look foolish, not daring even to agree with her, since her moods were so unaccountable that she might easily turn round and, with a great clamour, resent our saying what she had just said herself. After the performance, which Mahler had not been conducting because he disliked the work so much, we were all to meet in the Restaurant Hartmann. But there was a delay, for Strauss joined us in our box in great elation over the number of times he had been called before the curtain.

'Well, Pauksl what do you say to that for a success?'

He had better have held his tongue.

Mahler, unable to stand any more of it, pushed them into his large studio and we went into the room next door to await the end of the controversy. A confused clamour was audible and Mahler, who found it all very unpleasant, knocked on the door and called out that we couldn't wait any longer and were going ahead to the restaurant.

We preceded him to the restaurant without a word being spoken. He soon joined us, obviously worn out, and sat down next to me.

'My wife's a bit rough now and then,' these were his very words, 'but it's what I need, you know.'

That has the ring of authenticity, at least as far as the marital relationship of the Strausses is concerned, though Alma Mahler cannot have been describing the first Vienna performance of *Feuersnot*, for that was conducted by Mahler who claimed to admire the opera.

The singers at the Dresden première under Ernst von Schuch included Annie Krull as Diemut and Karl Scheidemantel as Kunrad. The Vienna principals, under Mahler's baton, were Margarethe Michalek and Leopold Demuth. The day before the Viennese first night, Strauss wrote to his parents from the Hotel Bristol in Vienna:

Here since Saturday! Yesterday, Monday, dress rehearsal of *Feuersno.* under Mahler's direction, which unfortunately, because of his terrible nervousness, did not go as well as I expected after Saturday's rehearsal, in which particularly the magnificent Vienna orchestra had delighted me in the highest degree. It is decidedly the best and finest-sounding orchestra in Europe. Décor is splendid, the costumes extremely original and unusual, the gifted Demuth well cast as Kunrad, Fräulein Michalek equally so as Diemut . . . Mahler is very nice, the whole staff are making every possible effort. Theatre fully sold out.

Though the first performance in Vienna went well, audiences did not flock to the second or third performances, receipts for which were very poor, and a fourth was cancelled at the last minute because fewer than a quarter of the seats had been sold. Mahler wrote to Strauss on 18 February, announcing that, for the present, he would have to withdraw the opera, and expressing his disgust with the attitude of the Viennese press and that of the public which had so tamely followed the press's lead. Nor did *Feuersnot* fare much better in Germany. There were productions in Berlin, Munich, and one or two other towns, but the opera failed to hold the stage. London first heard the work when it was conducted by Sir Thomas Beecham at Her Majesty's Theatre in an English translation in July 1910, with Maud Fay (Diemut) and Marc Oster (Kunrad). Alexander Smallens conducted the American première in Philadelphia in December 1927, with a cast which included a twenty-six-year-old baritone. Nelson Eddy, who five years later was to forsake opera to become a Hollywood film star. In recent years, there have been occasional productions of *Feuersnot*: a notable revival was the Vienna Festival production at the Volksoper in 1964, with Marcella Pobbe and Heinz Friedrich, conducted by Ernst Märzendorfer.

II

IN 1942, Strauss wrote of *Feuersnot*:

After the failure of *Guntram* I had lost the courage to write for the stage. It was then that I came across the Flemish legend, 'The Quenched Fires of Audenarde', which gave me the idea of writing, with personal motives, a little intermezzo against the theatre. To wreak some vengeance on my dear native town where I, little Richard the Third (there is no 'Second', according to Hans von Bülow) had, just like the great Richard the First [Wagner] thirty years before, had such unpleasant experiences. The good Ernst von Schuch had accepted *Feuersnot* and, in spite of some moral objections, it was very successfully performed in Dresden with the wonderful Karl Scheidemantel and Annie Krull. Its subsequent fate—especially in Berlin, where it had to be removed from the repertoire after the seventh performance at the instance of the Empress, whereupon the honest Generalintendant Count Hochberg handed in his resignation—is well known. Unfortunately, *Feuersnot* is comparatively difficult, requiring a superior baritone who can easily reach the heights, a good many solo singers capable of good characterization, and containing difficult children's choruses, which have always been a handicap in repertory performances. And then Kunrad's great address still fails to be appreciated by audiences used to *Il trovatore* and *Martha*. I wonder whether this will ever change. Ernst von Wolzogen, who wrote this pretty, truly popular libretto for me, later arranged a short story by Cervantes which I had already planned as a one-act opera. I have mislaid the libretto, I know not where.

(Wolzogen's libretto, eighty-four closely written manuscript pages, bearing the title, *Coabbradibosimpur, oder Die bösen Buben von Sevilla* [Coabbradibosimpur, or The Naughty Boys of Seville], was found among Strauss's effects after the composer's death.)

27

III

IN the Flemish legend, 'The Quenched Fires of Audenarde', as recounted in *Sagas of the Netherlands*, a young man who has been humiliated by the girl he loves seeks the assistance of a magician in planning his revenge. The youth had allowed himself to be pulled half-way up the side of the girl's house in a basket, in the expectation that he would thus reach her bedroom. She, however, left him hanging in his basket all night long to the amusement of the townspeople next morning. The magician extinguishes all the fires in the town, and announces that they can only be rekindled one at a time from the flame which will spring from the girl's backside when she is exhibited naked in the market-place.

Needless to say, this sensitive and engaging little story could hardly be transferred to the operatic stage without some alterations. But Wolzogen saw clearly its possibilities. Substituting, in his mind, Munich for Audenarde, he wrote in March 1900, to Strauss:

I have now got the following idea: *Feuersnot*—one act— scene of action Munich in legendary Renaissance times. The young hero lover is himself a magician, and the Grand Old Master, his mentor, who was once expelled by the people of Munich, never appears in person. The wicked young girl is forced to sacrifice her virginity at the end, to end the town's fire famine, at the urgent insistence of the High Council and the citizens. When love unites with the magic of genius, light dawns on even the most hopeless of the philistines!

The motto, which will be written behind the ears of the dear, narrow-minded townspeople and mixed with some ideal pan-pipe strains, will be something like this:

> Hold him right fast, that curious man
> Who'll magic you all a bit, if he can!
> You think of virtue he will tell
> And banish need and spite as well.
> Just swill away and fill your paunches
> And quarrel for the fattest haunches;
> To heaven he will never go,
> There must be magic there, you know;
> If bad from good you'll only learn,
> Then will your light forever burn.

That's just improvised, but you will already be able to get an idea from it. For the language, I have in mind a roughly jovial, somewhat archaic style, with a nuance of dialect.

28

In the minds of librettist and composer, the young lover was Strauss himself, and the old Master Magician was Wagner, who had suffered in Munich many years earlier. During the composition of his opera, Strauss described the score to his parents as pure Lortzing, very popular in style and melodious, with a liberal use of local folk-tunes to startle the Munich bourgeoisie. This is not a description which anyone knowing the completed work would recognize, for there is hardly a bar of *Feuersnot* which sounds in the slightest like Lortzing.

It was after attending a performance in Munich of Strauss's *Also sprach Zarathustra* at which the work was greeted with whistles and jeers from part of the audience that Wolzogen determined to proceed immediately with *Feuersnot*. In addition to the other changes that he made to the Flemish legend which he used as a basis for his libretto, Wolzogen introduced the element of the old Fire-Festivals which used to be a feature of life in several countries in mediaeval Europe.

IV

THE action of Strauss's *Singgedicht*, or poem for singing, takes place in Munich in legendary times, though the libretto specifies the twelfth century as a guide to anyone designing scenery and costumes for a stage production. The work is in one act, taking just over an hour and a half to perform. After a brief and lively orchestral introduction, when the curtain rises on the mediaeval Sentlingerstrasse (now spelt 'Sendlingerstrasse'), with its Gothic houses by the city gate, the scene revealed is one of bustling life. Young couples are promenading, arm in arm, while older citizens stand in front of their houses or look out of their windows. The most imposing house to be seen is that of the Burgomaster or Mayor, while close to it is a tavern, 'At the Sign of Great Christopher'. Two side streets can be seen, and through the city gate can be glimpsed an open space with trees. It is shortly before sundown on Midsummer Eve. From one of the side streets there appears a procession of children, headed by fife and drum, dragging a cart on which bundles of wood are piled. A crowd follows them. When they reach the Mayor's house, the children give a shout, and then, after a brief drum roll, begin to sing: 'Behold us here with fife and drummer./'Tis the feast of Midsummer./Therefore we beg of you/A piece of wood or two.'

Strauss's style here and throughout *Feuersnot*, though it nowhere suggests the melodic simplicity of Lortzing, is much lighter and livelier than in the heavily Wagnerian *Guntram*. In place of the earlier opera's thick orchestration, *Feuersnot* substitutes a brighter, more varied palette of colours, as well as, in the children's choruses and the comments of the

29

townspeople, a liberal use of Bavarian folksong. Though a number of themes from Wagner, and in particular from *Die Meistersinger*, are embedded in the score, Strauss is no longer subservient to the master, as he was in so much of *Guntram*. His own lighter and more varied style asserts itself, especially in *Feuersnot*'s waltzes, precursors of his *Rosenkavalier* manner. 'The chief features of this gay and audacious work', wrote Sir Thomas Beecham at the time of his London production of the opera, 'are the number and difficulty of the choruses and the indelicacy of the story.'

In response to the children's song, which has ended with the cheeky prediction that the Mayor's daughter, Diemut, will never win a man unless the children are given wood for their cart, the Mayor (bass) appears and jovially placates them. A basket attached by a rope to a beam and pully is let down, loaded with wood, while Diemut (soprano) and her three friends come out from the house with cakes and sweets which they distribute to the children. Diemut sings a cheerful little tune, which returns again at the end of the opera, after she has lost her virginity.

The comments of the children become increasingly ribald, until the Mayor and the citizens lose their patience and order them to go further off to look for wood. The children now approach the corner house opposite, hammering on the door and making farmyard noises. There is no answer from within, but the narrow-minded self-important Innkeeper, Jörg Pöschel (bass), emerges from his tavern and advises the children not to disturb the house's occupant, for he is a strange recluse who avoids company, even when he eats at the inn. Kunz Gilgenstock (bass), the cheerful and good-natured Baker and Brewer, speaks up for the house-owner, whom he believes to be a nobleman. Here Strauss makes use of an old Munich folksong, 'Der alte Peter'. Other neighbours now add their comments. The Haberdasher, Hämerlein (baritone), described as lively and elegant, speaks in favour of the recently arrived stranger, while Ortlieb Tulbeck (tenor), an elderly Cooper, tells a long story about the Crusader. Duke Henry, who brought back as his prisoner a giant Moor called Onuphrius who begat a long line of crippled, deformed creatures, the last of whom was a sorcerer. This tale of giants allows Strauss to quote an old Munich drinking-song, 'Mir san net von Pasing', in such a way that it recalls the motif of the giants Fasolt and Fafner from Wagner's *Das Rheingold*.

Tulbeck's wife (alto) supports his story, but another old man, Kofel the Blacksmith (bass), pours scorn on it, and the children resume their request for wood, threatening to knock a hole in the wall if they are not answered. The voice of Kunrad (baritone) is now heard inside the house, asking if the place is on fire. As he opens the door and appears on the threshold, the orchestra plunges into its bass depths, bringing the first section of the opera to a close.

With Kunrad, a more serious note enters the score. On his first appearance, rubbing his eyes, as though aroused from sleep, he is described as a pale young man, with long hair, and dressed in a dark but attractive costume. The theme, a sequence of chords, which accompanies him (Ex. 2) will be used as his motif and developed later in the work.

Ex.2

Kunrad gently asks the children why they are making such a noise, and they, surprised that he is not familiar with the traditional pastimes of Midsummer, repeat their request for wood, at first timidly, and then threatening him with a thousand years of hellfire if he should refuse them. When Diemut's companions begin to taunt him, he suddenly realizes that it is Midsummer's Eve. To the astonished disapproval of his neighbours, and the delight of the children, he now begins to break up his house for firewood, inviting the children to join him. (This is odd behaviour for someone whom the German libretto describes as an *Ebner*, which means leveller, or perhaps cabinet-maker or wood-worker of some kind. But Kunrad is also a student of alchemy, and usually described as such in English synopses of *Feuersnot*.)

Diemut's young friends think Kunrad extremely handsome, and they draw attention to the fact that Diemut herself appears to think so, too. To Diemut's increasing embarrassment and anger, they ask slyly who will leap with Kunrad through the flames at the Fire Festival. Kunrad, who has been quietly studying Diemut with great interest, now sings an ardent little aria in which he rejects book-learning and magic in favour of nature and life. 'As I leap over the flames, follow me there', he cries gaily to Diemut as he suddenly leaps towards her and kisses her on the lips. Some of the onlookers are delighted with his behaviour, though others are indignant. Diemut, in consternation, rushes to the door of her house, surrounding still by her laughing playmates.

Kunrad's arietta, with its orchestral accompaniment reminiscent of the Wagner of *Rienzi* or *Tannhäuser*, is lacking in individuality, though it plays its part in advancing a plot which, until now, has been somewhat thin in incident. Nor is the subsequent ensemble, in which the Mayor denounces Kunrad while Diemut's three friends continue to tease her, of very great musical interest. While the boys and girls now frolic around Kunrad in a quick waltz, Diemut reveals to her three friends a plan she has formed, to have her revenge against Kunrad. Strauss's waltz sequence makes use of a Munich drinking song, 'Guten Morgen, Herr Fischer', which bears an uncannily close resemblance to the waltz from Tchaikovsky's *Eugene Onegin* (Ex. 3). Is it possible that the Munich folk song was the provenance of Tchaikovsky's waltz?

Ex.3

The Mayor attempts to chase the children away, and they eventually move off cheerfully, with their cart full of wood. When the Bailiff appears, 'with sundry very stupid-looking constables', the Mayor informs him that little damage has been done, and only one or two hearts set aflame. Then, taking his daughter Diemut's hand, the Mayor tries to lead her indoors. The Bailiff is surprised to hear that Kunrad is the cause of the girl's distress, for he has never previously heard anything to that young man's discredit. But when Diemut has entered the house and her father has departed for the fire ceremony, the Bailiff suggests to Kunrad that he may have begun his courtship somewhat too abruptly.

It has slowly been getting darker, and the glow of the fire can now be seen in the distance. The children's song, too, can be heard. Kunrad, who has taken no notice of the Bailiff, now launches into a soliloquy, '*Feuersnot! Minnegebot!*' (Fire famine! The laws of love!) Shorn of its vocal line, which is no more than a series of disjointed phrases placed above the melodic interest which is all in the orchestra, this music will be heard again at the end of the opera. 'Who can coerce magic?' ('*Wer mag den Zauber zwingen?*'), Kunrad ends his abstruse outpouring of feeling, as the Bailiff runs off through the gateway, shaking his head.

Kunrad's outburst now gives way to Diemut's, softer, more poetic soliloquy. She emerges on to the balcony of the Mayor's house, where she stands combing her long hair as she sings of Midsummer, of the glowing fire, and of the glow from her cheeks as she recalls in shame the bittersweet memory of Kunrad's kiss. Kunrad now whispers to her from beneath the balcony, and a curious love duet ensues, which she begins skittishly, he with great ardour. Diemut's voice skips lightly over two octaves from the G sharp above the stave to that below middle C when she points out that Kunrad's ardent love of today will be ashes tomorrow. As it approaches its climax the duet begins to sound like a parody of the *Tristan und Isolde* love duet.

The distant voices of the children's song can be heard as Kunrad whispers to Diemut to let him enter the house. She tells him she will hoist him up in the basket, and as he gets into it her three girl-friends approach the house, creeping along in the shadows. They comment on the action as Kunrad slowly ascends in the basket only to stop short of the balcony. Diemut pretends he is too heavy for her to haul any further, and finally makes it plain to him that he has been tricked. By now her friends have brought the children and adults of the town along to witness Kunrad's humiliation. They all mock the unfortunate young man, except the Mayor who observes that it is not right to treat love with scorn.

It is not clear why Strauss directed that both Kunrad and Diemut should exaggerate the pathos in their duet, since Kunrad, at least, is meant to be sincere in his ardour. However, the point is an academic one: except in gross parody, it is difficult to convey an exaggerated degree of feeling in a love duet.

When the three friends of Diemut appear, their trio anticipates in mood and style the music Strauss was to compose for the discomfiture of Baron Ochs in Act II of *Der Rosenkavalier*. Suspended in his basket, Kunrad at first does not suspect that he is being made fun of, and embarks upon a further flight of romantic ardour. But the mood of the exchanges between him and Diemut soon alters as her purpose becomes clear, and the ensemble when the townfolk and the children arrive is lively and spirited.

The laughter of the citizens quickly subsides when Kunrad, still swaying in his basket half-way up the wall of the Mayor's house, calls on his dead Master to help him in his hour of need. Over a furious orchestral tremolo, Kunrad casts a spell, ordering all the fires in the city to extinguish themselves, since the town has scorned the power of love. He raises his arms, and instantly all the lights, torches, lanterns and candles, as well as the distant midsummer fire, are extinguished. The town is plunged into an impenetrable darkness.

A chorus follows in which the townspeople and the children express first their dismay and fear, although a few young couples sound as though they welcome the darkness; but the citizens soon become menacing, and threaten to hang Kunrad if he does not lift his curse. Strauss's writing here is oddly mechanical, as though he were anxious to hasten on to Kunrad's monologue, which provides the climax of the opera. As the ensemble ends, the moon appears from behind a cloud to reveal Kunrad who has managed to climb from the basket up on to the balcony of the Mayor's house. Smiling down upon the furious assembly, he addresses them on a theme whose relevance cannot have immediately been clear to them.

In the house in which he had been living, and which today he had started to wreck, there once lived '*Reichart der Meister*'. (This is clearly Richard the First, or Richard Wagner.) This great master was misunderstood by the foolish citizens of Munich who drove him from the town. '*Sein Wagen kam all zu gewagt Euch vor; da triebt Ihr den Wagner aus dem Thor*' (His daring was far too great for you, so you drove the darer from the door), he tells them, with heavy puns on Wagner, and '*wagen*' (to dare). At the first mention of Reichart, Strauss introduces the Valhalla motif from *Der Ring des Nibelungen*, while at the word-play on 'Wagner' he offers a familiar quotation from *Der fliegende Holländer*. The librettist manages next to insert the name '*Strauss*' into his text, in one of its old meanings of 'combat' or 'strife', and the composer obliges with a theme out of *Guntram*. He is unable, however, musically to match Wolzogen's mention of his own name, '*wohl zogen*' (somewhat far-fetched). It was for the honour of his departed Master, says Kunrad (alias Strauss) that he caused all the fires in Munich to be extinguished. In a surely inappropriate waltz rhythm he castigates the citizens for their conservatism. Finally, 'All warmth springs from woman', he proclaims. 'All light stems from love'. The fires will be relit only from the body of a passionate and loving maiden. 'Not a soul has understood the hidden sense of this allegory', the librettist complained in his memoirs more than twenty years later:

> The Philistines were naturally morally upset as usual, but even the professional art cognoscenti remained without any idea. Only art invests life, at least for men of culture, with light, colour, warmth and depth of meaning. Each true artist is a Prometheus who creates mankind in the likeness of God.

The early audiences for *Feuersnot*, however, can surely be forgiven for not having grasped the moral of the tale, embedded as it was in an unconvincing libretto, and obscured even further by Strauss's admittedly often engaging music. Kunrad's speech cannot have been easy for Strauss to set coherently, and indeed it fails to convince in performance, as a musical unit. It is best regarded as a repository of quotations and anticipations. The waltzes of *Der Rosenkavalier*, especially, seem just around the corner.

At the end of Kunrad's oration, the moon disappears and Kunrad is once more in darkness, under cover of which Diemut comes out onto the balcony and quickly drags the young man back into her room. An ensemble follows in which, to simple, folkish tunes, the citizens make their comments. It is now generally agreed that Kunrad is a paragon of all the virtues and that, for the sake of the community Diemut had better give in to him and restore fire and light to them all. The librettist has, in the lines '*Sein freier Gang/Seiner hohe Gestalt/Seiner Stimme Klang/Seiner Rede Gewalt*' (His easy gait, his fine features, his resonant voice, his powerful discourse), parodied Goethe's 'Gretchen am Spinnrade'. In his score, Strauss underlined this by adding a direct quote from Goethe's poem, '*Und, ach, sein Kuss*' (And, ah, his kiss) for Diemut's three friends to utter, though he asked that his contribution be omitted from the printed libretto.

This musically undistinguished ensemble ends with the full chorus echoing Kunrad's words, 'All warmth springs from women, all light stems from love', and calling on Diemut to end the fire-famine. When a faint glimmer of light is seen at Diemut's window, this is hailed by her father the Mayor as a wonderful sign. The final movement of the opera now begins, an orchestral description of what is happening in Diemut's room: Kunrad's passionate advances, her submission, and their act of love. At the orchestral climax, suddenly the lights in the houses and on the streets burst into flame, and the populace gives a great shout of joy while the orchestra blends Diemut's and Kunrad's themes in an easily understandable piece of musical symbolism. As the music sinks into detumescence, the voices of Diemut and Kunrad are heard tenderly assuring each other of their love. But the children are given the last noisy word of jubilation, and the citizens congratulate one another and the Mayor as the curtain quickly falls.

This last orchestral section of the opera is occasionally performed, without the not very important vocal parts, as a concert piece. It is by far the finest, and perhaps the only really attractive part of *Feuersnot*, an opera which offers too few opportunities to its principal characters, and too many difficulties with its children's choruses. If Strauss and Wolzogen believed that they were producing a hard-hitting satire on the bourgeois mentality as exemplified by the citizens of Munich, it was an extremely naïve belief. Wolzogen's libretto is weak, and Strauss's music uneven and, at times, trivial. Only in the opera's final pages does the composer rise above a level of jovial competence to something like the sustained musical inspiration of much of his later work.

Strauss himself retained his belief in *Feuersnot* to the end of his life. Three months before he died, he wrote in the last entry in his diary on 19 June 1949:

In nearly all the biographical articles which I now find myself reading in profusion, I miss the correct attitude, particularly towards the libretto of *Feuersnot*. One forgets that this admittedly by no means perfect work (especially in the all too unequal handling of the orchestra) still introduces into the nature of the older operas a new subjective style right at the beginning of the century. It is, in its way, a kind of prelude.

In another diary entry, some months earlier, he had also commented on *Feuersnot*:

There has always been criticism of the fusion of styles in *Feuersnot*: harmless jest mixed with Kunrad's admonishing speech. I concede that objection; without this mixture, though, the whole thing would have been too simplistic; and, anyway, Kunrad's address was the important thing for me; the rest of the plot was an amusing accessory.

An hour and a half (or more) is rather a long time for an audience to sit patiently, without an interval, and listen to an admonishing speech garnished with accessories which are really not as amusing as the composer imagined them to be. *Feuersnot*, though very different from *Guntram*, does not really mark an advance on Strauss's first opera; and, although its waltzes can now be heard to adumbrate those of *Der Rosenkavalier* which Strauss was to compose ten years later, it does not prepare one for the theatrical masterpiece, *Salome*, which was to be the composer's third opera. Though one might enjoy *Feuersnot* in the theatre if one is hearing it for the first time, this is not a work of which, having once heard it, one is likely to anticipate future performances with delight.

THREE

Salome

Drama in One Act
opus 54

Dramatis personae
Herod   (tenor)
Herodias, Herod's Wife   (mezzo-soprano)
Salome, Daughter of Herodias   (soprano)
Jokanaan (John the Baptist)   (baritone)
Narraboth, a young Syrian Captain   (tenor)
Herodias's Page   (alto)
Five Jews   (four tenors, one bass)
Two Nazarenes   (tenor, bass)
Two Soldiers   (basses)
A Cappadocian   (bass)
Herod's Page   (tenor)*
* or soprano. Strauss does not specify.

LIBRETTO an abridged German translation (by Hedwig Lachmann) of Oscar Wilde's play, *Salome*

TIME: during the lifetime of Christ, about AD30

PLACE: Herod's palace in Israel, to the east of the Dead Sea.

FIRST PERFORMED at the Königliches Opernhaus, Dresden, 9 December 1905, with Marie Wittich (Salome), Karl Perron (Jokanaan), and Carl Burrian (Herod), conducted by Ernst von Schuch.

I

OSCAR Wilde's play, *Salome*, written in French for Sarah Bernhardt but never performed by her, was published in Paris in 1893 and staged there the following year. (Britain did not see the play until 1905, in Lord Alfred Douglas's translation.) *Salome* was translated for the German stage by Hedwig Lachmann, and first performed in Germany in Breslau in 1901. The following year, it was produced by Max Reinhardt at his Kleines Theater in Berlin, where it had a remarkable run of 200 performances.

Strauss first made the acquaintance of Wilde's play when an Austrian poet, Anton Lindner, one of whose poems he had set to music a few years earlier, sent him a copy of *Salome* in 1902, with the suggestion that he, Lindner, should convert it into a libretto for the composer. Strauss expressed interest, and Lindner turned the play's opening scene into verse as an example which, however, failed to impress the composer. In November 1902, Strauss saw the Berlin production of the play in Hedwig Lachmann's translation, with Gertrud Eysoldt in the title-role. He had read her version, and was struck with its musical possibilities from the very first line, '*Wie schön ist die Prinzessin Salome, heute Nacht!*' (How beautiful the Princess Salome is tonight). When a friend suggested to him after the Berlin performance that he should set the play to music, he replied that he was already at work on it.

At this time, although he may have been actively considering *Salome*, Strauss was at work on a large-scale composition for orchestra, the *Symphonia Domestica*, which he completed in July 1903 while he was staying on the Isle of Wight after having conducted the Concertgebouw Orchestra at a Strauss Festival at the St. James's Hall, London. The following year, he made his American début conducting at Carnegie Hall. It was between his return from America and June of 1905 that the greater part of *Salome* was composed. Strauss had not yet written the music of Salome's 'Dance of the Seven Veils' when he played the score to Mahler and his wife Alma in a piano showroom in Strasbourg, and Mahler commented that surely it was risky to leave such an important part of the opera to be composed later, when he might not be able to recapture the right mood. Strauss's jaunty reply was 'Oh, don't worry, I'll soon fix that!'

Other writers have commented on the contrast between the violence of Strauss's *Salome* and the calm neatness of his manuscript score. He worked on the opera in every spare moment between conducting chores, confidently and methodically. When he played some of it to his father, shortly before the old man's death, his father said it made him itch as though he had ants in his pants: an understandable immediate reaction to an extremely neurotic score.

When *Salome* was finished, Strauss got in touch with Ernst von Schuch

38

at Dresden and offered him the première, reassuring the conductor that, this time, there were no difficult choruses as in *Feuersnot*, though there were a large number of small parts, and the principal roles as well as the orchestral score would be twice as difficult as the earlier opera. Schuch immediately accepted *Salome* for Dresden, and he and Strauss tentatively cast the principal roles and distributed scores to the singers. There was trouble, however, at the first rehearsal:

At the very first piano run-through [Strauss recalled later] the singers assembled in order to give their parts back to the conductor — all except the Herod, a Czech singer named Burrian who, when asked last of all, answered: 'I already know my role by heart.' Bravo! At this, the others felt rather ashamed and the work of the rehearsal actually started. During the rehearsals the dramatic soprano Frau Wittich went on strike. She had been entrusted with the role of the sixteen-year-old princess with the voice of an Isolde, on account of the strenuousness of the part and the thickness of the orchestration. 'One just doesn't write like that, Herr Strauss; either one thing or the other.' In righteous wrath she protested like any Saxon Burgomaster's wife, 'I won't do it, I'm a decent woman.'

She did do it, however, for *Salome* was far too good a part for her to refuse. But she apparently found the role difficult to learn, and Schuch was obliged to ask Strauss for a postponement of the première which had been planned for mid-November. Strauss's response was firm:

So now everything has come out blissfully just as I had feared. Editor, printer and myself, we have all fallen over ourselves to get you the piano score by September 1, and the high and mighty Frau Wittich has left the rotten thing lying around for five weeks and can't even do it in the end; but you mustn't be cross with me if, under the circumstances, I can no longer guarantee you the first performance.

In Leipzig, Nikisch is already hard at work at it. Mahler tells me today that, in Vienna, the piece has at least been pushed past the censor and that work is now forging ahead. He has got four singers covering the role of Salome; should he stage it before you there is nothing I can do about it. As I have already wired you, I will reserve the first performance for you until 9 December at the latest, and if you can't manage it by then, whoever is ready first can do it.

Strauss's letter had the desired effect, and *Salome* was given its première in Dresden on 9 December 1905. The composer's threat that Vienna might have got in first must have been a piece of bluff, for in Vienna Mahler was having difficulties with the Catholic Archbishop, a prelate burdened with the name of Piffl, whose objections to what he regarded as an immoral work succeeded in preventing the opera from being staged. Vienna was not to see *Salome* until 1918.

The Dresden première was a triumphant success, with thirty-eight curtain calls at the end of the performance, and, despite churchmen's warnings of the opera's immorality, it was quickly taken up by other German opera houses. *Salome*'s success, it should be noted, was with the public and with musicians. Music critics were, in the main, abusive, until the opera had established itself in the international repertory, after which they began to write respectfully of it. Mahler, forbidden to stage *Salome* in Vienna, wrote to his wife after he had seen it performed in Berlin: 'It is emphatically a work of genius, very powerful, and decidedly one of the most important works of our day. A Vulcan lives and labours under a heap of slag, a subterranean fire—not merely a firework! It is exactly the same with Strauss's whole personality.'

Salome reached Great Britain in 1910, when Sir Thomas Beecham included the opera in his autumn season at Covent Garden. There had, of course, been difficulties with the Lord Chamberlain, who had three years earlier forbidden performances of the opera and who now demanded that all biblical references be deleted. John the Baptist became a prophet named Mattaniah, the action was moved from Judaea to Greece, and the Jews and Nazarenes became Learned Men and Cappadocians. Salome's perverse desires were rendered in bowdlerized language, and of course there was no head of John the Baptist, or of anyone else, in the final scene. The young princess sang her climactic aria to a dish of blood. But ten performances were given before the end of the season, whereas the American première, in 1907 at the Metropolitan Opera House, New York, caused such a scandal that the production was withdrawn after the first performance.

II

IN his 1942 'Reminiscences of the First Performances of My Operas', Strauss wrote of *Salome*:

> Once, in Berlin, I went to Max Reinhardt's 'Little Theatre' in order to see Gertrud Eysoldt in Oscar Wilde's *Salome*. After the performance I met Heinrich Grunfeld who said to me: 'My dear Strauss, surely you could make an opera of this!' I replied: 'I am already busy composing it.' The Viennese poet Anton Lindner had sent me this exquisite play and had offered to turn it into a libretto for me. When I agreed, he sent me a few cleverly versified opening scenes, but I could not make up my

mind to start composing until one day it occurred to me to set to music *'Wie schön ist die Prinzessin Salome heute Nacht'* straight away. From then on it was not difficult to purge the piece of purple passages to such an extent that it became quite a good libretto. Now, of course, that the dance and especially the whole final scene is steeped in music it is easy to say that the play was 'simply calling for music'. Yes indeed, but that had to be discovered.

I had long been criticizing the fact that operas based on oriental and Jewish subjects lacked true oriental colour and scorching sun. The needs of the moment inspired me with truly exotic harmonies, which sparkled like taffeta, particularly in the strange cadences. The wish to characterize the dramatis personae as clearly as possible led me to bitonality, since the purely rhythmic characterization Mozart uses so ingeniously did not appear to me sufficient to express the antithesis between Herod and the Nazarene. This may well stand as a unique experiment with a peculiar subject, but it cannot be recommended to imitators. As soon as Schuch had had the courage to undertake to produce *Salome*, the difficulties began: during the first reading rehearsal at the piano, the assembled soloists returned their parts to the conductor with the single exception of Mr Burrian, a Czech, who, when asked for his opinion last of all, replied: 'I know it off by heart already.' Good for him. After this, the others could not help feeling a little ashamed, and rehearsals actually started.

During the casting rehearsals Frau Wittich, entrusted with the part of the sixteen-year-old Princess with the voice of Isolde ('One just does not write a thing like that, Herr Strauss: either one or the other'), because of the strenuous nature of the part and the strength of the orchestra, went on strike with the indignant protest to be expected from the wife of a Saxon *Bürgermeister*: 'I won't do it, I'm a decent woman', thereby reducing the producer Wirk, who was all for 'perversity and outrage', to desperation. And yet Frau Wittich, although of course her figure was unsuitable for the part, was quite right (if in a different sense): the capers cut in later performances by exotic variety stars indulging in snake-like movements and waving Jokanaan's head about in the air went beyond all bounds of decency and good taste. Anyone who has been in the east and has observed the decorum with which women there behave, will appreciate that Salome, being a chaste virgin and an oriental Princess, must be played with the simplest and most restrained of gestures, unless her defeat by the miracle of a great world is to excite only disgust and terror instead of sympathy. (In connection with this I should like to point out that the high B flat of the double bass during the killing of the Baptist does not represent cries of pain uttered by the victim, but sighs of anguish from the heart of an impatiently expectant Salome. The ominous passage proved so shocking during the dress rehearsal that Count Seebach, for fear of causing merriment, persuaded me to tone the double bass down by a sustained B flat on the English horns . . .)

The first performance in Dresden was, as usual, a success, but the critics gathered together in the Bellevue Hotel after the performance, shook their heads and agreed that the piece would perhaps be performed by a few of the largest theatres but would soon disappear. Three weeks later it had, I think, been accepted by ten theatres and had been a sensational success in Breslau with an orchestra of no more than 70 players. Thereupon there was a hullabaloo in the papers, the churches objected—the first performance in the Vienna State Opera took place in October 1918, after an embarrassing exchange of letters with Archbishop Piffl—and so did the Puritans in New York, where the opera had to be taken out of the repertoire at the instigation of a certain Mr Morgan. The German Kaiser permitted the performance of the opera only after Hulsen had had the bright idea of signifying the advent of the Magi at the end by the appearance of the morning star! William II once said to his intendant: 'I am sorry Strauss composed this *Salome*. I really like the fellow, but this will do him a lot of damage.' The damage enabled me to build my villa in Garmisch. In connection with this I remember with gratitude the Berlin publisher, Adolph Fürstner, who had the courage to print the opera, for which other colleagues (e.g. Hugo Bock) did not at first envy him in the least. But by doing so, this wise and kind Jew had also secured for himself *Der Rosenkavalier*. All honour to his memory!

An Italian impresario who could not pay Fürstner's fees and was unable to get hold of a printed score had commissioned a small Kapellmeister to make a new one from the piano score (!) and intended, without our authority, to perform the opera in this form in Holland, which, I understand, was outside the Berne Convention at that time. When Fürstner heard of this, he negotiated with the impresario, and eventually persuaded him to hand over his new score to us, and to perform the opera in accordance with my score, provided I conducted the performance in Amsterdam myself. I considered it my duty 'to save my opera' ('What an ass I was', to quote from *Ariadne*) and accepted the offer. But what I was to find in Amsterdam beggars all description. I had at my disposal for one dress rehearsal only a miserable Italian troupe hardly capable of managing more than a sixth-rate performance of *Il trovatore*, and which did not know its parts, and a beer-garden orchestra, which would have required at least twenty rehearsals to be made more or less presentable. It was dreadful, and yet I could not resign without risking an enormous indemnity. In the circumstances, it had to be carried through to the bitter end. I concluded the evening full of shame and annoyance and, believe it or not, my old friend, Councillor Fritz Sieger, who had been my patron in the Frankfurt Museum ever since my F minor symphony, and who had by chance attended the performance, told me afterwards that it had been quite a good performance and he had liked it very well indeed. Can it be that the hypnotism of my baton was such that even a connoisseur overlooked the shortcomings of the performance, or is it simply impossible to kill the opera? I think the latter must have been the case since, when I saw the piece in Innsbruck two years ago with redoubled woodwind, an orchestra of 56 players, and admittedly good soloists—including that excellent Swede, Madame Sonderquist—I had to admit that it made its effect in spite of these limitations. The moral of all this is: how many lines of the score could I not have saved myself from the beginning, had I written a score like the clever little Italian conductor whose orchestration was designed for seasons in Ferrara and Piacenza. But these '*l'art pour l'art*' artists who will never compose 'mysteries of the national soul' (*Münchner Neueste Nachrichten*, 9 February 1942) will heed no advice. The secret of the forty-line page of a score is after all greater than that of a 'romantic' purse.

III

THE source of the numerous versions of the story of Salome that are to be found in literature and art is the New Testament of the Bible. Both St. Matthew and St. Mark relate the tale: this is how it is told in the Gospel According to St. Matthew (chapter 14, verses 1 to 12):

1. At that time Herod the tetrarch heard of the fame of Jesus.
2. And said unto his servants, This is John the Baptist; he is risen from the dead; and therefore mighty works do shew forth themselves in him.
3. For Herod had laid hold on John, and bound him, and put him in prison for Herodias' sake, his brother Philip's wife.
4. For John said unto him, It is not lawful for thee to have her.
5. And when he would have put him to death, he feared the multitude, because they counted him as a prophet.
6. But when Herod's birthday was kept, the daughter of Herodias danced before them, and pleased Herod.

7. Whereupon he promised with an oath to give her whatsoever she would ask.

8. And she, being before instructed of her mother, said, Give me here John Baptist's head in a charger.

9. And the king was sorry: nevertheless for the oath's sake, and them which sat with him at meat, he commanded it to be given her.

10. And he sent, and beheaded John in the prison.

11. And his head was brought in a charger, and given to the damsel: and she brought it to her mother.

12. And his disciples came, and took up the body, and buried it, and went and told Jesus.

Nowhere in the Bible is there any mention of Salome by name: she is simply 'the daughter of Herodias'. According to medieval legend, Herodias had been in love with John. In modern treatments of the story, such as the plays, *The Fires of St. John* (1897) by Hermann Sudermann, and *Salome* by Oscar Wilde, Salome was obsessed with John the Baptist and Herod lusted after Salome. (Massenet's opera, *Hérodiade* (1881), is based on Flaubert's short story: John the Baptist, in this version, is in love with Salome. When he is killed by the jealous Herod, Salome stabs herself.)

Wilde added his own glosses upon the original story. For instance, in his play it is Salome rather than her mother Herodias who is the instigator of John the Baptist's execution. When Strauss decided to set Wilde's own prose text (in German translation) instead of a versification, although he may first have been attracted by the opening line of Hedwig Lachmann's German version he appears to have begun by composing the closing scene, in which he follows Wilde almost word for word. In the earlier part of the opera, there are numerous excisions of the play's text, made by Strauss in order to contain it within operatic length. Altogether, about one third of Wilde's play is omitted.

The story has been told by Wilde's biographers that his play was written in a single burst of creative energy, after which he went out to a nearby café to have a meal, and, having given his order, called the leader of the gypsy orchestra, saying to him, 'Play something in harmony with my thoughts, which are about a woman dancing with her bare feet in the blood of the man she has craved for and slain.' It is no less likely that many another anecdote about Wilde. His *Salome* was considered degenerate and offensive at the time of its creation. Later it was thought to be psychologically interesting, and now it reads and plays (when it is played at all) like an anthology of *fin de siècle* purple passages. However, behind the overwrought prose, there lies something of value in the play: an interesting juxtaposition of Christian and pagan values, the latter more convincingly portrayed by Wilde, as they were also to be by Strauss. In both play and opera, John the Baptist is a less well-rounded character than Salome, Herod or Herodias.

Although it was certainly not written with music in mind, Wilde's *Salome*, in one continuous act like Strauss's opera, is admirably suited to musical use, with its three climactic points, each of the latter two more dramatic than its predecessor. The first is Salome's enunciation of her desire for Jokanaan; the second the departure of Jokanaan back into the cistern, after the suicide of Narraboth (who is called simply 'A Young Syrian Captain' in the play's cast list); and the third, of course, is Salome's final soliloquy addressed to the head of the prophet. All seem to cry out for music.

For the most part, the cuts made in Wilde's text by Strauss do no harm to the drama. One regrets, however, the loss of the lament of the young page over the body of Narraboth, whom he loved. It would doubtless, had Strauss set it to music, have held up the action at a moment when the composer was keen to press forward to his second climax, but it would have given him an opportunity to convey a little unmorbid tenderness:

> The young Syrian has slain himself! The young captain has slain himself! He has slain himself who was my friend! I gave him a little box of perfumes and earrings wrought in silver, and now he has killed himself! Ah, did he not foretell that some misfortune would happen? I, too, foretold it, and it has happened. Well I knew that the moon was seeking a dead thing, but I knew not that it was he whom she sought. Ah! why did I not hide him from the moon? If I had hidden him in a cavern she would not have seen him.
>
> (Alfred Douglas's translation)

IV

THE entire action of the opera takes place on a wide terrace, which leads out of the banqueting hall of Herod's palace. It is night, and the moon is full. In the background can be seen an old cistern, with a cover of green bronze. Herodias's young Page (alto) and a group of soldiers are leaning against the balcony. Narraboth (tenor), the handsome young Syrian captain of the guard, looking into the banqueting hall, sings the opening line of the play, 'How beautiful is the Princess Salome tonight.' The soldiers discuss the guests at the banquet, and comment on the sullen look on the face of Herod, the Tetrarch (or ruler of the province, in this case Judaea). The opera is scored for a very large orchestra which establishes itself at the outset as a dominating element. There is no overture. After a swift upward run on a clarinet, the curtain rises. As Narraboth sighs, '*Wie schön ist die Prinzessin Salome heute Nacht*', a motif characterizing his desire for her is heard in the 'cellos (Ex. 4), the bass clarinet contributing a more sinister note in the last half of the phrase. When the Jews and rival sects at the banquet begin to quarrel, their dispute is mirrored in the dissonant snarling of different factions of the orchestra. 'What an uproar', a soldier comments. 'Who are those wild beasts howling?'

Ex.4

Two separate conversations are in progress. The soldiers continue to discuss the guests and Herod himself, whom they notice is looking grim, while the Page tries in vain to distract Narraboth's attention from the Princess Salome. 'You are always looking at her', he says to the young Syrian Captain. 'You look at her too much. It is dangerous to look at people in such fashion. Something terrible may happen.' But Narraboth continues to remark upon Salome's beauty and upon her paleness under the moon. As for the soldiers, although they cannot see whom Herod is looking at, the clarinet reveals who it is by repeating Salome's motif from Ex. 4. So far, with the exception of Narraboth's lyrical musing, the voice parts have been conversational in tone, with brief motivic phrases in the orchestra commenting on or emphasizing what is being sung. But now the voice of Jokanaan, or John the Baptist (baritone), is heard from the depths of the cistern in which he is imprisoned, proclaiming the coming of Christ. 'After me shall come another mightier than I. I am not worthy so much as to unloose the latchet of His shoes. When He comes, the desert places shall be glad, the eyes of the blind shall see, and the ears of the deaf shall be opened.' Jokanaan's grave legato is suitably solemn and majestic in tone, but it is clear even from this first brief utterance of the Prophet that Strauss's sympathies were not strongly engaged by this character. Strauss's genius was for creating characters in love, or in the grip of sexual obsession, but religious fervour was not within his range. He had managed cleverly to sidestep it in *Guntram*; in *Salome* the least convincing pages are those in which Jokanaan speaks of the coming Christ.

One of the soldiers wants forcibly to silence Jokanaan, but his companion speaks respectfully of the prophet, referring to him as a holy man, and gentle in his manner. He tells a Cappadocian standing nearby that the prophet came from the wilderness, and that his utterances are often difficult to understand. Here Strauss omits several lines from Wilde's play which contain information relevant to the action at a later stage:

The Cappadocian (pointing to the cistern): What a strange prison!
Second Soldier: It is an old cistern.
The Cappadocian: An old cistern! It must be very unhealthy.
Second Soldier: Oh no! For instance, the Tetrarch's brother, his elder brother, the first husband of Herodias the Queen, was imprisoned there for twelve years. It did not kill him. At the end of the twelve years he had to be strangled.
The Cappadocian: Strangled? Who dared to do that?
Second Soldier (pointing to the executioner, a huge Negro): That man yonder, Naaman.
The Cappadocian: He was not afraid?
Second Soldier: Oh no! The Tetrarch sent him the ring.
The Cappadocian: What ring?
Second Soldier: The death-ring. So he was not afraid.
The Cappadocian: Yet it is a terrible thing to strangle a king.
First Soldier: Why? Kings have but one neck, like other folk.
The Cappadocian: I think it terrible.

Narraboth, who has been gazing in the direction of the banquet, now notices that Salome has left the table and is approaching the terrace. His young admirer, the Page, again implores him, in vain, not to look at the princess. Almost immediately, Salome (soprano) appears. She is in a state of excitement and anger because her stepfather, Herod, has been gazing lustfully at her. She is keen, too, to escape not only the quarrelling of the Jews and Egyptians (and, in Wilde's play, the Greeks from Smyrna), but also the dull speech and coarse manners of the Romans. Salome drinks in the beauty of the moon, which she compares to that of a cold and chaste virgin.

The voice of Jokanaan is heard again, announcing that the Son of Man has come, and Salome demands to know who the prisoner is. When she is told, she remembers that he is the man of whom Herod is afraid, the man who has said monstrous things about her mother, Herodias. A slave now enters with a message from Herod: Salome is to return to the banquet. (Strauss did not bother to stipulate what singing voice the slave should have: he wrote the character's one line in the treble clef, at a pitch suitable for either tenor or soprano.) Salome refuses to go back, and continues to question the soldiers about Jokanaan. When the prophet's voice is heard again from the cistern, she says she wishes to speak to him, and orders that he be brought forth. The soldiers make it clear that they are afraid to disobey Herod's order that no one be allowed to speak to Jokanaan, so Salome changes her tactics and begins to work her wiles upon Narraboth, of whose hopeless devotion she is clearly aware, addressing him by name. If he will order the prophet to be brought before her, she tells Narraboth, she will drop a little flower from her litter as she passes by him tomorrow. Narraboth hesitates, and Salome now offers to look at him, on the morrow, through the muslin curtains of her litter if he will do as she asks. Unable to refuse her, Narraboth orders one of the soldiers to bring the prophet forth from the cistern.

An extended orchestral interlude prefaces Jokanaan's appearance, combining references to the prophet's piety and to Salome's latent passion. It is here that one first hears the phrase (Ex. 5) of which more extended use will be made in Salome's two long monologues later in the opera. When Jokanaan appears and begins to fulminate against Herod and Herodias ('Where is he whose cup of abominations is now full? . . . Where is she who gave herself unto the Captains of Assyria and the young men of Egypt?') Salome is both repelled and fascinated. Narraboth begs her not to stay, as she approaches Jokanaan and comments on the dark caves of his eyes, on his slim, ascetic figure, and on his skin which 'must be cool like ivory'.

Ex.5

Clearly it is necessary for the audience's suspension of disbelief that the interpreters of Salome and Jokanaan be, in their different ways, personable. Strauss made the role of Salome virtually impossible to cast plausibly when he wrote it for a dramatic soprano voice, pitting it against a huge orchestra. He himself admitted that the role, as written, called for a sixteen-year-old with the voice of Isolde: fortunately, in later years he reduced the volume of the orchestration, making the role available to the lyric-dramatic soprano who is often a less hefty creature than the *hoch dramatische* soprano. Similarly, Jokanaan requires to be performed by a young or youngish baritone who is reasonably slim, and not by a thick-waisted singer in middle-age.

'Who is this woman who is looking at me?' demands Jokanaan, and when she informs him that she is Salome, daughter of Herodias and Princess of Judaea, he exclaims, 'Back, daughter of Babylon! Come not near the chosen of the Lord!' His words fall like sweet invitations on the ear of the perverse Salome. The more he harangues, the stronger her desire for him becomes. When he orders her to repent and seek out the Son of Man, she innocently enquires, 'Who is he, the Son of Man? Is he as beautiful as thou art?'

Narraboth, meanwhile, has been pleading with Salome to return to the banquet within. Ignoring him, she launches into a monstrous confession of her lust for Jokanaan. She begins by extravagantly praising the beauty of his body. When the appalled holy man attempts to repel her, she changes her tune. 'Thy body is hideous', she tells him. It is his hair that she is enamoured of, his thick hair like the clusters of black grapes that hang from the vines of Edom. 'Back, daughter of Sodom', exclaims the prophet, at which Salome decides that his hair is horrible, like a crown of thorns. It is his mouth that she desires. After a long and erotic description of the redness of his lips, she ends, 'There is nothing in the world so red as thy mouth. Let me kiss thy mouth.'

Narraboth is by now in a frenzy of despair, but Salome can only repeat, 'Let me kiss thy mouth'. Jokanaan recoils in shocked horror, Narraboth stabs himself and falls dead at Salome's feet, but she continues to cry, 'Let me kiss thy mouth'. The soldiers attempt to draw her attention to the fact that their Captain has killed himself, but as Jokanaan retreats into his cistern Salome can only repeat 'I will kiss thy mouth, Jokanaan.'

At Jokanaan's mention of the Son of Man, and Salome's question about his beauty, the orchestra contributes a moment of tenderness and tranquillity, almost of regret for lost innocence. With her cry of 'Jokanaan', Salome begins the first of her two arias of lust for the prophet, a lust frustrated while he is alive, and perversely consummated only at the end of the opera when she caresses the head that has been severed from his body. This first aria is in three sections, devoted in turn to praise of the prophet's body, his hair, and his mouth, each outburst followed by a shocked reaction from Jokanaan. Strauss is much more successful in conveying the morbid passion of the depraved teenage princess than the pious utterances of John the Baptist, though he achieves a touching simplicity when, after Salome's insistent demands to be allowed to kiss his mouth, Jokanaan tells her to seek out the only man who can save her, one who is to be found in a boat on the sea of Galilee. The vocal climax Strauss gives the Prophet, however, is a cadence one more usually associates with the composer's heroines at their moments of greatest triumph or satisfaction.

The orchestra comes into its own as the prophet slowly descends into his cistern. It combines and juxtaposes various themes of Salome and Jokanaan, with those themes characterizing Salome's desire seeming to gain the upper hand, then lapses into near silence before becoming more lively again as it announces the entrance of Herod (tenor) and Herodias (mezzo-soprano) from the banquet. Followed by their guests and members of their court, Herod and Herodias now appear, Herod anxiously asking where Salome is, and being reproached by his wife for casting lustful glances upon his step-daughter. The neurotic Herod has drunk too much wine at supper: he imagines signs and portents in everything he sees, and is fearful of the moon which, he says, reels through the clouds like a drunken woman. When he slips in the blood of Narraboth, he is momentarily surprised to be told that the young Captain has killed himself. He remembers the young man as having been very handsome, and recalls that he, too, used to gaze longingly at Salome. Then, brusquely, he orders Narraboth's body to be removed. He now imagines there is a strong wind blowing, and a noise like the beating of vast wings, but Herodias tells him he is ill, and tries to persuade him to return to the palace.

Herod now turns his attention to Salome, attempting to persuade her to drink wine with him, which she refuses, and to share with him the fruit he has ordered to be brought. Again she refuses. He turns on Herodias, accusing her of having brought Salome up badly, but Herodias tartly reminds him that she and her daughter are descendants of a royal race, whereas Herod's father was a camel driver and a thief. The voice of the prophet is suddenly heard, and Herodias bids her husband silence him. When Herod refuses, calling Jokanaan a great prophet, she accuses Herod of being afraid of him, and asks why he does not deliver Jokanaan into the hands of the Jews. This sparks off a religious discussion among the Jews, to which two Nazarenes also contribute.

Jokanaan's voice is heard again, announcing that the day of the Lord has come, and the Jews and Nazarenes begin to argue about the Messiah who has been seen in Galilee, healing the blind, and even raising the dead. This disturbs Herod. 'I forbid him to do that', he cries. 'It would be terrible if the dead came back.' Jokanaan fulminates against 'the wanton daughter of Babylon', and Herodias again asks Herod to silence him. Herod, however, points out that the prophet has not actually mentioned her by name. He turns to Salome, and asks her to dance for him. Salome refuses, to the delight of her mother, but when Herod, growing increasingly excited, promises her whatever she may ask, if only she will dance for him, Salome makes him swear a solemn oath to that effect. Herod swears his oath, as Herodias continues to beg her daughter not to dance. Again Herod imagines an icy wind blowing around his head, and the beating of unseen wings. In the next instant, he feels feverish, and begins to tear at his mantle, and fling the festive garland of roses from his brow. Finally, 'I will dance for you, Tetrarch', says Salome. This entire scene is a gift to a fine character tenor, for Strauss has written the role of Herod superbly for the singer, and the orchestra most effectively aids the characterization by its constant comment.

Herodias makes one last attempt to prevent Salome from dancing, as the voice of the Prophet is heard again, fulminating against the immorality of Herod's court. 'Let us go within', Herodias insists. 'The voice of that man maddens me. I will not have my daughter dance while he is continually crying out. I will not have her dance while you look at her in this fashion. In a word, I will not have her dance.'

Salome now begins her Dance of the Seven Veils, the most famous striptease of all time, discarding her veils one by one until, at the end, she is supposedly naked. (Though not necessarily. Unlike the stout *prime donne* of earlier years, today's Salomes usually perform the dance themselves, rather than have a svelte ballerina deputize, and as often as not they simulate nakedness at the conclusion of the dance. But, in both the play and the opera's libretto, Salome removes only her sandals before putting on the veils to dance: Herod derives sensual gratification from the sight of her feet. 'Ah, you are going to dance with naked feet', he exclaims in Wilde's play. ' 'Tis well. Your little feet will be like white doves. They will be like little white flowers that dance upon the trees.')

It is thought that Strauss composed the Dance of the Seven Veils after completing the rest of the work. This would certainly explain the fact that it is virtually a potpourri of familiar themes, presented in a manner which robs them of any dramatic significance, and that its scoring is rather less imaginative than that of the rest of the opera. Given Strauss's wish to capture the real essence of the Middle East in his score, it is ironic (though doubtless inevitable) that, after a quasi-oriental beginning, Salome's sensual oriental dance should, for the most part, possess a thoroughly Viennese flavour.

When the dance is finished, Herod is beside himself with excitement. He repeats that he will give Salome whatever her soul desires, and is charmed by the way in which she phrases her request, as she kneels humbly before him: 'I would that they presently bring me in a silver charger . . . .' He laughingly interrupts her. 'In a silver charger? Surely yes, in a silver charger. What is it you would have in a silver charger, O sweet and fair Salome?' As she rises, Salome concludes her sentence simply: '. . . the head of Jokanaan'.

Herod is appalled, but his appalling wife, Herodias, is delighted. The Tetrarch tries to persuade Salome to accept alternative rewards, among them the largest emerald in the world, Herod's beautiful white peacocks, and all the jewels that he has hidden in his palace, jewels that Herodias has never seen. But Salome inexorably reminds him of the oath he has sworn, repeating 'Give me the head of Jokanaan!' Herod next offers her the mantle of the high priest, and even the veil of the sanctuary in the Jewish temple (which provokes a wail of shocked protest from the Jews), but she merely repeats 'Give me the head of Jokanaan!' Herod is terrified, for he believes the Prophet to be a holy man, and fears the anger of God. But he fears even more the misfortune which he is convinced would overtake him were he not to honour his oath. Realizing that it is hopeless to attempt to turn Salome aside from her insane desire, he sinks back in his seat, muttering, 'Let her be given what she asks! Of a truth she is her mother's child!' Herodias takes advantage of his state of collapse to remove the ring of death from Herod's hand, and gives it to a soldier who straightway bears it to the Executioner. ('The Executioner looks scared', one reads in Wilde's stage directions.)

As the Executioner descends into the cistern, Herodias expresses her pleasure in her daughter's enterprising behaviour, while Herod incoherently wonders who has taken the ring from his hand, and who has drunk the wine in his cup. He repeats that he is sure some evil will befall someone: it is presumably not the evil about to befall Jokanaan that he has in mind.

It is in this sequence of events, from the end of Salome's dance to the execution of Jokanaan, that Strauss's orchestral virtuosity reaches its highest peak, pushing to the limits of tonality, and expressing in masterly fashion the horror of the situation and Salome's final descent into a madness from which she cannot be reclaimed.

Salome leans over the cistern, attempting to listen to what is going on below. 'There is no sound. I hear nothing', she mutters to herself. 'Why does he not cry out, this man?' She hears something fall, but thinks it must be the executioner's sword. 'He is afraid, this slave. He has let his sword fall. He dare not kill him.' She turns to Herodias's Page, addressing him hysterically: 'Come hither, thou wert the friend of him who is dead, is it not so? Well, I tell thee, there are not dead men enough. Go to the soldiers and bid them go down and bring me the thing I ask, the thing the Tetrarch has promised me, the thing that is mine.' When the Page recoils, Salome turns to the soldiers, ordering them into the cistern, and calling to Herod to command his soldiers to bring her the head of Jokanaan.

As Salome eagerly listens, one hears emerging from a background of ominous silence (a silence conveyed musically by Strauss with a bass drum roll and deep tremolos in the basses), a succession of grisly sounds produced by four double basses instructed by the composer to pinch the string high up between the thumb and forefinger and strike it sharply with the bow. Sensitive listeners who suspect that they are hearing Jokanaan's head being sawed off may or may not accept the composer's assurance that these sounds 'do not represent cries of pain uttered by the victim, but sighs of anguish from the heart of an impatiently expectant Salome.'

The huge black arm of the executioner comes forth from the cistern, bearing on a silver shield the prophet's head. Salome seizes it, and begins her great final monologue, an arioso in which she addresses the severed head, taunting it even while she lasciviously contemplates her final act of perverse sexual lust. 'Thou wouldst not suffer me to kiss thy mouth, Jokanaan. Well! I will kiss it now. I will bite it with my teeth as one bites a ripe fruit . . . Wherefore dost thou not look at me? Art thou afraid of me, Jokanaan, that thou wilt not look at me? . . . Jokanaan, I still live, but thou, thou art dead, and thy head belongs to me. I can do with it what I will. I can throw it to the dogs and to the birds of the air . . . Ah, Jokanaan, thou wert beautiful . . . There was nothing in the world so white as thy body. There was nothing in the world so black as thy hair. In the whole world there was nothing so red as thy mouth . . . Well, thou hast seen thy God, Jokanaan, but me, me, thou didst never see. If thou hadst seen me thou wouldst have loved me . . . And the mystery of love is greater than the mystery of death.'

In disgust, Herod murmurs to Herodias, 'She is monstrous, thy daughter', while Herodias expresses approval of Salome's behaviour. Certain that some great evil will befall, Herod intends to hide in his palace. As he orders the lights to be extinguished, a huge black cloud crosses the moon, concealing it completely. Herod begins to climb the staircase, but is arrested by the voice of Salome emerging from the darkness. 'Ah! I have kissed thy mouth, Jokanaan', she exclaims in ecstasy. 'There was a bitter taste on thy lips. Was it the taste of blood? No! But perchance it is the taste of love. They say that love hath a bitter taste. But what of that? What of that? I have kissed thy mouth, Jokanaan.'

A ray of moonlight falls on Salome. As he sees her slavering with lust over the head of Jokanaan, Herod involuntarily cries out, 'Kill that woman!' The soldiers rush forward and crush Salome beneath their shields as the curtain falls.

Salome's final solo scene, beginning '*Ah! Du wollst mich nicht deinen Mund küssen lassen, Jokanaan!*', is perhaps one of Strauss's finest extended arias for the soprano voice. It is also, surely, one of the least engaging expressions of sexual desire in Strauss, or in the operas of any other composer! Example 5 and the other phrases which Salome used to extol Jokanaan's beauty while he was alive return again in altered form now that her desire is consummated. The end of the opera, after Herod's command that she be killed, comes with a brutal swiftness. Salome's themes sound kaleidoscopically as the shields of the soldiers pound upon her body.

Salome marks a distinct advance upon Strauss's earlier works for the stage. Its language is much more adventurous, and its characterization considerably more impressive: indeed, it remains to this day one of the masterpieces of twentieth-century opera. One can understand, and even sympathize with, the squeamishness of audiences subjected to it in the early years of the century. But now one's ears and one's sensibilities are exposed to more daring sounds and more disgusting acts of human behaviour. One can listen to Salome's final monologue for its lyricism, and to the entire opera for its dramatic force and for the brilliance with which its composer has convincingly recreated in twentieth-century sound the brutal pagan world of two thousand years ago.

FOUR

Elektra

Tragedy in One Act
opus 58

Dramatis personae
Klytemnestra, Widow of Agamemnon (mezzo-soprano)
Elektra (soprano)
Chrysothemis (soprano) } her Daughters
Aegisthus, Klytemnestra's Paramour (tenor)
Orestes, Son of Klytemnestra and Agamemnon (baritone)
The Tutor of Orestes (bass)
The Confidante of Klytemnestra (soprano)
The Trainbearer of Klytemnestra (soprano)
A Young Servant (tenor)
An Old Servant (bass)
The Overseer (soprano)
Five Maidservants (one contralto, two mezzo-sopranos,
two sopranos)

LIBRETTO by Hugo von Hofmannsthal, based on *Electra* by Sophocles

TIME: Antiquity

PLACE: Mycenae, Greece.

FIRST PERFORMED at the Königliches Opernhaus, Dresden, 25 January 1909, with Annie Krull (Elektra), Margarethe Siems (Chrysothemis), Ernestine Schumann-Heink (Klytemnestra) and Karl Perron (Orestes), conducted by Ernst von Schuch.

I

IN March 1900, while he was conducting in Paris, Strauss had met a twenty-six-year-old Austrian poet and playwright, Hugo von Hofmannsthal, who approached him with a suggestion for a ballet. Nothing came of this: six years were to pass before the great operatic partnership of Strauss and Hofmannsthal began. During those years Strauss composed *Feuersnot* and *Salome*. It had been at Max Reinhardt's Kleines Theater in Berlin in November 1902 that the composer had first seen Wilde's *Salome* on the stage, portrayed by Gertrud Eysolt; exactly one year later he saw the same actress at the same theatre, in another Max Reinhardt production, a new German version by Hugo von Hofmannsthal of the *Electra* of Sophocles. At the time, Strauss was about to begin the composition of *Salome*, and he was struck by the psychological, and even the formal similarities between the two plays. Early in 1906, some weeks after the première of his opera *Salome*, Strauss approached Hofmannsthal about the possibility of the poet's version of *Elektra* being used as the libretto of an opera.

The following is Strauss's account, written in 1942, of the genesis of the opera *Elektra*:

When I first saw Hofmannsthal's inspired play at the Kleines Theater with Gertrud Eysoldt, I immediately recognized, of course, what a magnificent operatic libretto it might be (after the alteration I made in the Orestes scene it has actually become one) and, just as previously with *Salome*, I appreciated the tremendous increase in musical tension to the very end. In *Elektra*, after the recognition scene, which could only be completely realized in music, the release in dance; in *Salome*, after the dance (the heart of the plot), the dreadful apotheosis of the end. Both operas offered wonderful musical points of attack:

Salome: the contrasts; the court of Herod, Jokanaan, the Jews, the Nazarenes.
Elektra: the possessed goddess of vengeance contrasted with the radiant character of her mortal sister.
Salome: the three seduction songs of Salome, Herod's three persuasive speeches, and Salome's ostinato: '*Ich will den Kopf des Jochanaan*' ('I want the head of Jokanaan').
Elektra: the first monologue; the unending climaxes in the scene between Elektra and Chrysothemis, and in the scene between Elektra and Klytemnestra (both unfortunately still extensively cut).

But at first I was put off by the idea that both subjects were very similar in psychological content, so that I doubted whether I should have the power to exhaust this subject also. But the wish to contrast this

trauss with Sir Thomas Beecham at the Theatre Royal, Drury Lane, London, during a rehearsal
reak in 1947

(left) Poster for the première of Strauss's first opera *Guntram*, Weimar, 1894

(below) Scene from the first production of *Guntram*

possessed, exalted Greece of the sixth century BC with Winckelmann's Roman copies and Goethe's humanism outweighed these doubts, and *Elektra* became even more intense in the unity of structure and in the force of its climaxes. I am almost tempted to say that it is to *Salome* what the more flawless, and stylistically more uniform *Lohengrin* is to the inspired first venture of *Tannhäuser*. Both operas are unique in my life's works. In them I penetrated to the uttermost limits of harmony, psychological polyphony (Klytemnestra's dream) and of the receptivity of modern ears . . .

The performance of *Elektra* had again been extremely carefully prepared by the conscientious Schuch. Once again he knew the score as well as if it were the twentieth performance. Schuch was famous for his elegant performances of Italian and French operas and as a discreet accompanist. He had perfected this praiseworthy art to such a pitch that, under him, even Wagner's scores sounded a little undistinguished. One hardly ever heard a real *fortissimo* from the brass of this exemplary Dresden orchestra. Since at that time, thirty-five years ago, I was still enamoured of the teutonic *ff*, I was stupid enough to find fault during rehearsals with Schuch's euphonious (but not incisive) brass, which annoyed him.

I insisted that, hearing my score for the first time, I should hear the whole complexity of the score, completely forgetting that such complicated polyphony will only become quite plastic and lucid after years, when the orchestra has it almost by heart. Schuch, being a friend of the poor 'declaiming' singers, had already toned down the orchestra in the first few rehearsals to such an extent that it sounded too colourless for my liking, although the singers at least could be heard. My continued insistence on secondary thematic parts annoyed Schuch so much that he played with such fury during the dress rehearsal that I was forced to make the humble confession: 'The orchestra was really a little too strong today.' 'You see', said Schuch triumphantly, and the first performance had perfect balance.

Only Frau Schumann-Heink (the famous Wagner singer) who gave a guest performance as Klytemnestra was shown to be miscast. I cannot use old 'stars'; I was beginning to realize at that time how fundamentally my vocal style differs even from that of Wagner. My vocal style has the pace of a stage play and frequently comes into conflict with the figuring and polyphony of the orchestra, so that none but the best conductors, who themselves know something of singing, can establish the balance of volume and speed between singer and baton. The struggle between word and music has been the problem of my life right from the beginning, which *Capriccio* solves with a question mark . . .

II

IN March, 1906, while Strauss was still undecided whether to attempt *Elektra*, or to turn to a subject further removed from *Salome*, perhaps a comedy, Hofmannsthal wrote from his villa outside Vienna. 'How goes it with you and *Elektra*?' he asked. 'I must say that what you have so unexpectedly aroused in me is the hope of considerable pleasure.' Strauss, in reply, wondered if Hofmannsthal might have some other subject he could use, something a little less like *Salome*. 'In any case', he ended,

I would ask you urgently to give me first refusal with anything that you write which is suitable for music. Your style has so much in common with mine. We were made for each other, and we are sure to do fine things together if you remain faithful to me. Have you got an entertaining renaissance subject I might use? A really wild Cesare Borgia or Savonarola would be the answer to my prayers.

Clearly, this was a case of artistic love at first sight. Both men looked forward to a long-standing relationship as creative partners: their only difficulty was in deciding with what subject to consummate the partnership. For several weeks Strauss continued to suggest other possibilities, while Hofmannsthal attempted to persuade him that *Salome* and *Elektra* were not so very similar. 'The similarities with the *Salome* plot', Hofmannsthal wrote,

seem to me, on closer consideration, to dwindle to nothing. (Both are one-act plays; each has a woman's name for a title; both take place in classical antiquity; and both parts were originally created in Berlin by Gertrud Eysoldt; that, I feel, is all the similarity adds up to.) The blend of colour in the two subjects strikes me as quite different in all essentials; in *Salome* much is, so to speak, purple and violet, and the atmosphere is torrid. In *Elektra*, on the other hand, it is a mixture of night and light, or black and bright. What is more, the rapid, rising sequence of events relating to Orestes and his deed which leads up to victory and purification—a sequence which I can imagine much more powerful in music than in the written word—is not matched by anything of a corresponding, or even faintly similar kind in *Salome*.

Hofmannsthal, as was so often to be the case throughout his twenty years of collaboration with Strauss, thought the composer's counter-suggestions deplorable:

You spoke of some plot to be taken from the renaissance. Allow me, my dear sir, to make you a frank reply. I do not believe there is any epoch in history which I and, like me, every creative poet among our contemporaries would bar from his work with feelings of such definite disinclination, indeed such unavoidable distaste, as this particular one. Subjects taken from the renaissance seem destined to transport the brushes of the most deplorable painters and the pens of the most hapless of poets.

In other words, this was the first of the many occasions on which poet was to say, in effect, to composer, 'Try not to be so vulgar.' On 9 June Strauss tried another suggestion. 'I have been reading Rückert's *Saul and David* today', he wrote. 'There's a lot in it that might be usable. And since the raving Saul has long interested me, I'd be glad if you would have a look at it.' He attempted flattery: 'Since I saw Rembrandt's 'Saul and David' in the Hague, the subject has haunted me, except that I can't shape it myself. But the creator of the dancing *Elektra* could!' A week later, however, Strauss seemed inexplicably to have capitulated. 'I am already busy on the first scene of *Elektra*,' he wrote, 'but I'm still making rather heavy weather of it.' He continued to suggest other ideas ('How about a subject from the French revolution for a change?') but, as he gradually became immersed in the world of *Elektra*, the other suggestions were made less frequently. By the end of the summer, it was accepted by both Strauss and Hofmannsthal that the composer's next opera would be his setting of the poet's version of the *Electra* of Sophocles.

III

HUGO von Hofmannsthal, poet, playwright and essayist, was born into an affluent banker's family in Vienna on 1 February 1874. (He was thus Strauss's junior by ten years: at the time of their first collaboration, he was in his early thirties, and the composer in his early forties.) Hofmannsthal's ancestry was Jewish on his mother's side, and half Austrian, half Italian on his father's. He was a man of wider culture than the shrewd Bavarian Strauss; he had made his name as a lyric poet while still in his teens, and his intellectual approach to language and the problems of communication led him to grapple with theories which would have seemed pointlessly abstruse to the composer whose creative life he was so memorably to share. In many ways, it was an unlikely marriage of minds, though it turned out to be, aesthetically as well as practically, an extremely successful one.

Hofmannsthal had written a few short plays before coming to the conclusion that he could best compensate for what he saw as the inadequacies of language by turning to traditional and mythical subject matter and using material that was a familiar part of European cultural heritage. It was in pursuance of this aim that he turned to the *Electra* of Sophocles, producing his own version of the myth in 1903.

In Greek mythology, the daughter of Agamemnon and Klytemnestra who avenges the murder of her father is Elektra. (The usual English spellings are Electra and Clytemnestra, but for the sake of consistency and convenience the German spellings of Strauss and Hofmannsthal are used here.). Elektra's story, and that of her family, the house of Atreus, is told by each of the three great dramatists of classical Greece: Aeschylus in his trilogy, the *Oresteia*, and Sophocles and Euripides in single plays, both given the name of their tragic heroine, *Elektra*. The plays of Sophocles and Euripides are vastly different from each other: the Sophocles version is the more direct and stark drama, concentrating on the character of Elektra and her qualities of heroism and tragic endurance. Its plot, like that of Hofmannsthal's version which does not diverge from it in outline, is simple. Elektra mourns the death of her father Agamemnon, who was murdered by her mother, Klytemnestra, and tries to persuade her sister Chrysothemis to help her avenge his death. Their brother Orestes, whom they had believed dead, returns home and kills both Klytemnestra and her lover, Aegisthus. The real climax of the drama in Sophocles, as in Hofmannsthal's play and in Strauss's opera, is the recognition scene between Elektra and her brother Orestes, a scene whose potentialities, as Hofmannsthal conceded, are most fully realized when conveyed through music.

As with Wilde's play, Strauss required not an adaptation of Hofmannsthal's *Elektra* for musical purposes but, for the most part, merely a reduction of the play's length, and this task the composer himself undertook, though the playwright also made valuable suggestions. 'During a walk recently', Hofmannsthal wrote to Strauss:

I strove to get thoroughly into the spirit of *Elektra* from your point of view, imagining the effect of the music, and in doing so came to the conclusion that the brief interlude of the cook and the young servant . . . is quite superfluous. If, therefore, you should want to cut it out, you have my consent in advance. For the mute (but important) scene . . . in which the old servant prostrates himself before Orestes and kisses his feet, I have the following proposal. Would not this scene be more effective for the music (and at the same time for the poetic mood) if many old servants, all the old servants of the house, were to come on to the stage? Three or four of them are bold enough to advance towards Orestes; the other fifteen or twenty old heads are huddled together at the gate to the courtyard; when these three or four fall at Orestes's feet, the others by the gateway also sink to the ground. Then the whole group scrambles to its worn-out feet and shuffles tremulously off the stage without a sound.

In the event, Strauss contented himself with no more than three additional servants. Hofmannsthal had also suggested leaving the character of Aegisthus out of the opera, but Strauss opposed this. He worked on the opera intermittently throughout 1907 and the first half of 1908, though his busy schedule with the opera company and the orchestra in Berlin, as well as conducting engagements throughout Europe and the understandable desire to acquaint himself with as many productions of *Salome* as possible, prevented him from concentrating his energies entirely upon *Elektra*. In February 1908, he wrote to Hofmannsthal from Warsaw, to say that he would be staying at the Hotel Imperial, Vienna, for two days in March, asking the playwright to meet him there to discuss some further small additions, and offering to play him what he had so far written of the opera.

In June, at his newly completed villa in the village of Garmisch in the Bavarian Alps (paid for by *Salome!*), Strauss was at last able to work uninterruptedly for a time on the new opera. It was at this point that he found he needed to ask Hofmannsthal to provide 'a few beautiful verses' for the moment of repose immediately after Elektra's recognition of Orestes. When he received these, he wrote, 'Your verses when Elektra recognizes Orestes are marvellous and already set to music. You are the born librettist—the greatest compliment, to my mind, since I consider it much more difficult to write a good operatic text than a fine play.'

Hofmannsthal had written a fine play which was also a good operatic text. According to the poet himself, his starting-point had been the character of Elektra as conveyed by Sophocles:

I read Sophocles' version of the drama in the garden and while walking in the woods during the autumn of 1901. I was struck by the reference in *Iphigenia* to 'Elektra with her tongue of fire', and while out walking I allowed my imagination free play with the character of Elektra, not without a certain pleasure in contrasting it with the 'devilishly human' atmosphere surrounding Iphigenia . . . I suddenly conceived a desire to write the piece as a result of contact with the theatre director Reinhardt; I had told him he ought to perform plays from ancient times, and he had replied that he was reluctant to do so owing to the 'plaster statue' character of the existing translations and adaptations.

In October 1908, Strauss was promoted from his Berlin position of Royal Kapellmeister to become General Music Director, despite the fact that the Kaiser, who had no taste for modern music, was known to have referred to him as 'that viper I have nourished in my bosom'. (Strauss thereafter became known in family circles as *Hofbusenschlange* or 'Royal Bosom-Viper'.) At the same time, he was given a year's leave of absence, ostensibly in order to complete the composition of *Elektra*, although, in fact, he had managed to finish the opera in September. The première was offered to and eagerly accepted by Ernst von Schuch in Dresden. 'The title-role', Strauss instructed, 'must above all be given to the highest and most dramatic soprano who can be found.' He visited Dresden in October to audition possible contenders, and chose Annie Krull who seven years previously had created the role of Diemut in *Feuersnot*. *Elektra* was given its première at the Königliches Opernhaus in Dresden on 25 January 1909. In addition to Annie Krull, the principal singers included Margarethe Siems (Chrysothemis), Ernestine Schumann-Heink (Klytemnestra) and Karl Perron (Orestes). Strauss himself has revealed that he was less than completely happy with the performance of Madame Schumann-Heink. That formidable contralto made it known, shortly after the première, that she was not at all happy with Strauss's music which she referred to publicly as a 'horrible din' (*furchtbares Gebrüll*), swearing that she would never sing the part of Klytemnestra again, 'not even for three thousand dollars a performance'.

The first night of *Elektra* was not unsuccessful, though it was certainly not the triumph that *Salome's* première had been. Jokes were made at the expense of Strauss's gargantuan orchestra, one cartoon showing the audience squeezed into the pit while the orchestra occupied the rest of the auditorium; a report circulated to the effect that in his next opera Strauss intended to augment the orchestra by four locomotives, ten jaguars, and several rhinoceroses. It was also alleged that, at one of the Dresden performances, half the orchestra played the score of *Salome* while the other half played *Elektra*, with neither musicians nor audience noticing anything amiss! Reviewing the *Elektra* première in the *Wiener Fremdenblatt*, the critic Julius Korngold commented wittily: *'Wie schön war die Prinzessin Salome, heute Nacht.'* Strauss took all this with good humour, merely remarking, in reply to the accusation that his music was needlessly ugly: 'When a mother is slain on the stage, do they expect me to write a violin concerto?'

Immediately after its intial Dresden performances, *Elektra* was produced in Berlin (in February), Vienna (in March) and Milan (in April). The Milan performances were in Italian, which is not surprising; but the New York production the following year was in French, which is inexplicable. (New York was not to experience *Elektra* in German until 1932). In February 1910 Strauss conducted the opera for the first time at its Dutch première in the Hague. He had on one occasion taken over from Schuch during a Dresden rehearsal, but had soon returned the baton to him, saying, 'I was able to compose it, but I'm not able to conduct it yet.' A few days after the Hague première, *Elektra* became the first Strauss opera to be heard in London. The composer travelled from the Hague to London for the first performance at Covent Garden which, conducted by Thomas Beecham, was an enormous success. A dissenting view was expressed by the critic Ernest Newman, who wrote in *The Nation* that

> there is a strong strain of foolishness and ugliness in [Strauss], that he is lacking in the sensitive feeling for the balance of a large work that some other great artists have, and that consequently there is not one large work of his, from *Don Quixote* onward, that is not marred by some folly or some foolery. If it were not for this strain of coarseness and thought-lessness in him, he would never have taken up so crude a perversion of the old Greek story as that of Hugo von Hofmannsthal.

This led to a reply by George Bernard Shaw, who thought Newman's response to the work 'ridiculous and idiotic'. The subsequent slanging match between Newman and Shaw enlivened the columns of *The Nation* on and off for four years. 'Not even in the third scene of *Das Rheingold*, or in the Klingsor scenes in *Parsifal*', wrote Shaw,

> is there such an atmosphere of malignant and cancerous evil as we get here. And that the power with which it is done is not the power of the evil itself, but of the passion that detests and must and finally can destroy that evil, is what makes the work great, and makes us rejoice in its horror.
>
> Whoever understands this, however vaguely, will understand Strauss's music, and why on Saturday night the crowded house burst into frenzied shoutings, not merely of applause, but of strenuous assent and affirmation, as the curtain fell.

IV

THE text of Hofmannsthal's drama, though in one continuous scene, divides into seven distinct sections, and Strauss in his musical treatment was able to preserve the identity of these sections, making the fourth of them, the dramatic confrontation between Elektra and Klytemnestra, the dramatic pivotal scene of the opera, preceded and followed by the con-trasting lyrical scenes involving Elektra and Chrysothemis. One might imagine the text as one vast sentence, with a semi-colon (in Strauss's musical sentence, a double bar-line) after the fourth scene. The sections could be described as follows:

1. Prelude—the servants.
2. Elektra.
3. Elektra and Chrysothemis.
4. Elektra and Klytemnestra.
5. Elektra and Chrysothemis.
6. Elektra and Orestes.
7. The Murders, and Elektra's Dance of Triumph.

What the audience is presumed to know before the rise of the curtain is that Agamemnon, King of Argos and supreme commander of the Greek forces in the Trojan War, had left his wife, Klytemnestra, to rule during his absence. Klytemnestra took as a lover Agamemnon's enemy Aegisthus, with whose help she murdered her husband on his return from Troy. The entire action of the opera takes place in the inner courtyard of the palace at Mycenae, against the gaunt walls, with a huge door, and windows running the length of a terrace inside the palace. After the murder of their father, Agamemnon, Elektra and her sister Chrysothemis have led miserable lives. Their brother, Orestes, is in exile, and they have not heard from him for many years. Elektra, obsessed with the idea of avenging her father's death, now lives like an animal and is treated as such by the servants.

When the curtain rises, with the orchestra blaring forth the motif which seems to embody the name of the murdered king, Agamemnon (Ex. 6), Elektra is seen scuttling across the courtyard while five maidservants, in the charge of a female overseer, draw water from a well. The servants discuss Elektra's degraded condition. When one of their number, the fifth maidservant, defends Elektra, reminding her colleagues that the princess is, after all, of noble birth, she is dragged into the servants' quarters on the order of the overseer, and savagely beaten. The general view of the servants is that Elektra is like a wild animal, and should be kept locked up.

Ex.6

This opening scene is a deliberately ugly cacophony of female voices shrieking their dialogue over a characteristically noisy Straussian orchestra. Motifs race across the score, references to Klytemnestra, to Elektra's mourning for her father, to her thoughts of revenge, and to the royal lineage of the House of Atreus. When the one gentle spirit among the servants is being beaten for having spoken up for Elektra, the orchestra viciously imitates the birch-strokes. Strauss was capable, behind his cheerful Bavarian exterior, of being as great a sadist as Puccini!

A rushing chromatic scale is heard in the basses, and Elektra now appears again, accompanied by a vehement orchestral statement of Ex. 7, which had been heard at her earlier brief appearance, and represents her hatred of Klytemnestra and Aegisthus. In this second scene, a great monologue, beginning with the words '*Allein! Weh, ganz allein!*' (Alone, alas, completely alone) Elektra addresses the spirit of Agamemnon, and the Agamemnon motif continually recurs in her vocal line and in the orchestra as she evokes her dead father. She relives his murder, when he was dragged from his bath and repeatedly stabbed, and she imagines the day when the blood of his murderers will in turn flow, while she and her sister Chrysothemis perform a royal dance of victory. The dance is heard in the orchestra, but it is not yet performed by Elektra, merely envisaged and eagerly anticipated.

Ex.7

When Elektra entreats Agamemnon to reveal himself, with the words 'Father, leave me not this day alone! Show thyself to thy child as thou didst yesterday, like a shadow in the recess of the wall!', another principal theme of the opera is heard in the orchestra (Ex. 8), a phrase of lyrical yearning which represents the children of Agamemnon, and which will appear again to great emotive effect later in the opera. This great solo scene establishes Elektra as the principal agent of retribution. She remains on stage until the end of the opera, and the entire series of events is experienced, as it were, through her eyes.

Elektra's wild dream of triumph and revenge is dispelled at the sudden appearance of her sister Chrysothemis, who enters hurriedly to warn Elektra that their mother intends to imprison her in a dark tower. In this third scene, Elektra pours scorn on the fears of her younger and weaker sister, but Chrysothemis, who is being driven almost to madness by the horror of the lives she and her sister are forced to lead, and by Elektra's

Ex.8 Langsam

obsession with revenge, yearns for a normal life and for children, far from the palace which has become a prison to her. The music which Strauss has given Chrysothemis is in effective contrast with that of Elektra, lighter and more lyrical in expression. But it is a generalized expression: Strauss has not been able to give this less strong character the individuality with which he has so memorably characterized Elektra.

From within the palace there can now be heard the sound of a crowd approaching, and torch-bearers appear in the terrace, lighting the way for a procession. Chrysothemis is frightened, for she knows that the bustle and the shouting herald the appearance of Klytemnestra on her way to propitiate the gods by a ritual sacrifice of beasts. Their mother, Chryso-themis tells her sister, had dreamed that she was being pursued by Orestes, and had awakened screaming with fear. 'When she trembles, sister, then is she most terrible. Do not cross her path today', Chryso-themis advises Elektra, whose only reply is that today she especially desires to speak with her mother. Chrysothemis flees, aghast, as the orchestra paints a graphic and horrifying sound-picture of the approach of Klytemnestra, her slaves, the beasts to be slaughtered, and the priests with their sacrificial knives.

The fourth scene begins with the arrival of Klytemnestra's entourage: first the stumbling cattle, driven forward by the whips of the slaves, then the priestly slaughterers, and finally the Queen herself, with her Confidante and her Trainbearer. Hofmannsthal has described Klytem-nestra: 'Her sallow, bloated face appears, in the lurid glow of the torches, all the more pale above her scarlet robe. She is leaning on her Confidante, who is dressed in dark violet, and also on an ivory stick decked with jewels and talismans. Her arms are hung with bangles, and her fingers glisten with rings. Her eyelids appear unnaturally large, and it seems to cost her a fearful effort to keep them open.' She is a woman tortured by the furies that rage within her, her mind ravaged with guilt and terror.

Seeing Elektra, who stands proudly before her, Klytemnestra reproach-es the gods for having burdened her with this child whom she sees as a nettle which she has no longer the strength or vigour to tear out and cast away. 'Why blame the gods? Are you not yourself a goddess?' Elektra asks her mother. Although her attendant women try to point out that her daughter is speaking sarcastically, Klytemnestra chooses to accept Elektra's words at their face value. Thinking to have found her daughter in a more amiable temper than usual, she dismisses both her Confidante and her Trainbearer, who depart only with reluctance, and then approaches Elektra. In the hope that this strange and disaffected child of hers may know of a way to dispel her bodily and mental torments, Klytemnestra describes her sleepless nights, the horror of the nightmares which infest what little sleep she can find, the evil eyes which seem always to watch her, and she asks Elektra to tell her of a cure. Surely, she exclaims in desperation, there is no evil spirit that cannot be exorcized, if one knows what kind of victim to sacrifice to the gods.

There follows a dialogue in which Elektra's answers to her mother's questions sound reassuring to Klytemnestra, although they all too clearly bear a different meaning to the audience. Klytemnestra promises she will slay any living creature in order to dispel the spectres that torment her, to which Elektra replies that, once the appointed victim has suffered under the axe, Klytemnestra will dream no more. The desperate questions and the enigmatic replies continue to succeed one another. Elektra reveals that the sacrifice should be a human one, that the chosen victim is a woman, not a servant or a child or a maiden, but a wife, and that she will be sacrificed by someone who is both a stranger and a kinsman. Throughout this fraught dialogue, the orchestra's thematic references have ranged widely, with the motif of Elektra's dance of triumph never far away. Now Klytemnestra becomes impatient with Elektra's temporizing replies, and demands more forthright answers. But Elektra herself has a question, whose significance at first her mother does not grasp: When will Orestes return home?

The abrupt change of pace and of tactics on Elektra's part, which is highly effective dramatically, is brought about by Strauss having made a cut at this point in Hofmannsthal's text, which approaches the subject of Orestes more gradually. But now Klytemnestra tries to avoid speaking of her son whom she has been told has become weak-minded, who stammers, who lives among animals, being no longer capable of distinguishing between man and beast. She claims to have sent gold to those who have been looking after him, to ensure that he is treated as the son of a royal house. Elektra accuses her of having sent the gold to pay for the death of Orestes whose return Klytemnestra has always feared, at which the Queen boasts that she has confidence in the servants who guard her. She turns again to the question uppermost in her mind. Who is to be sacrificed, to propitiate the gods? If her daughter does not tell her immediately, she will be locked up and starved until she does. Whose blood must flow in order that Klytemnestra may sleep again? A sustained top G sharp conveys the Queen's desperation.

Elektra now drops her ironic pretence. Adopting a threatening stance, she echoes her mother's last words. Blood will indeed flow. It will flow from the throat of Klytemnestra when the avenger captures her. Elektra gleefully describes the slayer creeping through the corridors of the palace until he comes upon the sleeping Klytemnestra. she awakens in terror, and flees, screaming, but he pursues her, and Elektra too joins in the chase, until the Queen is cornered close to a shadow in the darkness. The shadow is Agamemnon, and at his feet Klytemnestra is struck down, but not before she has had time to experience the horror of knowing that her doom is certain, that she is at the mercy of her executioners and that there can be no escape. Finally, the axe falls. With its fall all of Klytemnestra's bad dreams will end, nor will there be any further need for Elektra to dream. All who live will rejoice, cries Elektra with a triumphant top C.

The light of madness in her eyes, Elektra stands defiantly before Klytemnestra who now is cowering in fear. But suddenly a light appears from within the palace, and the confidante rushes out to whisper something in Klytemnestra's ear. At first the Queen fails to comprehend what she is being told, but when she does her fear leaves her and she makes a gesture of menace and triumph at Elektra. Meanwhile, her serving-maids have rushed into the courtyard with torches to light the Queen's way. Joyfully, Klytemnestra makes her way back into the palace, with the aid of her Confidante and her staff. No words are spoken, but the orchestra makes it clear that the Queen's sudden high spirits are due to news she has been given of Orestes. Elektra remains standing, mystified.

The pivotal point of the opera has now been reached, and the fifth scene begins as Chrysothemis runs out from the palace with a cry of 'Orest ist tot!' (Orestes is dead), while the orchestra plays the motif of the children of Agamemnon (Ex. 8), but now in the minor. Two strangers, an old man and a younger one, have arrived at the palace bearing the news that Orestes has been killed in a chariot race, dragged to death by his own horses. As Chrysothemis reveals all this to Elektra, a young slave hurries through the courtyard calling for the swiftest horse that can be found, for he has orders to bring the glad tidings to Aegisthus. Elektra, who at first has refused to believe Chrysothemis, now realizes that, if Agamemnon's murder is to be avenged, it is they, Elektra and her sister, who must do it. She reveals to Chrysothemis that she has kept hidden the axe with which their father had been killed, in order that one day it might be turned upon his killers by Orestes. Now that he is dead, she and Chrysothemis must use the axe, that very night, while the Queen and her lover are asleep. Elektra has not the strength to manage the deed alone: she begs Chrysothemis to help her, but her sister draws back in horror. In vain, Elektra promises that henceforth she will be the slave of Chrysothemis, if only she will help her avenge their father. Chrysothemis is unable to summon up in herself the spirit of vengeance which motivates Elektra. With a cry of 'I cannot', she rushes back into the palace, followed by her sister's curse.

The sixth scene has now been reached. Realizing that she will have to act alone, Elektra goes to the wall of the palace and begins to dig, with her hands, for the axe which she has buried there. As she does so, a man enters the courtyard from outside, and stands watching her, the orchestra making it clear that he is the bearer of sad tidings. When Elektra brusquely asks him his business, he assumes that she is one of the serving maids, and tells her that he and another man have a message which they must deliver personally to the Queen. He informs Elektra, to the accompaniment of the woeful theme which had announced his appearance, that he had been the companion of Orestes, and had seen him die. The grief-stricken Elektra asks why he must tell this to her, rather than to those who would rejoice to hear it. She cannot bear to think that he is alive and talking while her beloved brother is dead, and silent for ever.

The stranger solemnly announces that it was surely proper that Orestes should die, for he had loved life too much, which angered the gods. Elektra's grief now threatens to overwhelm her, to the surprise of the stranger who asks who she can be, to mourn so deeply the members of the royal household. Is she, perhaps, related to them? She reveals her identity, to the amazement of the stranger as he gazes on her wild, crazed condition. Softly, he whispers to her that Orestes is alive. In that case, she replies, save him before he is murdered. 'By the body of my father', the stranger announces, 'that is why I have come here.' The orchestra is by now making it clear that this is indeed Orestes, but Elektra asks, 'Who then are you?' Before he can answer, an old servant, closely followed by three others, enters the courtyard and, recognizing their master, all four of them fall on their knees before him, kissing his hands, his feet, and the hem of his garment. As the deeply moving recognition theme is heard in the orchestra the stranger answers, 'The very dogs in the courtyard know me, but not my sister.' The moment is a deeply affecting one, and Strauss makes the most of it, screwing the emotional tension to its heights and then slowly and gradually relaxing it. 'Orest', cries Elektra, on a rising fourth, all her madness and savagery drained from her in a great access of love for her brother. In a beautiful extended solo passage, she tells Orestes of her sufferings and of her determination that their father's death shall be avenged. Orestes promises that he will indeed avenge Agamemnon's death, and his sister blesses him for having brought her such relief. Roused to a state of frenzied joy, she sings a wild paean of praise to Orestes, and to all who aid him in his task. Suddenly, Orestes' Tutor appears in the doorway to the courtyard, to remind them that silence and cunning are necessary, if they are to be successful.

The seventh and final section of the opera now begins, as a servant with a torch appears, lighting the way for Klytemnestra's Confidante who gestures to the two strangers to follow her into the palace. When Orestes and his Tutor have gone, Elektra rushes to and fro like an excited animal, lamenting that she had forgotten to give her brother the axe of revenge. From within, however, she hears Klytemnestra shriek. 'Strike her again,' cries Elektra, and the cry is heard a second time, accompanied now in the orchestra by Agamemnon's theme as though to assure the dead king that he has been avenged.

Chrysothemis and a number of maids and attendants run into the courtyard, roused by the noises coming from the palace, but Elektra prevents them from going inside. They scatter as Aegisthus now returns from his hunt, strolling confidently towards the entrance to the palace and calling for attendants to light his way. He is disconcerted to be confronted by Elektra who, waving a torch, derisively offers to provide him with light. When he asks her where the strangers are, who had come with the news of the death of Orestes, Elektra replies that they are within, where they have found a friendly welcome. Aegisthus hurries into the palace, and the doors close behind him. After a few moments of anxious silence, he appears at the windows, struggling and calling for help. 'Does no one hear me?' he cries, as he is dragged away. 'Agamemnon hears you', Elektra shouts as she stands before the great doors, her excitement bordering on madness.

The cry now goes up that Orestes has slain Aegisthus and Klytemnestra. Chrysothemis and the attendants rush into the courtyard, calling that those faithful to the memory of Agamemnon are fighting to the death with the soldiers of Aegisthus. The others run off again, leaving the sisters alone. Elektra exclaims that her great hour has come and that she must lead the dance of triumph. Chrysothemis, in growing excitement, sings of the new life which is returning to the land. When Chrysothemis runs into the palace to embrace a now victorious Orestes, Elektra, whose mind has finally snapped under the strain of her emotions, breaks into a wild dance. Chrysothemis returns, surrounded by a crowd of retainers, and calls her sister by name, but Elektra bids everyone be silent and join her in the dance. As the others watch in horror, she takes a few more ungainly steps, and then collapses, lifeless, as Chrysothemis runs to the door of the palace, beating upon it, and calling for Orestes. The orchestra thunders out the name of Agamemnon for the last time, and the curtain falls.

By comparison with the colourful, glittering savagery of *Salome*, *Elektra* is both more violent and, somehow, more single-minded in its relentless thrust. Its score can still sound absolutely shattering, and its dissonant harmonies must have seemed unutterably barbaric to the ears of its early audiences. Written for so huge an orchestra, and with such complexity of thematic cross-referencing, it batters at one's senses with a vehemence which, one imagines, must be not unlike that with which the classical Greek drama assaulted its audiences. *Elektra* is one of the most remarkable operas of the twentieth century, and Strauss's most Wagnerian in its ability to communicate on more than one level of consciousness.

FIVE

Der Rosenkavalier

Comedy for Music in Three Acts
opus 59

Dramatis personae
The Princess of Werdenberg (The Marschallin)   (soprano)
Baron Ochs of Lerchenau   (bass)
Octavian (called Quinquin), a Young Gentleman
                                    of Noble Family   (mezzo-soprano)
Herr von Faninal, a Rich Man, newly ennobled   (baritone)
Sophie, his Daughter   (soprano)
Mistress Marianne Leitmetzerin, her Duenna   (soprano)
Valzacchi, an Intriguer   (tenor)
Annina, his Partner   (contralto)
A Police Inspector   (bass)
The Marschallin's Major-Domo   (tenor)
Faninal's Major-Domo   (tenor)
A Notary   (bass)
An Innkeeper   (tenor)
A Singer   (tenor)
Three Orphans of Noble Family
                    (soprano, mezzo-soprano and contralto)
A Milliner   (soprano)
A Vendor of Animals   (tenor)
Four Servants of the Marschallin   (two tenors, two basses)
Four Waiters   (one tenor, three basses)

LIBRETTO by Hugo von Hofmannsthal

TIME: The first years of Maria Theresa's reign (i.e. mid-eighteenth century)

PLACE: Vienna.

FIRST PERFORMED at the Königliches Opernhaus, Dresden, 26 January 1911, with Margarethe Siems (The Marschallin), Minnie Nast (Sophie), Eva von der Osten (Octavian), Karl Perron (Baron Ochs) and Karl Scheidemantel (Faninal), conducted by Ernst von Schuch.

I

AFTER the horrors of *Salome* and *Elektra*, Strauss wanted his next opera to be an elegant eighteenth-century comedy, something in the manner of Mozart, as he suggested to Hofmannsthal. Less than three weeks after the January 1909 première of *Elektra*, Hofmannsthal wrote from Weimar,, where he had been visiting his friend Count Harry Kessler, diplomat and journalist, to tell Strauss that he had spent three quiet afternoons drafting the scenario for an opera, 'full of burlesque situations and characters, with lively action, pellucid almost like a pantomime.' The opera would contain two big roles, one for baritone and the other 'for a graceful girl dressed up as a man, à la [Geraldine] Farrar or Mary Garden. Period: the old Vienna under the Empress Maria Theresa.' The libretto would be very concise, and the opera would probably last no longer than two and a half hours or, as Hofmannsthal put it, 'half the length of *Die Meistersinger*'.

Though *Der Rosenkavalier* (The Rose Cavalier), as the opera came to be called, turned out to be considerably longer than two and a half hours, due mainly to Strauss's reluctance to be concise, but also, to some extent, to Hofmannsthal's own tendency towards prolixity, neither composer nor librettist ever completely lost sight of what they had envisaged it to be at the outset, a light, Mozartian comedy of manners, perhaps in the style of *Le nozze di Figaro* or *Così fan tutte*. Hofmannsthal began to write his libretto in the spring of 1909, and Strauss professed himself to be delighted with the opening scene which he said would set itself to music 'like oil and melted butter'. 'You're da Ponte and Scribe rolled into one', he told his librettist.

Hofmannsthal was a difficult man to compliment. 'It seems to me', he replied, 'that Scribe as well as da Ponte worked perhaps within a somewhat simpler convention.' He warned Strauss that not all of the libretto would be as easy to set to music as this first, purely lyrical scene. 'There are bound to be sticky patches', he prophesied, ending his letter by asking the composer to 'try and think of an old-fashioned Viennese waltz, sweet and yet saucy, which must pervade the whole of the last act.' Strauss, when he had received the remainder of Act I, expressed his fear that, though it was charming and delicate, it might be 'a little too delicate for the mob', but his collaborator hastened to allay the composer's anxiety, and also to lecture him a little 'Your apprehension lest the libretto be too "delicate" does not make me nervous', he wrote:

Even the least sophisticated audience cannot help finding the action simple and intelligible: a pompous, fat, and elderly suitor favoured by the father has his nose put out of joint by a dashing young lover—could anything be plainer? The working out of this plot must be, I feel, as I have done it; that is, free from anything trivial and conventional. True and lasting success depends upon the effect on the more sensitive no less than on the coarser sections of the public, for the former are needed to give a work of art its prestige which is just as essential as its popular appeal.

For the second act, Strauss asked for 'a contemplative ensemble passage, to follow the moment when some dramatic bomb has just gone off, when the action is suspended and everybody is lost in contemplation.' Such moments of repose, he realized, were most important, and he offered Hofmannsthal some examples of the kind of thing he had in mind, among them the Quintet in Wagner's *Die Meistersinger von Nürnberg* and the beginning of the ensemble at the end of Act I of Rossini's *Il barbiere di Siviglia*. If Hofmannsthal did not provide him with quite this kind of opportunity in Act II, he certainly did in Act III, and Strauss responded marvellously with the great Trio for the three female voices.

It was Act II which gave the most trouble. Strauss's theatrical instincts being at least the equal of those of his more literary colleague, he wrote a long letter, criticizing the librettist's initial draft of the second act, and setting out in detail his suggestions for improving its shape and its dramatic thrust. Hofmannsthal accepted this in good humour, and slowly the second act was moulded into its final form, although, when Strauss asked for a more impassioned duet for Octavian and Sophie than the librettist had given him, Hofmannsthal replied that what he wanted at all costs to avoid was 'to see these two young creatures, who have nothing of the Valkyries or Tristan about them, bursting into a Wagnerian kind of erotic screaming.'

Hofmannsthal had more than one way of using Wagner as a stick with which to beat his composer. Gently ridiculed when he imitated Wagner, Strauss was also castigated by his collaborator for failing to emulate his great predecessor. 'One more thing, if you will allow me to speak quite frankly', Hofmannsthal wrote to Strauss in June,

a detail in the aria of Ochs distressed me profoundly when I heard it. The line '*Muss halt eine Frau in der Nähe dabei sein*' can never conceivably be acted or sung in any but a sentimental manner. Ochs must whisper it to the Marschallin as a stupid yet sly piece of coarse familiarity, with his hand half covering his mouth; he must whisper, not bawl it, for God's sake! . . . Wagner differentiates such things in declamation with marvellous nicety.

One of the most delightful scenes in Act II, that of the disgruntled Ochs licking his wounds after the skirmish with Octavian, was suggested to the

composer by his recollection of Verdi's *Falstaff* in which, as Strauss wrote
to Hofmannsthal, 'there is an amusing monologue at the beginning of the
last act; it starts with the words "Mondo ladro". I picture the scene of the
Baron, after Faninal's exit, similarly: the Baron on the sofa, the surgeon
attending to him, the mute servants lined up behind the couch, and the
Baron talking in snatches, partly to himself and partly to the others, in
turn boastful and sorry for himself, always interrupted by orchestral
interludes . . .'

Work on *Der Rosenkavalier* continued throughout 1909 and into 1910.
It was not until the end of September 1910, that Strauss finally completed
his score. The first performance of the opera in Dresden on 26 January
1911 was hugely successful, an outcome which had been confidently
anticipated, for several other German opera houses had already begun to
rehearse the opera. The first performance of *Der Rosenkavalier* in Nurem-
berg took place the day after the Dresden première, a few days later the
opera was staged in Munich, and in the following weeks it was produced in
Hamburg (where a new young soprano, Lotte Lehmann, who was to
become the greatest of Marschallins, understudied the role of Sophie),
Vienna, Berlin and Milan. *Der Rosenkavalier* remains to this day Strauss's
most popular opera.

II

IN 1942, Strauss recollected the first performances of *Der Rosenkavalier*
thus:

> . . . When, in Dresden, I listened to the first stage rehearsal with
> orchestra, I realized during the second act that the producer of the old
> school [Georg Toller] who was in charge was completely incapable of pro-
> ducing the opera. Alfred Roller's stage designs were excellent and have
> remained exemplary to this day. All honour to his memory! Remember-
> ing a kind offer made by Max Reinhardt, I asked Generalintendant
> Count Seebach whether I could invite Reinhardt to come and help us.
> Seebach reluctantly permitted this on the condition that Reinhardt
> would not set foot on the stage. Reinhardt came without making
> demands and, Jew and art enthusiast that he was, even accepted the
> above condition, and thus we all met on the rehearsal stage, Reinhardt
> as a modest spectator, whilst I in my clumsy way showed the singers as
> best I could how to play their parts. After a while, Reinhardt could be
> observed whispering to Frau von der Osten [Octavian] in a corner of
> the hall, and then again with Fraulein Siems [the Marschallin], Perron
> [Baron Ochs] etc.

The next day they came to the rehearsal transformed into fully-fledged actors. Thereupon Seebach graciously permitted Reinhardt to direct operations on the stage instead of watching the rehearsal from the stalls. The result was a new style in opera and a perfect performance in which the trio in particular (Siems, von der Osten, Nast) delighted everybody.

The evening was somewhat long drawn out, since, in my enthusiasm, I had composed the whole of the rather talkative text without alteration, although even the author had expected me to make cuts. Cuts were Schuch's [the conductor's] speciality; he never, I believe, conducted an opera without cuts, and was particularly proud when he could leave out a whole act of a modern opera. Immediately after my departure he proceeded to make the most dreadful cuts in *Der Rosenkavalier*, which were immediately copied by the thoughtless directors of other theatres; I had to fight for years against this stupidity. It is not true that a well-composed and dramatically carefully arranged opera is made shorter by cuts. For example, a year later, Seebach's friend, Baroness Knorring, came to Berlin and saw 'my' *Rosenkavalier*. Afterwards she told me the opera had seemed to her shorter than in Dresden. I replied: 'Yes, because there were fewer cuts in it.' The proportions were better, and light and shade were better distributed.

After I had borne my annoyance at Schuch's ineradicable cuts for some time, I wrote to him saying that he had forgotten one important cut; the trio in the third act only impeded the action, and I suggested the following cut: D major: '*Ich weiss auch nix, gar nix*' to G major: beginning of the last duet. This offended him, but at last he was cured to some extent of the Dresden disease. Schuch's predecessor once came to Draeseke and said: 'I hear you have completed a new opera.' Draeseke replied: 'Well, the opera itself is finished, only the cuts have still to be composed . . .'

Two important hints to the performers: Just as Klytemnestra should not be an old hag, but a beautiful proud woman of fifty, whose ruin is purely spiritual and by no means physical, the Marschallin must be a young and beautiful woman of thirty-two at the most who, in a bad mood, thinks herself 'an old woman' as compared with the seventeen-year-old Octavian, but who is not by any means David's Magdalene, who, by the way, is also frequently presented as too old. Octavian is neither the first nor the last lover of the beautiful Marschallin, nor must the latter play the end of the first act sentimentally as a tragic farewell to life, but with Viennese grace and lightness, half weeping, half smiling. The conductor should not slow down too much, starting with the F major 2/4. The figure which has so far been most misunderstood is that of Ochs. Most basses have presented him as a disgusting vulgar monster with a repellent mask and proletarian manners, and this has rightly shocked civilized audiences (the French and Italians). This is quite wrong: Ochs must be a rustic beau of thirty-five, who is after all a member of the gentry, if somewhat countrified, and who is capable of behaving properly in the salon of the Marschallin without running the risk of being thrown out by her servants after five minutes. He is at heart a cad, but outwardly still so presentable that Faninal does not refuse him at first sight. Especially Ochs's first scene in the bedroom must be played with the utmost delicacy and discretion if it is not to be as disgusting as the love affair of a general's elderly wife with a cadet. In other words, Viennese comedy, not Berlin farce.

III

DER Rosenkavalier was to prove the most popular by far of the works on which Strauss and Hofmannsthal collaborated, and it has come to be regarded as the most Viennese of operas, although only its librettist was Viennese: its composer was thoroughly German despite the prevalence of waltzes in this, the first of his two operas to be set entirely in Vienna. Actually, *Der Rosenkavalier* combines Viennese melancholy and light irony with German earnestness and heavy-handed humour. A comparison of the Austrian and the Prussian characters which Hofmannsthal once drew up is instructive, for, although Strauss was not Prussian but Bavarian, Hofmannsthal's two columns do give a general indication of the differences in personality between composer and librettist.

The Prussian	The Austrian
Modern in his views (cosmopolitan around 1800, liberal around 1848, now Bismarckian, almost lacking a memory for past phases).	Traditional in his views, stable almost for centuries.
Lacks a sense of history.	Possesses an instinct for history.
Strong on abstraction.	Little talent for abstraction.
Incomparable in orderly execution.	More mercurial.
Acts according to instructions.	Acts according to a sense of fitness.
Strong on dialectic.	Rejects dialectic.
More skill in expression.	More balance.
More consequential.	More ability to adapt to conditions.
Self-reliance.	Self-irony.
Seemingly masculine.	Seemingly immature.
Makes everything functional.	Gives a social twist to everything.

Asserts and justifies himself.	Prefers to keep matters vague.
Self-righteous, arrogant, hectoring.	Shamefaced, vain, witty.
Forces crises.	Avoids crises.
Fights for his rights.	Lets things go.
Incapable of entering into other people's thoughts.	Enters into other people's thoughts to the point of losing his character.
Willed character.	Playacting.
Every individual bears a part of authority.	Every individual bears a part of all humanity.
Pushing.	Pleasure-seeking.
Preponderance of the occupational.	Preponderance of the private.
Extreme exaggeration.	Irony to the point of self-destruction.

Unlike Strauss, Hofmannsthal was quick to take offence. On one occasion, having discovered that Strauss had played to a friend some music which he had not offered to play to his collaborator, Hofmannsthal wrote to the composer, airing his grievance. 'You are a real Viennese', Strauss replied. 'Instead of saying simply, "Dear Doctor, please play me something from *Joseph*", you wait for a propitious turn in the conversation. When that doesn't happen to arrive, you write me a letter later. Serves you right.'

That Strauss and Hofmannsthal met only very infrequently was due largely to the librettist's fastidiousness. Though he admired Strauss as a composer, Hofmannsthal considered himself his colleague's superior both socially and intellectually, and in addition could not stand the impossible Pauline Strauss for whose behaviour Strauss found himself apologizing to Hofmannsthal more than once. The unfortunate Strauss was looked down upon by his wife as well as by his librettist. As the years went by, Pauline (who thought nothing of interrupting Strauss while he was composing *Elektra*, to send him to the village to buy milk) became ever more shrewish and more convinced of the necessity continually to remind others of her superior breeding. As he had indicated, Strauss seems to have acquiesced in being dominated by her, and perhaps actively enjoyed his role in the marital comedy.

The fact that their operas were brought into being with Strauss composing methodically in Bavaria while Hofmannsthal wrote moodily and fitfully in Austria led to the collaborators' working methods and their personal relationship being well documented in correspondence. The letters of both composer and librettist are fascinating and revealing, especially of the dramatic as distinct from the musical aspects of the operas. This is specially true in the case of *Der Rosenkavalier*.

IV

HOFMANNSTHAL'S first rough synopsis differs somewhat from the plot of *Der Rosenkavalier* as we know it. The notes which he made in collaboration with Count Harry Kessler while he was staying with Kessler in Weimar read as follows:

1. The house of Geronte. Geronte awaits arrival of son-in-law from good country nobility. Sophie with the pretty Faublas talks of her forthcoming marriage. She is astonished that it angers him. Arrival of Pourceaugnac and elderly aunts, animals, and marvellous luggage (marriage bed). He sends for the Intriguers. Marquise. Rendezvous at night with Faublas, at which Faublas is delighted but with reservations. Sophie begs for rescue. The Intriguers.

2. Bedroom of the Marquise. A night of love. Morning. Gratitude. Pourceaugnac announced. Faublas remains disguised in women's clothes. Faublas so similar: yes, all natural children of the noble lady. Hairdresser, servants, etc., importuning Pourceaugnac. They depart. While the Marquise is having her hair dressed, Pourceaugnac invites the chamber-maid to supper. Pourceaugnac parsimonious (detailed discussion where supper is to be). Pourceaugnac departs. Intriguer comes and tells how it should be done.

3. Room at the tavern. The charade is rehearsed. Faublas's boots under his frock. The supper. Arrest. Geronte compromised in front of courtiers. The Marquise appears. Geronte wants to enter bridal chamber. The disguised Faublas reveals himself. The Marquise confirms he is a man.

The names of the characters and some elements of the plot derive from three French plays: *Monsieur de Pourceaugnac* and *Les Fourberies de Scapin* by Molière, and *Les Amours du Chevalier de Faublas* by Louvet de Couvray, a contemporary of Beaumarchais. In due course Hofmannsthal moved the locale to Vienna, and changed the names of the characters as well as the disposition of the scenes. Geronte became Faninal, Pourceaugnac by a process of metamorphosis turned into Baron Ochs auf Lerchenau, and 'the pretty Faublas' was renamed Octavian. The plot was finally shaped jointly by Strauss and Hofmannsthal, and named *Ochs auf Lerchenau*. Three weeks later it had become *Der Rosenkavalier*.

V

THE action of *Der Rosenkavalier* takes place in Vienna in the middle of the eighteenth century or, as Strauss and Hofmannsthal describe it, 'in the early years of the reign of Maria Theresa'. Act I is set in the bedroom of the Princess von Werdenberg, referred to as the Marschallin (or wife of the Marshal, her husband being a *Feldmarschall* or Field Marshal). It is morning, and the curtain rises on a large and elegant bed-chamber containing, amongst other furniture, a huge four-poster bed, the curtains of which are half-drawn. On the bed, concealed except for her arm which protrudes from the curtains, lies the Marschallin, and kneeling on a footstool by the side of the bed is the seventeen-year-old Octavian, half embracing the Marschallin. Before the curtain has risen, however, the orchestra has played an impassioned Prelude (or Introduction, to use Strauss's term) clearly intended to represent the love-making of the previous night. Beginning with the motifs of the lovers, a rising, masculine phrase on the horns for Octavian and a gentler, feminine, falling phrase for the Marschallin, the Introduction portrays Octavian's raging passion. When he reaches his climax, the exultant horns most graphically depict the young man's orgasm, after which the Introduction subsides into a detumescent, sad and wistful mood. That the middle-aged Strauss took a slightly jaded view of such youthful ardour is suggested by his direction that the passages leading to the climax be played with strongly parodied expression.

When the curtain rises, the lovers are indulging in affectionate post-coital conversation. Marie Therese, the Marschallin (soprano), is a beautiful woman in her thirties, while her handsome teenage lover, Count Octavian Maria Ehrenreich Bonaventura Fernand Hyacinth Rofrano (he reveals all these given names in Act II) is, we are to assume, one of a succession of lovers she has taken to amuse herself during the frequent absences of her husband. It is odd that Strauss should have decided to write the role of the virile young Octavian for a female mezzo-soprano voice *à la* Cherubino, though presumably he wanted to stress the Mozartian parallel. Anyone unacquainted with the opera might easily mistake the situation at the rise of the curtain, and think he was witnessing a lesbian relationship. This adds a certain irrelevant picquancy to the flavour of the scene, but it is difficult not to feel that Strauss ought perhaps to have risen above his lack of interest in the tenor voice, and written the role of Octavian for a youthful lyric tenor.

The dialogue between the Marschallin and Octavian is interrupted by the arrival of the Marschallin's little negro servant with her breakfast chocolate. At his approach, Octavian is made to hide behind a screen. The Marschallin has to remind him to take his sword with him, and after the negro servant has left she rebukes Octavian for being so careless as to leave a tell-tale sword in a lady's bedroom. Octavian is young enough to sulk a little at this, but soon he and the Marschallin are exchanging tender phrases. When Octavian boasts of his good fortune in spending a night with her while her husband is away hunting in the Croatian woods, the Marschallin asks him not to mention her husband for she had dreamed of him during the night. That she should have dreamed of the Feldmarschall while she was in bed with him is another affront to Octavian's *amour propre*, but while the Marschallin is describing her dream a commotion is heard in the ante-chamber, heralding the arrival of someone. Thinking her husband has returned unexpectedly, the Marschallin quickly directs Octavian to hide in an alcove behind the bed, while she herself continues to listen anxiously to the noises in the next room.

When she realizes that the male voice she can hear imperiously demanding admission to her boudoir is not that of her husband, the Marschallin's relieved exclamation, '*Quinquin* [her pet name for Octavian] *es ist ein Besuch*' ('It's someone visiting'), introduces a light-hearted waltz tune in the orchestra. The visitor is a relative of the Marschallin, the countrified, rough-mannered Baron Ochs auf Lerchenau who now forces his way past the servants outside the Marschallin's door, and enters her bedroom. By this time, Octavian has reappeared. Dressed in a chamber-maid's frock and cap, he makes a mock curtesy to the Marschallin and addresses her in a country girl's accent. Before the Marschallin can insist he change back into his own clothes, Ochs has entered. He collides with Octavian, and is obviously attracted by, as he thinks, the new maid. Indeed, he is so busy flirting with her, that it is only with difficulty that the Marschallin manages to extract from him the reason for his visit. He had written to her about it, but the Marschallin had been so occupied with Octavian that she had paid no attention to his letter. It transpires that Ochs is planning to marry Sophie, the daughter of a wealthy and recently ennobled supplier to the army, Herr von Faninal, and wishes the Marschallin to nominate for him the Knight of the Rose (*Rosenkavalier*) who will carry the silver rose, the traditional symbol of their betrothal, to the young lady.

Until now, although there have been no extended melodic passages, the dialogue of the Marschallin and Octavian has been carried on in a lyrical parlando style, a kind of arioso. The Baron introduces a rougher note, and Strauss's huge orchestra which has been making delightful sounds in support of the lovers now has to adopt a harsher manner, especially when accompanying the Baron's more outspoken comments.

Agreeing to choose one of their cousins as a Knight of the Rose, the Marschallin attempts to get rid of Ochs, but he also wishes to consult her notary regarding the marriage settlement, so she reluctantly allows him to stay, since her morning levee, which the notary will attend, is about to begin. While awaiting the appearance of the notary, Ochs continues shamelessly to flirt with the maid, Mariandel (Octavian in disguise), who recklessly leads him on. Lightly rebuked by the Marschallin, Ochs unabashedly embarks upon a lengthy recital of his country pleasures, which are predominantly sexuฺ¹ his lewd reminiscences punctuated by occasional comments from the Marschallin who seems not to take offence at either the style or the content of her country cousin's utterance. The final section of Ochs's monologue turns into a trio with the Marschallin and Octavian.

Ochs attempts to persuade the Marschallin to part with Mariandel, whom he would like to take into his service as a maid for his bride-to-be. The Marschallin will have none of this, but Ochs's request gives her an idea. She sends 'Mariandel' to fetch a locket-portrait of her young cousin, Count Octavian Rofrano, whom she recommends as Knight of the Rose. Ochs is astonished at the likeness between the young nobleman of the portrait and the maid, Mariandel, and the Marschallin allows him to believe that Mariandel is an illegitimate child of Octavian's father. Ochs gladly accepts Octavian as bearer of the silver rose, 'Mariandel' makes her escape from the room, and the Marschallin's levee begins as the curious assemblage of people who had been waiting in the ante-chamber now crowds into the boudoir.

The scene of the levee allows Strauss to compose one of his large and complex ensembles. In addition to the notary, the characters include the chef and a boy carrying the menu of the day, a milliner, a scholar carrying a folio, an animal-dealer with dogs and a small monkey for sale, the Marschallin's hairdresser, a distressed widow with her three children, an Italian tenor accompanied by a flautist, and finally two Italian intriguers, Valzacchi and Annina. All try to interest the Marschallin in their immediate concerns, the intriguers attempting to sell her a scandal-sheet which she rejects, while Ochs begins to discuss his marriage arrangements with the notary, a discussion in the course of which he loses his temper and bangs the table, interrupting the second verse of the Italian tenor's aria, a charming eighteenth-century pastiche, 'Di rigori armato il seno'. Eventually, the Marschallin instructs her major-domo to clear the room, and everyone leaves, even Ochs and his ragged retinue of servants, though not before the Baron has asked the Italians to help him to procure an assignation with Mariandel. At the Marschallin's request, Ochs leaves with her the casket containing the silver rose which it is agreed Octavian will present to Sophie von Faninal.

Left alone, the Marschallin embarks upon a monologue in which the distasteful thought of the boorish Ochs marrying a young virgin leads her to muse on her own life, and the sad miracle by which the young girl she used to be has been transformed by time into a mature woman, and will, in due course, become '*die alte Frau, die alte Marschallin*' (the old woman, the old Marschallin). Composed in Strauss's conversational, quasi-arioso style of melodic recitative, this contemplative aria is both moving and memorable. At its conclusion, Octavian re-enters, having changed into morning clothes and riding boots. A kind of love duet ensues, one in which the Marschallin's mood becomes increasingly autumnal, to the confusion of her young lover who, in his immaturity, interprets her words as meaning that she no longer loves him. In another quasi-aria, '*Die Zeit, die ist ein sonderbar' Ding*' (Time is a strange thing), the Marschallin muses on the transience of all things and the relentless passage of time. Sometimes, she says, she awakens in the middle of the night, and stops all the clocks. Yet one must not fear time, for it is a creation of God. This is one of Strauss's most beautiful arias, and in context extremely moving.

Octavian is almost reduced to tears when the Marschallin tells him that, one day, he will leave her for someone younger or more beautiful than she—she is vain enough, or human enough, to hesitate slightly before '*schöner*' (more beautiful)—and Octavian protests that neither today nor tomorrow could he ever think of leaving her. In a memorable phrase (Ex. 3) which will recur in the third act, the Marschallin insists that she is not mistaken: '*Heut' oder morgen oder den übernächsten Tag*' (Today or tomorrow or the day after that). She explains (and here librettist and composer are completely in harmony, the words and music inseparable from each other) that one must take life lightly, and not cling to what must be released:

> *Leicht will ich's machen dir und mir.*
> *Leicht muss man sein,*
> *mit leichtem Herz und leichten Händen,*
> *halten und nehmen, halten und lassen.*
> *Die nicht so sind, die straft das Leben, und*
> *Gott—und Gott erbarmt sich ihrer nicht.*

(I want to make it light between you and me. One must be light, light of heart and light of hand, holding and taking, holding and letting go. Those who are not so are punished by life, and God—and God shows them no mercy.)

The Marschallin now tells Octavian that he must leave her, for she is about to go to church, and then she will visit her Uncle Greifenklau who is old and crippled. If she decides to drive in the Prater in the afternoon, she will send a message, and Octavian may come and ride by the side of her carriage. Octavian leaves swiftly, still upset, and as soon as he has gone the Marschallin realizes she has not kissed him goodbye. She rings for her servants, and sends four footmen after him, but they return to report that the young Count had ridden off too quickly for them. Dismissing them, the Marschallin calls for her little negro page, and gives him the casket to deliver to Octavian. 'Tell the Count that inside is the silver rose', she instructs her page, lingering on the high G of 'Rose' as though unwilling to let the rose, and by implication Octavian, slip from her grasp. The page runs off and, as she sits alone, the Marschallin rests her head in her hands. The closing bars in the orchestra most poignantly convey her mood of bitter-sweet introspection.

It is difficult for the singer portraying the Marschallin to play this scene 'without the slightest trace of sentimentality', as Strauss many years later suggested, for the mood and the music are sentimental, though not cloyingly so. The conclusion of this act, if played and sung with the right feeling, can be one of the most affecting scenes in opera.

Act II takes place in the grand salon of Herr von Faninal's lavishly decorated town house where excited preparations are in hand to receive Sophie's future bridegroom, Baron Ochs, who will be preceded by his rose-bearer, Octavian. A short and bustling orchestral prelude leads into the opening scene in which Faninal (baritone) is preparing to leave the house to meet and escort Ochs back to it, while his daughter, Sophie (soprano), accompanied by her duenna or chaperone, Marianne Leitmetzerin (soprano), eagerly awaits the arrival of her suitor's Knight of the Rose. Faninal's Major-Domo (tenor) at last manages to get his master out of the house, and Sophie tries to prepare herself for the solemnity of the occasion while Marianne, who is peering out of the window to observe Faninal's departure, keeps chattering away about the splendour of the family's coach and horses, taking delight in the fact that all of their neighbours in the street are witnessing the scene. As Faninal drives off, Octavian arrives. Marianne describes the two coaches, the first of which, drawn by four horses, is empty, while in the second, drawn by six horses, sits the handsome *Rosenkavalier* himself. The voices of footmen running in the street in front of Octavian's carriage, calling 'Rofrano, Rofrano' are heard, as Marianne, still at the window, informs Sophie of Octavian's progress into the house. The excitement on stage and in the orchestra grows to a climax: on a clash of cymbals and a triumphant F sharp chord the double doors are flung open and Octavian enters, an elegantly glittering figure in white and silver, holding the silver rose and followed by an impressive retinue. His entrance is described thus in the score: 'Behind [Octavian] his servants in his colours, white and pale green. The Footmen, the Heyducks with their crooked Hungarian swords at their side; the

Couriers in white leather with green ostrich plumes. Immediately behind Octavian a black servant, carrying his hat, and another Footman who carries the casket of the silver rose in both hands. Behind these, Faninal's servants. Octavian, taking the rose in his right hand, advances with high-born grace towards Sophie; but his youthful features bear traces of embarrassment and he blushes. Sophie turns pale with excitement at his splendid appearance. They stand opposite each other, each disconcerted by the confusion and beauty of the other.'

The presentation of the silver rose, one of the most enchanting scenes in the whole of Strauss, is a duet for the two sopranos, a love duet although neither character as yet recognizes the fact. They begin, on Octavian's part formally, and on Sophie's hesitantly, as he asks her to accept the rose, on behalf of his kinsman Baron Ochs, as a token of his love for her. Then, in an ecstatically soaring phrase (Ex. 9) as Sophie smells the artificial scent of the rose (*'Wie himmlische, nicht irdische'*; How heavenly, not earthly), the duet proper begins. The two youngsters sing of the bliss of the moment they are sharing. It is the dawning of their love, though at the conclusion of the duet they lapse again into formal and embarrassed conversation, seated facing each other on two chairs, with Sophie's chaperone between them. The ingenuous girl tells Octavian she has looked him up in the *Ehrenspiegel Österreichs* (the Austrian Debrett), and knows he is seventeen years and two months old. (She, incidentally, is barely fifteen.) She proceeds to rattle off Octavian's long list of Christian names, and confesses that she is aware, too, of the pet name, 'Quinquin', by which he is known to beautiful women. She tells him that she is looking forward to being married (she has, of course, not yet seen her future bridegroom, for her marriage into the nobility has been arranged by her father), but Octavian hardly hears her words, so confused is he by her beauty.

Ex.9

Wie himm – – – lische, nicht ir-di-sche

Their *tête-à-tête* is suddenly interrupted by the arrival of Faninal with Baron Ochs and the Baron's disreputable-looking servants. Sophie is understandably dismayed at her first sight of Ochs, and his boorish, over-bearing condescension and coarse behaviour lead her to remark to Marianne that he has the manners of a horse-dealer. ('And, my God, he's pockmarked as well', she adds in consternation.) Meanwhile, Ochs has been treating Faninal *de haut en bas*, and giving Octavian advice on how to address the middle classes. When Ochs pulls Sophie on to his knee and attempts to begin a decidely *risqué* conversation with her, the poor girl can no longer conceal her fury. Faninal at first appears not to notice that anything is amiss, so delighted is he at this imminent further step up the social ladder for his family, while Marianne continues to make excuses to Sophie for Ochs's behaviour, and to tell her what a fortunate girl she is to be marrying so splendid a nobleman.

To Sophie's outraged outburst, 'No man has ever spoken to me like this. What can you think of me, and of yourself? What are you to me?', Ochs replies leeringly that overnight she will discover what he is, to quote his favourite song. And he begins to hum the song, a delightful waltz which, ironically, has become Strauss's best-known waltz tune (Ex. 10): ironically, because there can be no doubt that Strauss plagiarized Josef Strauss's quite well-known waltz, *Dynamiden* op. 73. Richard Strauss never acknowledged his debt to the earlier Strauss, brother of Johann, though presumably his excuse for having lifted the tune of Ochs's waltz from the Viennese composer's *Dynamiden* would have been that his intention was to parody the idea of the Viennese waltz rather than to write an example of it.

Ex.10

Ochs now retires with Faninal and a Notary to an adjacent room to attend to the drawing-up of the marriage contract, leaving Sophie with Octavian whom Ochs invites to flirt with her in order to make her more pliable for him. As soon as Ochs has left, Octavian asks Sophie if she really intends to marry such a creature. Upon receiving her heart-felt reply, 'Not for all the world', he attempts to express his feelings for her, despite being somewhat inhibited by the presence of Marianne Leitmetzerin. The chaperone, however, is called away to deal with a commotion caused by Ochs's servants who have been drinking Faninal's brandy and are now chasing his housemaids all over the house. Left alone together, Sophie and Octavian are free to indulge in a real love duet. This begins as an urgent discussion of the immediate situation, but soon gives way to a more lyrical tone of voice. Strauss directs that this latter section of the duet be sung tenderly, with careful observation of the expression marks, especially the *p* and *pp*. The composer is anxious at this point to avoid a note of passion: it is Octavian's tender protective feeling for the inexperienced girl that he wishes to convey, as the greatest possible contrast to the coarse insensitivity of Ochs.

As the duet nears its climax, the Italian intriguers, Valzacchi and Annina, appear, and gradually creep closer to the young couple who are now in each other's arms. At the final cadence, they leap forward, Valzacchi grabbing Octavian while Annina pounces upon Sophie, and call loudly for Baron Ochs who arrives quickly upon the scene. Ochs is amused rather than annoyed, and congratulates Octavian on being so fast a worker. Octavian attempts to give Sophie an opportunity to tell the Baron that she will have none of him, but she is too nervous to speak, and finally Octavian himself has to do it for her. At this, Ochs shows understandable signs of annoyance, and is about to lead Sophie from the room when Octavian angrily prevents him. Ochs whistles for his servants who come running, but Octavian draws his sword, forcing the Baron to do likewise, and in the ensuing skirmish Octavian not only manages to keep the servants at bay but also lightly pricks Ochs's arm, causing the cowardly Baron to drop his sword and begin shouting 'Murder' at the top of his voice.

Ochs is helped to an improvised sofa in the middle of the room, and a doctor is summoned. Before long, the Faninal and Lerchenau servants are milling about, and at the height of the commotion Faninal returns with the Notary. In a fury at the treatment Ochs has received in his house, Faninal threatens Sophie with instant despatch to a nunnery if she does not marry Ochs, and orders Octavian out of the house. Octavian quietly assures Sophie that she will hear from him, and leaves, but not before having an urgent and furtive conversation in a corner of the room with the two Italian intriguers whom we are to understand he is engaging to assist him in a plot to discredit the Baron. That Valzacchi and Annina instantly change sides is not necessarily surprising (though Strauss and Hofmannsthal agonized over it in their correspondence). The services of the intriguers are, after all, available to whoever is willing to pay for them.

The chaotic ensemble scene, much of it in waltz rhythm, is sheer delight. The act ends, however, in comparative quietness. When the crowd has dispersed and Ochs is lying on the sofa with his arm in a sling, sipping a glass of wine, Annina returns to give him a note which purports to be from the Marschallin's maid, Mariandel, agreeing to an assignation with Ochs. The delighted Baron despatches Annina to find pen and paper for his reply, and then slowly leaves the room, humming the tune of his favourite waltz (Ex. 10). This makes a splendid end to the act, the strings drawing the last drop of schmaltz from Strauss's waltz parody, and Ochs ending his song on a sustained low E as the curtain slowly falls and the orchestra offers the first phrase of the waltz three times, the first two softly, the last *mezzo forte*.

The third act begins with a substantial orchestral prelude, lasting about six and a half minutes in performance and described by Strauss (who directs that it be played as quickly as possible) as *'Einleitung und Pantomime'* (Introduction and Pantomime), for about half-way through it (at figure 27 in the vocal score) the curtain rises on a scene which is played in mime. At this point the scuttling *fugato* of the first part of the Introduction gives way to the rhythm of the waltz, which pervades the whole of Act III, set in a private room at an inn. At the back of the room, to the left, is a recess which contains a bed, hidden by a curtain which can be drawn. A supper table laid for two stands in the centre of the room which, as the curtain rises, is in semi-darkness. Elaborate preparations are in hand for Octavian's revenge upon Ochs, and the precise moments at which each piece of business is to be performed is noted in the score. Piecing these notes together, one arrives at the following narrative:

Annina is discovered, dressed as a lady in mourning. Valzacchi is arranging her veil, putting her dress to rights, and perfecting her make-up. Octavian arrives dressed in female clothes, and it is only when he lifts his skirts to feel in his pockets that one sees his riding boots beneath. He throws a purse to the Intriguers who thank him profusely. Five dubious-looking characters arrive, and are given their instructions by Valzacchi who positions them outside the room behind various trapdoors in the floor and concealed windows in the walls. Octavian leaves to begin his role in the affair, while Valzacchi rehearses his helpers. When he claps his hands, the various doors and windows open and heads appear, gazing into the room from the most unlikely places. At another sign from Valzacchi, they disappear and the secret panels close. Valzacchi now begins to light the candles in the room, and waiters arrive to complete the preparations for supper. Baron Ochs is now ushered in, his arm still in a sling, leading Octavian (as Mariandel) and followed by one of his servants. The waiters continue lighting the room, but Ochs follows them and extinguishes most of the candles.

As the pantomime ends, the Landlord of the inn rushes forward to ask if all is to His Lordship's liking. Ochs gets rid of the Landlord and the waiters with difficulty, and attempts to settle down to his *tête-à-tête* supper with Mariandel. His intention, of course, is to get the girl drunk and steer her in the direction of the bed in the alcove.

The supper scene is extremely amusing, with Octavian alternately keeping Ochs at bay and leading him on, while a succession of charming waltzes is played in a nearby room, their rhythm pervading the dialogue

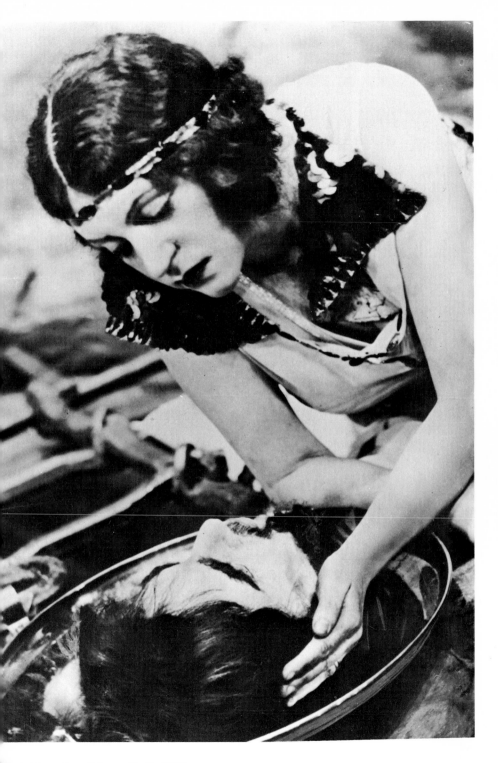

Maria Nemeth as Salome, Berlin 1933

(above) Birgit Nilsson as Elektra, at the Royal Opera House, Covent Garden in 1969

(below) Barbara Bonney (Sophie) and Ann Murray (Octavian) in *Der Rosenkavalier*, at Covent Garden in 1987

of Ochs and Octavian. Ochs leans closer to Mariandel to kiss her, but is momentarily disturbed by her extraordinary resemblance to Octavian, and postpones his kiss. The off-stage musicians now strike up Ochs's favourite waltz (Ex. 10), at which Mariandel tearfully exclaims '*Die schöne Musi*' (Such lovely music) and lapses into a sentimental mood. When the girl appears to be overcome with sentiment and wine, Ochs decides the moment has come for him to act. He removes his wig, and turns to Octavian, only to notice suddenly that faces are peering at him from the wall, and even from the floor. Beside himself with fright, he grabs a hand-bell and rings it distractedly, at which a concealed door opens and Annina, dressed in mourning, appears, exclaiming that the Baron is her husband who has deserted her. She calls the Landlord and the staff who rush in, as also do four children who run towards Ochs, screaming 'Papa! Papa!'. At the height of the confusion, Ochs foolishly flings open a window that looks on to the street, and calls loudly for the police without consider-ing the consequences to himself. When a police officer arrives, Mariandel cleverly manages to reveal the bed in the alcove, and to avoid arrest on a charge of debauchery Ochs attempts to pass her off as his fiancée, Sophie von Faninal. However, he has no sooner pronounced Faninal's name than that gentleman himself enters, having been summoned by the conspirators.

Asked by the police officer to confirm that Mariandel is his daughter, a shocked and enraged Faninal sends for Sophie who has been waiting outside the inn in her father's carriage. Sophie is delighted to find her unwanted bridegroom in an awkward situation, but the thought of the scandal that will attach to his name from this escapade causes Faninal to faint, and he is carried into an adjoining room, followed by Sophie who is concerned for his health. Ochs now attempts to leave with Mariandel who he still insists is his fiancée, and to whom he mutters that if she behaves herself he will marry her and make her his Baroness. Mariandel, however, murmurs to the police officer that she has something to say which the Baron must not overhear. Two police constables detain Ochs on one side of the room, while Mariandel, after a whispered conversation with the officer, goes behind the curtain to the alcove which contains the bed. From the alcove, her clothes are thrown out, piece by piece, to the amusement of the police officer and the consternation of Ochs. While Ochs is struggling with the constables, the Landlord rushes in to announce the arrival of the Marschallin.

The Marschallin's presence at this disreputable inn takes some explain-ing, and the explanation is to be found in the stage directions in Strauss's score, though it is not easy for a director to reveal it clearly to the audience. What has happened is that Ochs's servant has slipped out and hastily summoned the Marschallin, on the assumption that she will be able to extricate his master from the mess in which he has landed himself.

Recognizing the Police Commissary as her husband's ex-orderly, the Marschallin persuades him to retire from the scene with his constables, and proceeds to take command of the situation herself. Octavian, now fully dressed *in persona propria*, emerges from the alcove to the stupefaction of Ochs who, however, soon recovers his *sang froid* and says he had suspected something of the kind. Sophie returns from the adjacent room and makes it clear to Ochs that neither she nor her father wish ever to see him again. The thick-skinned Baron makes a final attempt to effect a reconciliation with Faninal, and the Marschallin's iron hand has to emerge from its velvet glove before he finally realizes that he has lost his betrothed, and that the only thing he can do is leave with as little fuss as possible. His departure, however, turns out to be a noisy one, for he is pursued by the Landlord who presents his bill, Annina and the children who resume their screams of 'Papa', and various waiters, musicians and assorted lackeys, all demanding payment. Strauss the composer sends Ochs packing with a superb ensemble in which the various waltz themes already heard are gathered up to magnificent effect.

What remains now is the finale of the opera, an extended lyrical scene for the Marschallin, Octavian and Sophie, into which Strauss has poured his most inspired music. Always at his best when writing for the soprano voice, he here indulges himself with twenty minutes of glorious lyricism for not one but three soprano voices. (Octavian is officially a mezzo soprano-role, but Strauss seems not to have distinguished between mezzo and soprano tessituras, and the role is as often as not sung by a soprano. Lotte Lehmann, before she became the greatest of Marschallins, was a successful Octavian, and more recent soprano interpreters have included Lisa Della Casa, Sena Jurinac and Irmgard Seefried, the first two of whom went on to become successful Marschallins.)

The Marschallin now accepts that the two young people are in love. Her parting from Octavian has merely come a little sooner than she had anticipated. In the great Trio (Ex. 11), a richly textured, moving and ecstatic piece introduced by the love theme from Act II, she accepts the situation. At its conclusion, she joins Faninal in the adjacent room, and leaves the inn with him between the two verses of a final love duet sung by Octavian and Sophie. As the two young people leave, Sophie drops her handkerchief. For a moment the stage is empty. Then the Marschallin's little black page comes running in, finds the handkerchief, and dances out with it. The curtain falls quickly.

So ends Strauss's best-loved opera. No one who responds to the music of Richard Strauss can fail to fall a little in love with the Marschallin,

Octavian and Sophie. Admittedly, few can fail to find Baron Ochs some-what too much of a good thing, for Strauss has not completely solved the problem of how to present a boorish character amusingly. But even Ochs has his attractive moments, in Act II and the beginning of Act III. (He is surely allowed rather too much breathing-space in Act I.) *Der Rosen-kavalier* may not be Strauss's finest work for the theatre, but it is the one which is received with the greatest affection by audiences, and it has come to be accepted as the most Viennese of operas, despite the fact that it was composed by a German. At least its other creator, Hofmannsthal, was genuinely Viennese.

SIX

Ariadne auf Naxos

Opera in One Act with Prologue
opus 60

Dramatis personae
Characters in the prologue:

The Major-Domo   (speaking part)
A Teacher of Music   (baritone)
The Composer   (soprano)
The Tenor (later Bacchus)   (tenor)
An Officer   (tenor)
A Dancing Master   (tenor)
A Wig Maker   (bass)
A Lackey   (bass)
Zerbinetta   (soprano)
Prima Donna (later Ariadne)   (soprano)
Harlequin   (baritone)
Scaramuccio   (tenor)
Truffaldino   (bass)
Brighella   (tenor)

Characters in the opera:

Ariadne   (soprano)
Bacchus   (tenor)
Naiad   (soprano)
Dryad   (contralto) } Three Nymphs
Echo   (soprano)
Zerbinetta   (soprano)
Harlequin   (baritone)
Scaramuccio   (tenor)
Truffaldino   (bass)
Brighella   (tenor)

Ariadne auf Naxos

LIBRETTO by Hugo von Hofmannsthal

TIME: Prologue: The first half of the eighteenth century
Opera: The mythical past

PLACE: Prologue: Vienna. Opera: the island of Naxos.

FIRST PERFORMED at the Hofoper, Vienna, 4 October 1916, with Maria
Jeritza (Ariadne), Selma Kurz (Zerbinetta), Lotte Lehmann (Composer)
and Béla Környey (Bacchus), conducted by Franz Schalk. (An earlier
version of the opera, in one act without prologue, was first performed at
the Kleines Haus of the Hoftheater, Stuttgart, on 25 October 1912, with
Maria Jeritza (Ariadne), Margarethe Siems (Zerbinetta) and Hermann
Jadlowker (Bacchus), conducted by the composer.

I

WHILE *Der Rosenkavalier* was still in rehearsal, Hofmannsthal was already
giving thought to the next opera he and Strauss would create, for Strauss
now seemed to want to devote almost all of his creative energies to the
theatre. At first Hofmannsthal favoured a treatment of 'Das Steinerne
Herz' (The Heart of Stone), a fairy story by Wilhelm Hauff set in the
Black Forest, but when Strauss responded with a naïve eagerness to this
the librettist then withdrew his suggestion with characteristic hauteur:
'What a confounded fool I was to tell you the title and the subject, and
thus direct your imagination to Hauff's fairy tale which, except for the
central germ, has nothing in common with what exists in my own imagination. In this way I have raised definite images and desires in your mind
which my scenario is bound to disappoint. I am really quite inordinately
vexed. What makes it worse is that my scenario is in fact very beautiful.
. . .' He directed Strauss's attention instead to another project. He,
Hofmannsthal, would make a new German translation and adaptation of
Molière's play, *Le Bourgeois Gentilhomme* (known in German as *Der Bürger
als Edelmann*), compressing Molière's five acts into two, and dispensing
with the secondary plot. Strauss would provide incidental music, and,
instead of the Turkish ceremony with which the play ends, there would be
an opera on the theme of Ariadne, 'performed after dinner, in the presence
of Jourdain, the Count and the dubious Marquise, and . . . punctuated
now and then by brief remarks from these spectators.'

'The playbill', Hofmannsthal wrote to Strauss in May 1911, 'will look
like this:'

DER BÜRGER ALS EDELMANN
A comedy with dances, by Molière, adapted by
Hugo von Hofmannsthal from the old translation
by Biering (1751).

Cast . . .

At the end of Act II,
Divertissement:

ARIADNE AUF NAXOS
(Music by Richard Strauss)

Ariadne   Harlequin
Bacchus   the first Scaramouche
Echo   the second Scaramouche
first Nymph   Tartaglia
second Nymph   Brighella, and so on

The short dances in the play will be preserved (not all of them, but certainly the tailors' dance and the brief scene of the musicians). During the dinner I should like instrumental music: no singing, since the opera is just about to begin.

Strauss's reaction to the outline which Hofmannsthal sent him was this time somewhat lukewarm. He thought the first half 'nice' and the second half 'thin', but supposed that he could write 'some pleasant salon music'. The correspondence of poet and composer during the gestation of this new work reveals them behaving like caricatures of themselves. Hofmannsthal was at his most portentous: 'When two men like us set out to produce a "trifle", it has to become a very serious trifle', he wrote, and went on to explain to Strauss, *de haut en bas*, the symbolism of the Ariadne story. The composer replied that Hofmannsthal's symbolism was such that a mere superficial musician could not hope to understand it. And, that being the case, might not audiences and even critics fail to grasp it as well?

When he actually began to set Hofmannsthal's text for *Ariadne auf Naxos*, Strauss said he envisaged Zerbinetta as the star role, which he would write for a high coloratura soprano, and that he intended Ariadne to be a contralto. He suggested that, if Hofmannsthal needed to learn about the form of the coloratura aria, he should ask the famous Viennese soprano Selma Kurz to sing him arias from *La sonnambula* or *Lucia di Lammermoor*, or some Mozart rondos. Hofmannsthal reacted rather coolly to this. 'I shall make myself acquainted with the formal requirements of coloratura', he told Strauss, 'though not through Mme Kurz with whom I am

94

not on those kind of terms and whom I would definitely not like to bring into anything.'

With a certain amount of compromise on either side, poet and composer managed to complete their project, Strauss finishing the music in April 1912. The play, with its operatic appendix, was to be produced by Max Reinhardt, not at his theatre in Berlin but in Stuttgart. Rehearsals began in June, though the première was not until October. Friction between Reinhardt's company and the resident singers and actors at the Stuttgart Hoftheater came to a head at the dress rehearsal when several key members of the stage staff were sent off by the Stuttgart management to work on a production at another theatre. The first night, on 25 October, was something of a disaster. Though the press reports were in general favourable, the audience received the Molière-Hofmannsthal-Strauss mélange without enthusiasm. Those who had come to enjoy Molière were bored by the opera which was tacked on at the end of the comedy, while the operagoers who had come to hear Strauss's latest opera were vexed at having first to sit through a play by Molière. One critic, Richard Specht (who was later to write a biography of Strauss), made the useful suggestion that the opera should be performed on its own, preceded by an explanatory prologue. This was eventually to happen, but meanwhile Strauss and Hofmannsthal were content to let their hybrid work be produced in other cities, in the hope that it would in due course find the public success that had been denied it in Stuttgart.

II

A more detailed and highly subjective account of the events leading to the première of the Hofmannsthal-Strauss version of Molière's *Der Bürger als Edelmann*, and beyond to the eventual creation of *Ariadne auf Naxos* as a separate opera, was given by Strauss in his 1942 'Reminiscences':

Intended by Hofmannsthal as a thanks offering to Max Reinhardt in the form of an epilogue to a comedy by Molière, Ariadne, split into three parts—provided (like a well-known mythological snake) with nine heads—was eventually resolved into two new comedies. The first idea was fascinating: beginning in the most sober of comic prose and proceeding via ballet and *commedia dell'arte* to the heights of the purest symphonic music, it finally failed due to a certain lack of culture on the part of the audience. The play-going public felt it did not get its money's worth, while the opera public did not know what to make of Molière. The producer had to present dramatic and operatic casts

95

simultaneously and instead of two box-office successes he had one dubious one.

But let us start with the history of the opera. I enjoyed composing the incidental music to the play which—like almost everything else I dashed off, as it were, 'with my left hand'—turned out so well that it continued to survive successfully as a small suite for orchestra. The little opera, too, went very well up to the appearance of Bacchus, when I began to fear that the small chamber orchestra would be inadequate for my dionysiac urges. I informed Hofmannsthal of my fears and asked him whether I could not change over at this point to 'full orchestra', if necessary behind the stage. This was admittedly a stupid idea. Hofmannsthal implored me to give it up, and under this benevolent compulsion the second half of the opera has turned out to be characteristic enough in spite of everything.

Next there followed the choice of a small theatre. The beautiful theatre in Dresden, which was where I usually had my first performances, seemed to me to be too large. When Max Schillings accepted all my conditions—Reinhardt with his Berlin ensemble, for Molière, and for the opera a cast to be chosen by me (I was thinking of Madame Jeritza whom I had seen in Munich in *La belle Hélène* (!!!), of the splendid tenor Jadlowker and the coloratura Frieda Hempel)—and offered me the small theatre in Stuttgart which was to be reopened, I accepted gratefully. Everything went well until the dress rehearsal. To this day I am unable to doubt the good intentions of the Generalintendant Baron von Putlitz and of Schillings, who was my friend; but I had not counted on certain 'forces of destiny' which were smouldering in the jealousy of the Stuttgart operatic and dramatic casts, upset because they were only to come into action after the first performance as a second cast, although they had been responsible for all the preliminary rehearsals before the arrival of the guest artists. I had apparently offended the producer Gerhauser when I had replied, somewhat rashly, to one of his technical questions: 'Reinhardt will settle all that.'

In short, was it malice—or chance? A performance of *Undine* [an opera by Lortzing] had been scheduled to take place in the big theatre simultaneously with the dress rehearsal of *Ariadne* in the small theatre, and a number of important members of the technical staff (stage managers etc.) whom I needed urgently had been detailed to take part in the *Undine* performance. In consequence everything was turned upside down at my dress rehearsal. The scene-designer Stern acted as stage manager, although he had no idea of stage management. Singers made their entrances either too late or at the wrong time, the sets were all wrong, and in short it was a mess. I was fuming with rage and exploded

in an outburst against Schillings, who was of course completely innocent. I felt foolish and later I even had to apologise to Putlitz.
The evening itself went off all right. But two things could not have
been anticipated. Firstly, that the audience was looking forward to the
Strauss opera so much that it did not show sufficient interest in the
splendid Molière, played admirably by Reinhardt's actors, especially by
the inspired Pallenberg; and secondly that after the Molière the amiable
King Karl of Wurttemberg, with the best of intentions, held a reception lasting three quarters of an hour, which meant that *Ariadne*, which
lasts an hour and a half, began about two and a half hours after the
beginning of the play, so that the audience was somewhat tired and ill-
tempered. In spite of this the result was good, although the evening on
the whole was too long. thereafter, the Molière was shortened more and
more: apart from the superb Pallenberg there was no actor who could
have done justice to the difficult leading role on which the success of
the evening depended. In the performance of Hofmannsthal's newly
revised version of *Le Bourgeois Gentilhomme* (to which he had added
a third act) in the Deutsches Theater in Berlin the orchestra was
inadequate.

In short, we had no end of trouble. The charming initial idea—to
move from the most sober of prose comedies to the experience of pure
music—had proved a practical failure. To put it bluntly, this was
because the play-going public had no wish to listen to opera and vice
versa. The proper cultural soil for this pretty hybrid was lacking. Thus
Hofmannsthal and I were forced, four years later, to undertake the
operation of separating Molière and Hofmannsthal-Strauss, although
the work had been successfully performed on many stages (among
others in the Munich Residenztheater and the Berlin Schauspielhaus).

Hofmannsthal's inspired introduction, which had been cut almost in
its entirety in Stuttgart, owing to the length of the evening's programme, was composed afresh by me, and in this new version the opera
was first performed in Vienna in the autumn of 1916. As the Composer,
we had the splendid Lotte Lehmann, whom I had just discovered (and
who was later to sing Ariadne, the Dyer's Wife [in *Die Frau ohne
Schatten*], Arabella, Octavian, an unparalleled Christine [in *Intermezzo*]
and an unforgettable Marschallin). Lehmann combined a warm voice
and excellent diction with inspired acting ability and a beautiful stage
appearance, all of which made her a unique interpreter of my female
roles.

The Molière play was also completed by Hofmannsthal with a charming third act (with the Turkish comedy) and in this new version of the
play I incorporated parts of Lully's music which I had revised. This is

97

a work whose performance, provided it was adequate in all respects, would grace any stage with opera, play and ballet at its command, in company with *Egmont, A Midsummer Night's Dream* and *Manfred*. But to discuss that would lead us to a new and sad topic, that of cultural tasks for the German operatic stage.

III

IN general, productions of the Molière-Hofmannsthal-Strauss hybrid were no more successful elsewhere than the Stuttgart première had been. One conductor who remained faithful to the work, however, was Sir Thomas Beecham who first staged it at His Majesty's Theatre, London, in the spring of 1913, only some months after the Stuttgart première, and who conducted it again with the Glyndebourne opera company at the Edinburgh Festival in 1950. In 1913, the Molière play was performed in an English translation by Somerset Maugham, and the role of Monsieur Jourdain was played by Sir Herbert Tree. Thirty-seven years later, the translation Beecham used was a new one by Miles Malleson who played Monsieur Jourdain. In his autobiography, *A Mingled Chime*, Beecham wrote that, in his view, it was in this first version of *Ariadne* that the musical accomplishment of Strauss attained its highest reach. 'It has to be admitted', Beecham continued,

> that it is neither an easy nor practicable sort of piece to give in an ordinary opera house, as it postulates the employment of a first-rate group of actors as well as singers; and for this reason, no doubt, the authors re-wrote it at a later period, making a full-blown opera of the old medley and thinking probably that they were making a very good job of it. The result has been doubly unfortunate, for the later version has not only failed to hold the stage, but has dimmed the public recollection of the far superior and more attractive original.

Beecham wrote those lines during World War II. In the four or five decades since then, the second version of *Ariadne*, unencumbered by Molière, has become one of Strauss's more popular operas, while the first version remains something to be performed only under special festival conditions. But Strauss and Hofmannsthal did not, in any case, immediately proceed to revise the work after its disappointing première in 1912. They considered doing so, but Hofmannsthal's first suggestion that the Molière play be replaced by a Prologue to the opera, to be set entirely in *secco* recitative, fortunately did not commend itself to Strauss. It was not until 1916, when he was at work on his next opera, *Die Frau ohne Schatten*, that, after discussing the idea in Berlin with the conductor Leo Blech,

Strauss became intrigued by the character of the young Composer, who dominates Hofmannsthal's Prologue. On May Day, he began to set the Prologue to music: not as recitative unaccompanied by orchestra, but as a rich-textured musical dialogue which expands, where required, into lyrical arioso.

At one stage, Strauss tended to see the character of the Composer as the young Mozart; Hofmannsthal, of course, had the young Hofmannsthal in mind. However, when he wrote the Composer's moving outburst in which he declares that music is a holy art, Hofmannsthal told Strauss that 'this struck me as the kind of text Beethoven might have liked to use.' Strauss then decided, 'since tenors are so terrible', to write the part of the adolescent composer for a young soprano.

It took Strauss less than seven weeks to compose the Prologue and make what changes he and Hofmannsthal considered necessary to the opera itself. The première of the new *Ariadne* took place at the Vienna Hofoper in the autumn of 1916. Maria Jeritza, the Ariadne of the 1912 version, sang the role again, and the Zerbinetta was the superb Viennese coloratura soprano, Selma Kurz, whom Hofmannsthal had earlier not wanted to 'bring into anything'. The role of the Composer in the Prologue was to have been undertaken by another distinguished Viennese soprano, Marie Gutheil-Schoder, and a new young soprano named Lotte Lehmann, recently arrived in Vienna from the Hamburg Opera where she had sung the small role of Echo in the first version of *Ariadne*, was engaged to understudy her. When Gutheil-Schoder, apparently suffering from a cold, absented herself from the first rehearsal, Lotte Lehmann was asked to sing through the part. Before she had sung more than a few phrases, Strauss realized that here was the perfect Composer. At his insistence, the role was taken away from the famous Gutheil-Schoder, and given to Lehmann, whose performance at the première on 4 October 1916, made her overnight the idol of Vienna, and marked the beginning of her long association with the operas of Strauss of whose soprano roles she was to become one of the greatest interpreters. (In the London première of the revised *Ariadne* eight years later, Lotte Lehmann sang the title-role, with Elisabeth Schumann as the Composer.) The new *Ariadne auf Naxos* was favourably received in Vienna, and in subsequent productions elsewhere, and it is this version which has endured.

IV

THE incidental music which Strauss had composed for the Molière play was not wasted. Having separated *Ariadne* from *Le Bourgeois Gentilhomme*, Strauss and Hofmannsthal now turned their attention again to the play, which Hofmannsthal re-cast in three acts, and which was performed, with Strauss's music, at Max Reinhardt's Deutsches Theater in Berlin, on 9 April 1918. For the Vienna production six years later, in the Redoutensaal, Strauss himself conducted the orchestra. This adaptation of Molière by Hofmannsthal with music by Strauss has, however, failed to hold the stage, and must be accounted one of the collaborators' rare complete failures. Nevertheless, the ever practical Strauss contrived to salvage much of the music, forming it into a nine-movement orchestral suite which he conducted in Salzburg in 1920 and which is still occasionally to be heard in the concert hall.

In the catalogue of Strauss's music, the opus number 60 is shared by four works: (i) the 1912 hybrid, which was described on the playbills of the Stuttgart Hoftheater as '*Ariadne auf Naxos*, Oper in einem Aufzuge von Hugo von Hofmannsthal. Musik von Richard Strauss. Zu spielen nach dem *Bürger als Edelmann* des Molière.' (*Ariadne on Naxos*, an opera in one act by Hugo von Hofmannsthal. Music by Richard Strauss. To be performed after Molière's *The Would-Be Gentleman*.); (ii) the 1916 Vienna version of the opera alone, the form in which it is best known today; (iii) the version of the Molière play alone, adapted by Hofmannsthal, with music by Strauss, which was first performed in 1918 in Berlin; (iv) Strauss's 'Suite from *Der Bürger als Edelmann*', put together in 1918 and first performed at a concert in Salzburg in 1920.

Although, for the purposes of this present study of Strauss's operas, the definitive Vienna *Ariadne auf Naxos* of 1916 must be the version to discuss in detail, a brief description of what was presented to audiences in Stuttgart in 1912 might also be helpful. Molière's delightful comedy, *Le Bourgeois Gentilhomme*, was written in 1670, three years before the playwright's death, and proved immensely popular when it was first performed before Louis XIV and a court audience. In five acts, with a ballet after each act, the play describes the antics of Monsieur Jourdain, a ridiculously snobbish member of the bourgeoisie, as he attempts to make a gentleman of himself. He is seen studying fencing, dancing and philosophy, is duped by an unscrupulous nobleman, Dorante, and opposes his daughter Lucile's marriage to Cléante, or to any other commoner. Cléante outwits Jourdain by disguising himself as the son of the Grand Turk and gaining Jourdain's permission to marry his daughter.

In adapting the play so that it could serve as the introduction to a one-act opera by Strauss, Hofmannsthal decided to eliminate that part of the plot which concerns Lucile and her suitor Cléante, and to concentrate on the character to M. Jourdain and his involvement with the nobleman, Dorante, who uses Jourdain to aid the progress of his affair with the Marquise Dorimène. In place of the Turkish Ceremony with which

Molière ends his play, Hofmannsthal substituted the performance of an opera (*Ariadne auf Naxos*) which Dorante persuades Jourdain to mount. A situation is contrived whereby a number of *commedia dell'arte* performers find themselves obliged to present their comedy simultaneously with the serious opera, in order not to delay the grand display of fireworks which Jourdain intends to be the finale to the evening's entertainment.

In addition to the music of the opera, Strauss also composed incidental music to accompany the play in Hofmannsthal's adaptation. After an Overture, the first musical number is a brief piece to herald the appearance of Jourdain in the first scene of the play with his Music Master and his Dancing Master. During this scene, the Music Master introduces his pupil, a composer (whose opera *Ariadne auf Naxos* is to be performed at Jourdain's house that evening). This character, who is not in Molière's original play, was later to be given the leading role in the Prologue which Hofmannsthal and Strauss wrote for the 1916 *Ariadne* in Vienna.

Strauss's contributions, scattered throughout the play, consist mainly of songs and music for dancing. The *Bürger als Edelmann* Suite which he put together in 1918 for concert performance (after a revised version of the play alone, with Strauss's music, also revised, had been staged unsuccessfully in Berlin earlier in the year) contains the following nine movements:

1. Overture to Act 1
2. Minuet: the Dancing Master
3. The Fencing Master
4. Entrance and Dance of the Tailors
5. Minuet (from Lully's incidental music to *Le Bourgeois Gentilhomme*)
6. Courante
7. Entrance of Cléante (based on Lully)
8. Prelude to Act 2 (Intermezzo)
9. The Dinner Music

V

THE version of *Ariadne auf Naxos* that is performed today is the opera in a Prologue and one act which was first staged in Vienna in 1916. The action of the Prologue takes place, not in Paris at the house of M. Jourdain, but in eighteenth-century Vienna, in the mansion (to use the words of his Major-Domo) 'of the richest man in Vienna'. (Though he is unnamed, and never appears, he could easily be Herr Faninal from *Der Rosenkavalier!*) This *nouveau riche* Viennese gentleman engages an opera company and a *commedia dell' arte* troupe to entertain his guests on the same evening. At the last moment, the performers are told that the entertainments must be given simultaneously. The comedienne Zerbinetta (soprano) and her troupe cleverly insinuate themselves into the opera which is about Ariadne (soprano) and Bacchus (tenor).

The Prologue begins with a brief orchestral introduction in which a number of themes to be heard later pass quickly in review, themes relating to the Composer, his Music Master, the *commedia dell' arte* troupe, and the Ariadne-Bacchus love duet. This prelude does not draw to a full close but dwindles into an accompanying role as the curtain rises on an elegant and spacious salon. The room has been fitted up for use as a makeshift theatre, of which the backstage area is now visible. The Major Domo enters to find the Music Master (baritone) in an excitable state, for he has just heard a rumour that his pupil's *opera seria*, *Ariadne auf Naxos*, to be performed after dinner that evening, is now to be followed by a vulgar Italian comedy. The Music Master can hardly believe this to be true, but he would certainly not allow it.

The Major Domo haughtily points out to the Music Master that it is not for him, a mere musician, to allow or disallow anything. 'It rests solely with His Lordship, my master, to decide what kind of entertainment he will offer his guests', he continues. *Ariadne* is to be followed by the Italian comedy, and the evening will end precisely at nine with a display of fireworks. His tone makes it abundantly clear that the fireworks are to be the major event of the evening. The Music Master's contributions to this dialogue are sung in *secco* recitative, sometimes accompanied by harmonium continuo, and punctuated by orchestral comment, while the Major Domo's replies are always spoken. His is a non-singing role, to emphasise the fact that he represents the rich philistine employer and does not share the language of the arts.

The orchestral interjections are always apt, quoting the appropriate themes. A snippet of Zerbinetta's dance music accompanies the Major Domo's reference to the Italian comedy, and, when the Music Master wonders despairingly how he is going to inform his pupil, the Composer, that he must share the evening with a comic afterpiece, the Composer's theme underlines his dilemma.

The Music Master rushes off and a servant enters, showing a young officer the way to the dressing-room of Zerbinetta, the leading lady of the troupe of Italian comedians. As the servant is brusquely dismissed by the officer, the young Composer enters hurriedly, to an announcement of his theme in the strings, and asks that the fiddle players be sent to him for a short final rehearsal. The servant informs him plainly that this is impossible, since his musicians are at present playing for the guests in the dining-hall. The Composer decides instead to rehearse his Ariadne, and goes to the door of the dressing-room occupied by Zerbinetta, only to be told by the servant that it is not his prima donna who is in there, but another lady, who is very busy. The servant leaves, and the Composer's anger dissolves as a musical theme, first announced hesitatingly by a flute, comes into his head. (It is a tune which Strauss had used in his incidental music for Molière's play.) He tries to capture it, though his mind is preoccupied with last-minute details to be communicated to the cast of his *Ariadne*, whose performance is due to begin in fifteen minutes.

The Composer particularly wants to remind his tenor that he is meant to represent a god, not a clown, and is about to knock on the door of the tenor's dressing-room when it is suddenly flung open. The Wig Maker staggers out followed by the tenor, already in his Bacchus costume but with a bald head, flourishing his Bacchus-wig with which he is dissatisfied. When the Composer, still trying to hold in his mind the melody which had come to him, asks the Wig Maker if he has a piece of paper, he receives a curt negative reply.

The stage now becomes somewhat animated. The Prima Donna makes a brief appearance, and Zerbinetta emerges from her dressing-room with her admirer. She and her Dancing Master exchange views about the boring *opera seria* which their performance is to follow. When the Composer asks who the entrancing young lady is, his Music Master decides this is as good a moment as any to break the news to him, and tells him that she is Zerbinetta, whose troupe will be singing and dancing in a comedy to be performed immediately after *Ariadne*. (He quotes a phrase from the clowns' dance: one wonders how he comes to know it.) The Composer's fury erupts in an impassioned monologue, in the course of which, however, he remembers the melody he was earlier attempting to compose, and breaks off to rehearse it to himself, ending with another request for a piece of music-paper.

Zerbinetta's male companions, Harlequin (baritone), Scaramuccio (tenor), Truffaldino (bass) and Brighella (tenor) now emerge from Zerbinetta's dressing-room. According to Strauss's score they march in, doing a goose-step: a detail which post-World War II directors of the opera are usually tactful enough to suppress. The Music Master attempts to console his pupil, and to assure the Prima Donna that her portrayal of Ariadne will be the highlight of the evening, while the Dancing Master flatters Zerbinetta.

The commotion is interrupted, first by a servant who announces that the guests are about to rise from the dinner-table, and then by the Major Domo who arrives with the news that his master has changed his mind about the evening's programme. In order to ensure that the firework display will begin punctually at nine, the Dance Masquerade of Zerbinetta and her troupe will be performed, neither before nor after *Ariadne*, but simultaneously with the *opera seria*. An additional reason for His Lordship to have reached this decision is that for some days he had been greatly displeased to consider that, in a mansion so magnificently equipped as his, no better setting for an opera could be found than a desert island. The island would now at least be populated by the characters from the masquerade.

Several of the performers exclaim that his Lordship must be demented, but the Major Domo repeats that, having ordered two entertainments, his master now wishes them to be served up simultaneously. How that is to be achieved is a detail he is prepared to leave to the professionals.

Zerbinetta and the Dancing Master are not at all dismayed by this change of plans, and are quite prepared to improvise their way into the opera *Ariadne* at appropriate moments. They begin to discuss their strategy, while the Music Master attempts to console his pupil, the Composer. The Dancing Master suggests to the Music Master that he persuade his pupil to delete the least interesting parts of his opera, to allow time for the comedians. He points out the practical advantages of compromise, the alternative to which is that the Composer will not hear his opera performed at all.

Reluctantly, the Composer begins to make his cuts. In the course of this he is approached confidentially by Prima Donna and Tenor in turn, each insistent that the other's music be cut. The Dancing Master gives Zerbinetta a somewhat flippant account of the opera's plot, while the Composer attempts to explain to her its deeper significance. Deserted by Theseus, he tells her, Ariadne waits on her desert island for death, and mistakes Bacchus for the God of Death. This strikes Zerbinetta as ridiculous and unlikely behaviour for any sensible woman. She instructs her four fellow-performers that they are to play a lively band of travellers who come by chance to the desert island and attempt to cheer up a Princess who has been jilted by her lover.

The Composer's phrases are romantic and elevated in style, while Zerbinetta's are lightly frivolous. As he continues to explain Ariadne's situation, the Composer's arioso adumbrates the mood and musical material of the aria, '*Es gibt ein Reich*', which Ariadne is to sing in the opera. Unimpressed by this, Zerbinetta begins to flirt with the Composer, and in a tender duet she proves adept at projecting her coquetry in a musical language which cleverly simulates his own, albeit somewhat more sentimental in tone. The Composer would have to have been much older and less naïve to have withstood the appeal of '*Ein Augenblick ist wenig*' (Ex. 12).

(above) Paul Knüpfer (Baron Ochs) and Frieda Hempel (The Marschallin) in the first Berlin production of *Der Rosenkavalier*

(right) Maria Jeritza in the title-role of *Ariadne auf Naxos*

(above) Lotte Lehmann as the Dyer's Wife in *Die Frau ohne Schatten*, Vienna, 1919

(opposite) Hildegard Hillebrecht (Empress) and James King (Emperor) in *Die Frau ohne Schatten*, at Covent Garden in 1967

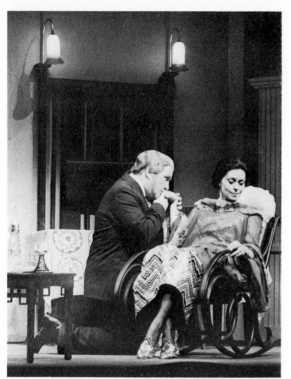

(left) Alexander Oliver (Baron Lummer) and Elisabeth Söderström (Christine) in *Intermezzo*, Glyndebourne, 1974

(below) Strauss with the cast of the *Intermezzo* première: Margarethe Kraus (Anna, the maid), Karl Ziegler (Baron Lummer), Lotte Lehmann (Christine), Alfred Jerger (Storch), and the designer, Lothar Wallerstein

Ex.12

Ein   Au – – – – –   gen-   blick —— ist   we – –

-nig   ein Blick ———— ist   viel ————————   *etc.*

When the Music Master comes to call him, the Composer is in a state of
ecstasy and sings of the redeeming power of music in an arioso, '*Musik ist
eine heilige Kunst*'. Here, in what is effectively the climax of the Prologue,
Strauss has composed his own hymn of heart-felt gratitude to the art of
music, just as surely as Schubert had done in his setting of Schober's
poem, '*An die Musik*'. The Composer has barely finished singing it before
he is interrupted by a shrill whistle from Zerbinetta to call her troupe on to
the stage. Brought back to earth with a sharp jolt, and regretting bitterly
the compromise he has been persuaded into, which Strauss emphasizes in
the general cacophony, the Composer runs off in despair as all around him
prepare for the immediate rise of the curtain upon his opera, *Ariadne*.

After an interval, the opera itself begins. The background to the young
Composer's opera is the classical Greek myth of Ariadne, daughter of
Minos, King of Crete. Ariadne fell in love with an Athenian youth,
Theseus, and helped him slay the Minotaur and escape with her. On their
voyage to Athens they landed on the island of Naxos where Theseus, for
reasons of his own, abandoned her.

The scene is Naxos. An overture sets the sorrowful mood, anticipating
phrases later to be sung by Ariadne, and then quickens before the curtain
rises to reveal Ariadne lying motionless near the entrance to a cave,
surrounded by three nymphs, Naiad, Dryad and Echo, who watch over
her and comment on her incessant grieving. Their flowing G major trio
brings to mind the music of the Rhinemaidens in Wagner's *Ring*, perhaps
deliberately.

Ariadne awakens, and laments the fact that she is still alive. Her
heartfelt cries of woe are repeated (but 'soullessly', the score insists) by
Echo, and Zerbinetta's troupe of comedians emerges briefly from the
wings to comment upon her misery. They disappear again as Ariadne
begins her monologue, '*Ein schönes war*', in which she recalls her happiness with Theseus, and anticipates her death almost joyfully. The comedians now return, muttering that she must be mad. Ariadne rather
surprisingly reacts to their comment, remarking that she may well be
made but is also wise. Harlequin, the romantic comedian of the troupe,
and thus given by Strauss the voice of a lyric baritone, sings a little song,

'Lieben, Hassen, Hoffen, Zagen', whose burden is that the human heart is a resilient organ, and that any kind of feeling, whether of pleasure or pain, is preferable to a numb lack of feeling. Echo wordlessly repeats Harlequin's musical phrases.

Unmoved, Ariadne sings of the land of death to which she hopes soon to be led by the messenger, Hermes. Her beautiful aria, *'Es gibt ein Reich'*, begins solemnly, progressing to an ecstatic climax as Ariadne begs Hermes to take this burdensome life from her. The aria falls to a graceful close from the soprano's high B flat. The four male comedians now return in an attempt to console Ariadne with a cheerful dance (*'Die Dame gibt mit trübem Sinn'*), in the latter part of which Zerbinetta joins them.

Seeing that Ariadne is unresponsive, Zerbinetta dismisses her companions and addresses the princess in a brilliant coloratura recitative and aria (*'Grossmächtige Prinzessin'*) in which she advises Ariadne to adopt a more worldly attitude to men. Zerbinetta herself has had many lovers: Pagliaccio, Mezzetino, Cavicchio, Burattino, Pasquariello. Expect deceit from men, enjoy what they have to offer, and pass on to the next experience: this is her advice to Ariadne. The aria has become a coloratura's virtuoso showpiece, even in the slightly modified form in which it appears in the revised *Ariadne* (the original 1912 version having been even more difficult). The role of Zerbinetta calls for an agile voice with a reliable sustained F above high C.

Harlequin reappears with the comment that Zerbinetta's pretty sermon has been preached to deaf ears, for Ariadne has retired within her cave. He then proceeds to flirt with Zerbinetta. The other three clowns return and, after much byplay, Harlequin makes off with Zerbinetta while the others begin a comical search for her. The music for the clowns is light and attractive, Zerbinetta repeating some of the material from her aria, and the men cavorting to a pleasant but unmemorable waltz tune of the kind which flowed so easily from Strauss's pen.

Finally, Zerbinetta and her troupe disappear, and Ariadne's nymphs return in some agitation to announce that a ship bearing the handsome young god, Bacchus, is approaching the island. Their trio begins and ends with a trumpet fanfare, heralding the approach of Bacchus, about whom the nymphs have produced a great deal of information (which, as they are all singing at once, is unfortunately never clearly heard).

Having only recently escaped the clutches of Circe and survived the effects of her magic potion, Bacchus is making his way to Naxos. His youthful tenor voice is now heard in the distance, calling *'Circe, Circe, kannst du mich hören?'* (Circe, Circe, can you hear me?), not in an attempt to find her again, but in remonstrance. Ariadne, in the belief that he is Hermes, messenger of death, emerges from her cave to listen, and the three Nymphs, also listening, withdraw to one side. Ariadne tells herself, quietly, that the god's voice strikes through all her suffering, easing her pain, while the nymphs exhort Bacchus to continue his song in a gentle trio, '*Töne, töne, süsse Stimme*' (Sing on, sweet voice), whose tune surely derives from Schubert's 'Wiegenlied'.

Still calling on Circe, the voice of Bacchus now sounds much closer. When Bacchus himself appears, Ariadne in a moment of terror fears that it is Theseus who has returned, but quickly realizes her mistake and comes to the conclusion that this must, after all, be Hermes, come to conduct her to the land of the dead. Bacchus, in turn, assumes Ariadne to be a goddess or sorceress, and a lengthy (perhaps too lengthy) love duet ensues, based on a mutually beneficial misunderstanding: '*Ich grüsse dich, du Bote aller Boten . . . Bin ich ein Gott*' (I greet you, messenger of messengers . . . I am a god). Ariadne, still confused, accepts that she is to be transformed, either by death or by some other experience, and Bacchus happily places himself in thrall to, as he thinks, an enchantress not unlike Circe. He entreats Ariadne to come with him, and a canopy descends to veil them both from sight as the nymphs continue their gentle encouragement. Zerbinetta appears from the wings and, pointing over her shoulder to Ariadne and Bacchus, mockingly repeats her recipe for earthly happiness: when a new god appears, surrender without a word. Bacchus and Ariadne can be heard, accepting their need of each other, and as the curtain falls the voice of Bacchus is raised in rapturous salutation to Ariadne.

Ariadne auf Naxos, while not a complete success, has remained popular in its final version as much as for the sympathetic character of the Composer in the prologue, as for the Ariadne-Bacchus opera itself. The arias for Ariadne and Zerbinetta have established themselves beyond the confines of the opera, and, although the love duet has not, it can nevertheless be made to sound effective in the theatre provided that its performers have stamina as well as fine voices. Much of Ariadne's music has both charm and a certain nobility, contrasting well with Zerbinetta's cheerful vulgarity. Though by no means the finest of the operas which Strauss wrote with Hofmannsthal, *Ariadne auf Naxos* is still an attractive, if uneven work.

SEVEN

Die Frau ohne Schatten

Opera in Three Acts
opus 65

Dramatis personae
The Emperor   (tenor)
The Empress, his Wife   (soprano)
The Nurse   (mezzo-soprano)
A Spirit Messenger   (baritone)
A Guardian of the Threshold of the Temple
                    (soprano or counter-tenor)
Apparition of a Youth   (tenor)
The Voice of the Falcon   (soprano)
A Voice from Above   (contralto)
Barak, the Dyer   (bass-baritone)
His Wife   (soprano)
The One-Eyed (high bass) ⎤
The One-Armed   (bass)   ⎬ Brothers of Barak
The Hunchback   (tenor) ⎦
Six Children's Voices   (sopranos and contraltos)
Voices of the Nightwatchmen   (three basses)

LIBRETTO by Hugo von Hofmannsthal

TIME: The mythical past

PLACE: The South Eastern Islands, a mythical region.

FIRST PERFORMED at the Hofoper, Vienna, 10 October 1919, with Lotte Lehmann (Barak's Wife), Maria Jeritza (The Empress), Karl Oestvig (The Emperor), Richard Mayr (Barak), and Lucie Weidt (The Nurse), conducted by Franz Schalk.

I

THE subject of their next opera, *Die Frau ohne Schatten*, had first been suggested by Hofmannsthal in 1911, but had been put aside at that time in favour of *Ariadne auf Naxos*. After the première of the first version of *Ariadne* in 1912, their next collaboration was on a ballet, *Josephslegende*, which was given its first performance in Paris in 1914. The two men had spent a four-day motoring holiday in Italy in April 1913, discussing *Die Frau ohne Schatten*, but Strauss was to complete his Alpine Symphony and the *Ariadne* revision before beginning to compose the new opera.

That the work had a particularly long gestation period is hardly surprising, for Hofmannsthal's libretto is an extremely complex work, and Strauss clearly did not find it easy at first to enter its symbolic world. On his fiftieth birthday on June 11 1914, Strauss was in London. On the following day, in Oxford, he was given an honorary degree of Doctor of Music. He had by this time received the first two acts of *Die Frau ohne Schatten* from Hofmannsthal, and he began to compose the opera shortly before the outbreak of World War I on 4 August. It was not until April of the following year that he received a completed Act III from the librettist: he did not manage to complete his composition until September 1916. Realizing that so huge and difficult a work could not be staged until the end of the war, Strauss and Hofmannsthal then put their opera aside and worked on other projects.

While he was still at work on the music of Act III, Strauss had written his librettist a letter which clearly reveals the difficulties he was experiencing in coming to grips with Hofmannsthal's ideas. 'My own inclination', Strauss confessed,

is for realistic comedy with really interesting people—either like *Der Rosenkavalier* with its splendid Marschallin, or with a burlesque, satirical content, somewhat in the manner of Offenbach's parodies . . . Characters like the Emperor and Empress [in *Die Frau ohne Schatten*], and also the Nurse, can't be filled with red corpuscles in the same way as a Marschallin, an Octavian, or an Ochs. No matter how I rack my brains—and I'm toiling really hard, sifting and sifting—my heart's only half in it. When the head has to do the major part of the work, you get a breath of academic chill (what my wife very rightly calls 'note-spinning') which no bellows can ever kindle into a real fire. Well, I have now sketched out the whole ending of the opera (the quartet and the choruses), and it's got verve and a great upward sweep—but my wife finds it cold and misses the heart-touching, flame-kindling melodic texture of the *Rosenkavalier* trio . . . I shall make every effort to shape Act III in line with your intentions, but let's make up our minds that

Die Frau ohne Schatten shall be our last romantic opera. I hope you'll very soon have a fine, happy idea to help me definitely to set out on the new road.

Although his English earnings which he had banked in London were sequestered at the beginning of the war, Strauss was now a rich man. The new paths along which music was being led by the younger Viennese composers Berg and Schoenberg, and by Stravinsky, were antipathetic to him, and since he no longer needed to earn his living by composition, when it was suggested that he might assume the directorship of the Vienna Opera, Strauss was interested. 'It has been my devoutest wish for the past thirty years', he told Hofmannsthal, 'to assume the *de facto* supreme direction of a huge Court Opera House on the artistic side.' In 1919, with the collapse of the Austrian monarchy, the Court Opera was renamed the Vienna State Opera, and Strauss became its artistic supervisor, in partnership with Franz Schalk who was nominally the head of the Opera House.

Strauss's appointment was announced in March 1919. He did not take up his duties in Vienna until December, but before then he appeared as a guest conductor at a festival in May to celebrate the Opera House's fiftieth anniversary. On 10 October, as though to herald his new relationship with the Staatsoper, *Die Frau ohne Schatten* was given its première there, conducted by Franz Schalk, with a superb cast headed by Maria Jeritza as the Empress, Lotte Lehmann as Barak's Wife, Richard Mayr as Barak, Lucie Weidt as the Nurse, and Karl Oestvig as the Emperor. The production by Hans Breuer was well received, but although *Die Frau ohne Schatten* was shortly afterwards staged in Dresden and Berlin, it did not become one of Strauss's more popular works until more than forty years later, when it was conducted in Vienna by Herbert von Karajan and Karl Böhm. It has now secured a firm place for itself in the operatic repertory.

II

HERE is Strauss's 1942 recollection of the events leading to the work's première:

. . . When, in the summer of 1918, we were staying at Aschau in the Salzkammergut with friends, Frau Nossal and the Kammersänger Franz Steiner (who was to become an excellent interpreter of my songs during many concert tours which took us as far as Bucharest, Stockholm etc.), Baron Andrian called me to Vienna where, under Franz Schalk in October 1919 (sets: A. Roller, production: Wymetal*) *Fr-o-Sch* was first lavishly produced with a grand cast (Emperor: Oestvig;

Empress: Jeritza; Nurse: Weidt; Dyer's Wife: Lehmann; Barak: Mayr). After this first great success, its way over the German stage was fraught with misfortune. In Vienna itself, owing to the strain imposed by the vocal parts and to the difficulties over the sets, the opera had to be withdrawn more often than it was performed. At the second theatre (Dresden) it came to grief because of the imperfections of the *mise en scène* (Eva von der Osten had meanwhile ruined her voice with dramatic roles) which forced me to ask Count Seebach after the dress rehearsal to postpone the first performance for several days. Although the orchestra under Fritz Reiner was excellent, the performance suffered from the inadequate Dyer's Wife. It was a mixed pleasure.

It was a serious blunder to entrust this opera, difficult as it was to cast and produce, to medium and even small theatres immediately after the war. When, on another occasion, I saw the Stuttgart post-war production (on the cheap!) I realized that the opera would never have much success. But it has succeeded nevertheless and has made a deep impression, especially in the Vienna-Salzburg performance (Krauss-Wallerstein) and finally in Munich (Krauss-Hartmann-Sievert). Music lovers in particular consider it to be my most important work.

III

LIKE one or two other Strauss operas, *Die Frau ohne Schatten* is a work one can easily dislike in advance, for a synopsis of its plot is bound to appear more than somewhat pretentiously obscure. Similarly, the *donnée* of *Capriccio* is apt to strike one as being too flimsily theoretical to be viable dramatically; and the domestic small-talk of *Intermezzo* suggests an unbearable cosiness. In fact, however, both *Capriccio* and *Intermezzo*, despite their unlikely provenance, are among Strauss's most successful works for the stage: aesthetically successful, at any rate, even if not as popular as such earlier operas as *Salome*, *Elektra*, and *Der Rosenkavalier*. And so it is with *Die Frau ohne Schatten*. Hofmannsthal's libretto may be pretentious, but its pretensions are, for the most part, legitimate.

The assertion has been made that, though Hofmannsthal may have known what it all meant, the composer did not, and that consequently Strauss's score is less persuasive than on other occasions when the partnership was functioning more evenly. But a study of the score and the libretto hardly supports such a contention. Strauss's understanding of his librettist's intentions may well have been intuitive: it was also, surely, complete.

---

* *(facing page)* Strauss was mistaken. It was not Wilhelm von Wymetal but Hans Breuer who produced the opera.

111

In no other opera of the collaboration did he so closely and accurately follow the changing moods of the text.

It was, as usual, Hofmannsthal who had suggested the project, just after *Der Rosenkavalier* had been given its first performance in Dresden, and he and Strauss were about to plunge into *Ariadne auf Naxos*. Hofmannsthal was keen to work, at some time, on a much bigger scale, and wrote to Strauss about an idea he had for what he called a 'magic fairy-tale with two men confronting two women'. One of the women, he informed the composer, might well be based on the character of Strauss's wife, well-known for her bad temper and shrewishness. 'A bizarre woman with a very beautiful soul *au fond*' was Hofmannsthal's reasonably tactful description.

Curiously, Strauss failed to react to his collaborator's nod in the direction of Pauline. Much later, when actually composing the opera, he complained that he was having difficulty in bringing the Dyer's Wife imaginatively to life. Hofmannsthal professed himself surprised, and tried hinting again. 'I must say', he wrote, 'it would go somewhat against the grain if I had to comment on a character whose sharp and definite contours speak for themselves.' He reminded Strauss that he had frequently expressed the desire to depict in music the capricious and flighty aspects of such a 'basically good woman', and ended by stating rather primly that he would prefer not to say more.

So the Dyer's Wife is something of a split personality: the librettist used the composer's wife as a model, but the composer was unable to view his wife with sufficient artistic objectivity to notice the fact. Nevertheless, with his superb musical characterization of Hofmannsthal's creation, Strauss probably came closer to a portrait of Pauline in *Die Frau ohne Schatten* than in the more sentimental deliberate portrait he was to compose in *Intermezzo*.

Referring to *Der Rosenkavalier* as their *Figaro*, Hofmannsthal told Strauss he hoped *Die Frau ohne Schatten* would be their *Zauberflöte*. Certainly *Die Frau*, or *Fr-o-Sch* (a character in *Die Fledermaus*) as Strauss liked to call it, has parallels with *Die Zauberflöte*: both are quest operas in which characters fulfil themselves by facing great danger; both are concerned with two pairs of lovers, patrician and plebeian; both contain apparent villains, Sarastro and Keikobad, whose actions finally appear to have been for the general good; both are set in a time and place of fable; and both derive to some extent from oriental mythology.

The meaning of the libretto of *Die Frau* is explicit. Hofmannsthal, in explaining it to Strauss, made use of a couple of lines from Goethe: '*Von dem Gesetz, das alle Wesen bindet,/Befreit der Mensch sich, der sich überwindet.*' (From the law that governs all life, man is freed by rising above himself.) The action takes place on three levels of existence: the spirit world, the world of mankind, and an in-between state in which the Emperor and Empress live, hovering between the earthly and the spiritual.

The Empress is the daughter of Keikobad, the spirit ruler, and in order to prevent her husband from being turned into stone by Keikobad, she must procure a shadow. The shadow is fecundity. It is also, as the Empress learns, humanity. It cannot be acquired by trickery: it can only be earned at overwhelming cost.

Mankind is represented by Barak the Dyer and his wife. Barak's wife is coaxed into agreeing to sell her shadow by the Empress's Nurse, a fearsome old hag whose prime allegiance is to Keikobad. Barak's wife is given no name in the opera (the only characters with names are Keikobad, who does not actually appear, and Barak). She is disgruntled and shrewish out of disappointment, for although she has been married to Barak for two and a half years he has not yet got her with child. Bitterly, she renounces all prospects of childbearing and prepares to sell her shadow. But the Empress, who has been progressing from a state of cold, unfeeling immortality, to a humanity which feels precisely because it is mortal, is finally unable to accept the sacrifice offered by Barak's wife. Even when she sees her husband the Emperor turned to stone, she cannot bring herself to release him at the expense of the unhappy mortals with whom she has become involved. It is at the moment when she imagines she has lost her husband that, in fact, she frees him and the human couple as well.

The Empress's acquisition of humanity is the real point and meaning of the work. Not only is this perfectly clear from Hofmannsthal's libretto, it is also unmistakably there in the music which Strauss wrote for the Empress. She moves from the glitteringly cool utterance of her first aria to the emotional warmth of the scene in Act III in which she makes her agonized choice and exhibits a fully human sympathy for the first time. It is she who is the central figure of the opera, although the Dyer's wife may appear to be more dramatically active. For much of the time the Empress has little to do, but she is the one character who appears in every scene.

IV

THE opera is set in the mythical past, and in a mythical place, described by Hofmannsthal as the South Eastern Islands. The first scene of Act I takes place on a flat roof overlooking the Imperial gardens, with the dimly lit entrance to the royal apartments on one side. There is no overture: the curtain rises immediately to reveal the Empress's devoted Nurse crouching in the shadows before the entrance. Noticing a glimmer of light on the lake below, the Nurse imagines that it is her master, Keikobad, ruler of the spirit world, approaching. She hastens to assure him that she is faithfully watching over his daughter. It is, however, not Keikobad himself who appears, but his Spirit Messenger, clad in armour and encompassed with a blue light. He reminds the Nurse that eleven messengers have already visited her, a new one with every waning moon, to ask the same question. Does the Empress cast a shadow? If she still does not, then woe betide them all.

The Nurse is forced to answer that the Empress casts no shadow, and that light passes through her body as though she were glass. When the Messenger chides her for having allowed the daugher of Keikobad to be stolen by the Emperor, the Nurse defends herself by asking how she could possibly have kept close watch on a child to whom her father had given the power of transforming herself at will into a bird or a gazelle. The Messenger asks to see the Empress, but the Nurse informs him that she is not alone. The Emperor is with her, for there has not been one night in the twelve months which have passed since their meeting when he did not desire her. The Emperor, the Nurse continues, is a hunter and a lover, and nothing else. He spends every night with his Empress, and then at dawn steals away from her to spend his day hunting.

The Messenger now issues Keikobad's stern edict. The Empress has three days more in which to acquire a shadow. Should she fail to do so, she will be returned to the arms of her father, Keikobad. This pleases the Nurse, who would like nothing better than for her mistress and herself to be able to return to the spirit world. But what, she asks, will happen to the Emperor? 'Er wird zu Stein' (He will be turned to stone), the Messenger announces, and the Nurse, in awe, repeats his grim descending phrase (Ex. 13). Warning her to guard her mistress well, the Messenger departs. As the Nurse once again repeats to herself in wonderment 'Er wird zu Stein', the Emperor suddenly appears in the doorway of the royal apartments, calling her roughly and asking if she is awake. 'Awake, and lying like a faithful dog across your threshold', the Nurse answers obsequiously.

Ex.13

114

Throughout the opera, Strauss weaves into his orchestral texture the numerous themes, melodic fragments or phrases, which represent characters or ideas. The omnipotent Keikobad is evoked by the tubas in the opening bars, and such concepts as the Empress's shadow and the threatened petrification of the Emperor are identified in the orchestra whenever they are mentioned. The melodic arioso in which the action is advanced broadens into more extended lyrical sections at appropriate moments, the first of these occurring now with the appearance of the Emperor who, after bidding the Nurse to keep watch until the Empress should call her, prepares to depart for the day's hunt, but not before recalling, in an aria, the events of that day twelve months past when he first encountered his beloved.

He had been hunting in the moon-mountains with his favourite red falcon with whose aid he had captured a white gazelle which, as he was about to spear it, turned into the woman whom he has made his wife. As he describes the occasion, the orchestra bursts forth with the lyrical tune which it has adumbrated throughout his aria (Ex. 14). In his anger at the red falcon which had dared to perch on the forehead of the gazelle and to strike at its eyes, the Emperor had thrown his dagger at the bird and frightened it away. He has sought his favourite falcon ever since, but without success. He now tells the Nurse that he will be away, hunting, for three days, and instructs her to say to the Empress that, whatever falls to his arrow or spear, it is she, his Empress, who is his greatest prize.

Ex.14

As the Emperor departs, the ominous Ex. 13 is heard again in the orchestra, warning of the fate that could befall him at the end of three days. The Nurse now brusquely dismisses those of the Emperor's servants who have lingered behind, for she hears her mistress approaching. The Empress's entrance is heralded by a brilliant and eloquent orchestral passage which immediately characterizes her as a creature of light and air. Her high-lying and darting vocal line emphasizes her affiliation with the elements, as she sings of her desire to transform herself again into the form of a bird or a gazelle.

Suddenly, in the sky above her the Empress sees the red falcon hovering, and greets him as he settles, weeping, upon a tree. She is able to understand the bird's utterance, and therefore so are we. In a soprano voice, the falcon asks why he should not weep, for the Empress casts no shadow and so the Emperor must be turned to stone. Remembering now that she had once heard this curse long ago, and forgotten it, the Empress implores the Nurse to help her find a shadow.

The Nurse makes it clear that it is because the Emperor, who had presumed that he could transform his bride into a fully human state, has failed to do so, and specifically has failed to implant a child in her womb, that he must pay the price. It is her infertility which causes the Empress to cast no shadow. The Nurse admits she might know how to procure a shadow, but the Empress herself would have to go and fetch it from the world of mankind, a lower world, says the Nurse, of stagnant smells and long-dead corpses, a world which would fill the Empress with horror and loathing.

Impatiently, the Empress exclaims that day is breaking, and that the Nurse must immediately lead her down into the world of men. The Nurse continues to describe the horrors of the human world and its greedy, senseless and joyless inhabitants, but the Empress, although she is fearful, is determined to procure a shadow and save her husband. She and the Nurse sing in duet and, as they descend to earth, their journey is described vividly in the orchestra.

During the orchestral description of their flight, the scene changes to a poorly furnished room in the house which Barak, the Dyer, shares with his wife and his three brothers. The room, which serves as both workshop and dwelling, contains a bed, a primitive oriental hearth, and a number of tubs, buckets and other appurtenances of the dyer's trade. Vats of dye stand on the none too clean floor, and dyed cloths are stretched on racks to dry. Barak's three brothers are quarrelling. The One-eyed Brother (bass) is on top of the One-armed Brother (bass), attempting to throttle him, while the youngest brother, the Hunchback (tenor), is doing his best to separate them. The skirmish ends only when the Dyer's Wife (soprano) approaches with a bucket of water which she throws over the brothers, who then begin to rail at her.

Barak (bass-baritone) arrives home and, at his wife's urging, sends his brothers to work outside. However, when she threatens to leave him unless he gets rid of the brothers, Barak calmly points out that there is nowhere else for them to go, and that he has always looked after them. He recalls the time when they were happy and attractive children, and gently asks his wife when she is going to give him children of their own. A love theme earlier associated with the Emperor and Empress is briefly heard, only to vanish as the shrewish wife tells her husband that, since she has been fruitless in the two and a half years of their marriage, she has now put all thoughts of parenthood from her. She gruffly advises her husband to do likewise.

Barak reacts calmly and amiably to his wife's words, assuring her that he is not angry with her and that he will await patiently the blessings which he is convinced will in time come to them. He has been parcelling up a huge bundle of skins which he now hoists onto his back to take off to market. As he leaves, he sings a few bars of a cheerful folk-like tune. A new quality has appeared in the score with the introduction of Barak, a simple, good-natured soul whose goodness Strauss has, rather surprisingly, conveyed most effectively, indeed movingly, in slow, lyrically expansive music, warmly scored and providing a sharp contrast to the discontented nagging of the Dyer's Wife.

The orchestra now recalls the motifs of the flight to earth of the Empress and the Nurse, who suddenly and magically appear in the room, dressed as serving-maids. The Nurse pretends that she takes the Dyer's Wife to be a princess, and asks if the man who has just departed is one of her lackeys. She professes astonishment when told by his wife that he is Barak the Dyer and her husband. The Empress begs to be allowed to kiss the woman's shadow, and slowly Barak's wife is persuaded that her shadow is a thing of great worth which she could sell in exchange for riches, everlasting beauty, and a nightly throng of lovers.

The Nurse momentarily conjures up jewels, servants who adorn the Dyer's Wife with richly woven garments, and the apparition of a handsome young lover. When all these samples of future delights disappear, the Dyer's Wife asks how she can sell her shadow. She is told that she must renounce motherhood forever: the appropriate theme is heard at this point in the orchestra. The two strangers will stay in the house for three days, and will act as her servants during the period in which the shadow is to be relinquished.

Barak's wife gives her tacit consent, but suddenly hears her husband returning. She has neglected to prepare his supper, but this is taken care of by the Nurse who conjures five little fishes into the frying pan, and magically divides the bed, causing Barak's half to move to the other side of the room. She and the Empress take their leave, the Nurse promising that they will return the following day at noon.

As the visitors depart, the voices of unborn children are heard wailing, the sound appearing to come from the fish in the pan. 'Mother', the voices beg, 'let us come into the house. We are in the dark, and frightened.' The Dyer's Wife mutters 'I wish I could find some water to silence this fire', at which the children's voices, fading away, justifiably complain of her hard-heartedness. When Barak enters, singing his cheerful song, his wife gestures to his supper and his newly positioned bed, and retires behind her bed-curtains. In resignation, Barak prepares to eat his meal, while outside in the street the voices of night-watchmen can be heard solemnly exhorting married couples to love one another, to be fruitful and to multiply. Barak asks his wife if she hears their message, but she does not reply. Sadly, he stretches out to sleep as the curtain slowly falls.

Act II consists of five short scenes, with the action alternating between Barak's house and the upper spheres. The act begins in Barak's house as the Dyer and his brothers are setting out for the market. As soon as they have gone, the Nurse who has installed herself and the Empress in the house as maid-servants to Barak's wife begins to tempt that discontented woman by reminding her of the handsome young man who had been conjured up the previous day. The Nurse produces him again, but as the Dyer's Wife, encouraged by the Nurse and an invisible chorus, reaches out to embrace the youth, the Empress suddenly exclaims that she can hear Barak returning. By the time he enters, the youth has been made to vanish.

Barak has brought with him his brothers and a mob of begging children, for he has been successful at market and has purchased food and wine in abundance. He offers food to the Empress, and asks her to take some to his wife who angrily rejects it, declaring that she does not want to sweeten the bitterness in her mouth. The scene ends with an ensemble in which several themes are heard jostling for supremacy. As the orchestra alone continues with Barak's theme, the curtain falls. When it rises again the scene has changed to outside the Emperor's falcon-house in a lonely part of the wood. The cry of the falcon is heard in the orchestra, punctuating a long and gently melancholy cello solo which utilizes themes associated with the Emperor who now appears. The falcon has led him to this place, and the reason soon becomes clear, for the house in which the Empress had assured the Emperor she would spend his three days' absence is empty. As he watches, his suspicion mounting, he eventually observes the Empress and the Nurse returning from the world of humankind. His wife has lied to him, and so she must die. But he cannot bring himself to use his arrow which had first transformed her into a woman by grazing her, nor his sword which had loosened her girdle, nor his bare hands. Sadly, the Emperor implores his falcon to lead him away to some desolate place where neither man nor beast will hear his lamenting. The curtain falls, and during the ensuing thirty-two bars of orchestral interlude, in which the threatening notes of '*Er wird zu Stein*' are heard as well as the mournful cry of the falcon, the scene changes back to Barak's hovel.

As the curtain rises again, Barak is working while his wife stands aside, complaining to herself. When Barak asks her to pour him a drink, she reminds him that there are now servants to do this, and the Nurse immediately pours a drink for him, slipping a drug into the glass as she does so. Barak quickly falls asleep, and although his wife is somewhat anxious about him, she does not demur when the Nurse again calls forth the apparition of the handsome youth on whom her thoughts had been dwelling since his last appearance. But once again she draws back at the last moment, and when the Nurse causes the youth to fall before her as if overcome, the Dyer's wife rushes to her husband and attempts to awaken him, shouting at him that he should be guarding his wife and his house from robbers, instead of sleeping. Meanwhile, the Nurse has hurriedly dematerialized the handsome vision.

Hearing talk of robbers, Barak finally shakes himself awake, and leaps to his feet calling for his brothers, and for a hammer to attack the thieves. His wife scornfully quietens him, and Barak confusedly wonders what is happening to him. He is aware that things are occurring which he does not understand, and he does not know what to make of his wife's comments on his intelligence and his ability to provide for her. He sits in utter dejection as she leaves with the Nurse. The Empress remains, and when she replies to Barak's 'Who's there?' with 'It is I, my lord, your servant', an orchestral reference to the theme of Barak's goodness conveys that the Empress is beginning to feel sympathy for these humans and their plight. The curtain falls, while an orchestral interlude continues this train of thought in an increasingly agitated manner.

When the curtain rises again, the scene has changed to the Empress's bedroom in the falcon-house. The Empress lies on her bed in restless slumber, with the Nurse asleep at the foot of the bed. Murmuring in her sleep, the Empress begins a dream, which one sees enacted while she sleeps. Led on by his falcon, the Emperor enters a rocky cave and approaches a bronze door leading into the interior of a mountain. Voices from within the mountain call, 'To the water of life' and 'To the brink of death', and the falcon repeats its grim warning: 'The woman casts no shadow. The Emperor must be turned to stone.' As the Emperor passes through the door which closes behind him, the Empress awakens suddenly from her dream, aware now of the danger which threatens her husband, aware too of what she perceives to be her own guilt, and conscious of the harm she is inflicting upon Barak and his wife. Her agitation takes her to a high D flat at the climax of her outburst. The curtain falls, while the orchestra continues to explore these questions, the motif of Keikobad now thrusting itself to the fore.

The final scene of Act II takes place in Barak's house. Although it is only midday, the room grows darker and darker, to the consternation of Barak's brothers. The Nurse mutters to the Empress that higher powers have joined the game, by which she presumably means the mighty Keikobad. In a powerful ensemble the various characters give voice to their conflicting thoughts, Barak confused, his brothers terrified, his wife bad-tempered, the Nurse confident, and the Empress grateful that she has been allowed to encounter so good a man as Barak, and determined to share his burdens.

Suddenly, Barak's wife turns to him and, in an hysterical outburst punctuated by sounds of thunder and flashes of lightning, confesses that she has entertained a lover in the house. She announces that she is now selling her shadow for great riches, and that in token of this she forswears motherhood forever. An appalled Barak calls for the fire to be kindled, so that he can see his wife's face clearly. The light of the fire reveals her to be shadowless, but when the Nurse tells the Empress to seize the shadow, she refuses, and swears that somehow she will save Barak's wife from the consequences of her rash action.

Barak is about to kill his wife with a flaming sword which has flown through the air into his hand, when she cries out to him that she has not betrayed him, that she has been faithless only in thought, but that she is willing to die by his hand. Barak lifts the sword, but it is miraculously snatched from him. The room trembles, the ground opens, and water pours in through the walls. The three brothers make their escape but Barak and his wife are swallowed up by the earth. The Empress and the Nurse have retreated to a safe distance, from which the Nurse mutters once again that higher powers are in play.

Act III begins with solemn brass chords in the orchestra, followed first by an *angst*-ridden passage for solo bassoon, and then by the lamenting voices, on flutes, clarinets and celesta, of unborn children. When the curtain rises, the scene revealed is an underground vault, divided into two by a thick wall. On the right, Barak crouches on the hard stone floor. On the left side of the wall sits his wife, in tears, with her hair loose. Each is unaware of the other's presence. As she hears the voices of the unborn children, the Dyer's Wife calls on them to be quiet, for she has not, after all, renounced them. In an affecting arioso, she implores Barak, wherever he may be, to hear and to forgive her, for she realizes now that she loves him.

Her voice subsides, and on the other side of the wall Barak begins to ponder, in the most beautiful melody of the entire opera (Ex. 15), on his

Krauss and Maria Jeritza (Helen), after her first performance of *Die Aegyptische Helena*

(above) Scene from Act I of *Die Aegyptische Helena*

(below) Act III of *Arabella*, Covent Garden, 1965. On the right are Lisa Della Casa (Arabella) and Dietrich Fischer-Dieskau (Mandryka)

Ex.15

Mir   an – ver-traut   –   dass ich sie

he-   ge,   –   dass ich sie   tra –   ge –

– auf die –   sen   Hän –   den.

obligation to cherish and to protect his wife. His solo, '*Mir anvertraut*' (Entrusted to me), turns into a fervent duet as his wife's voice joins his. At its conclusion, a shaft of light in Barak's dungeon reveals a staircase leading upwards through the rock, and a voice (contralto) is heard urging him, 'Make your way upwards, man, for the way is open'. As Barak stands and begins to climb, his wife again calls on him to come to her, even if he means to kill her. The shaft of light now shines down on her side of the dungeon, and the magic voice guides her, too, upwards.

The vault begins to sink, and the lights to fade. The changes of scene in this final act are directed in Strauss's score to be effected without the curtain being lowered: when the scene becomes visible again after about fifty bars of increasingly urgent orchestral comment, what is revealed is a rocky terrace, with steps leading up from water to the wall of a huge temple with a bronze door which stands open. Near it, the Spirit-Messenger waits with attendant spirits. A boat carrying the Nurse and the sleeping Empress floats downstream, coming to a stop at the foot of the steps.

The Empress awakens and hastens to leave the boat, for she recognizes the scene of her recent dream. The Nurse tries to persuade her to leave what she claims is an evil place. When she discovers that the boat will move no further, the Nurse suggests abandoning it and taking to a road which will lead down from the mountain. However, the Empress is adamant. Trumpets are heard sounding from within the mountain, which she interprets as a summons to judgment by her father, Keikobad. She realizes that her husband, the Emperor, is on trial, and she intends to share his ordeal. When the Nurse continues to insist that she will find her a shadow, the Empress loses patience with her former mentor, for she suddenly understands that beyond the door lies not the water of life but the brink of death, to which she must travel if she is to save her husband. 'All is now clear to me', she exclaims as she turns determinedly to the entrance of the temple. 'I must go to him.'

In desperation, the Nurse warns the Empress that Keikobad, whom his daughter hardly knows, is terrible in his wrath, and that he will punish her for having given herself into human hands. But the trumpet call is heard again, sounding the phrase which had summoned Barak and his wife from their dungeon, and the Empress now banishes her Nurse for ever, her vocal line poignantly sad, as she moves to the door, which opens to admit her and closes again behind her. The well-meaning Nurse tries to follow her, willing to die in an attempt to save her beloved charge, but she is turned away by the Spirit-Messenger who seizes her and throws her into the boat, ordering it to carry her down to the world of men. (The voices of Barak and his wife are heard to join the ensemble in a passage which is frequently cut in performance.)

As the boat is borne away, the scene gradually changes again to a hall containing a curtained recess. Barak and his wife can still be heard lamenting their fate as the Empress is led in by the attendant spirits. A solo violin plays a long, winding, typically Straussian melody as she approaches the recess, humbly submitting herself to the judgment of Keikobad. A fountain of golden water springs up, but she rejects this, the water of life, for she possesses within her that which is greater: love. A spirit, the Guardian of the Threshold (who can be either a soprano or a male voice singing falsetto) urges her to drink, promising that the shadow which belonged to Barak's wife will then be hers. But the Empress can hear the voices of Barak and his wife, still desperately calling to each other. 'There is blood in the water', she cries. 'I will not drink.'

The fountain subsides, and the Empress addresses the shadowy figure seated in the curtained niche, assuming it to be Keikobad. As the light grows brighter, however, the seated figure is revealed to be the Emperor, completely petrified except for his eyes. The petrification motif thunders out, and, horrified, the Empress reverts to the spoken word: 'Woe is me, the curse is fulfilled. My guilt is punished in him!' Unearthly voices are heard chanting the curse, and the image of the Emperor disappears as the fountain rises again. 'Say "I will". That woman's shadow will be yours, and your husband will return to life and depart with you', the Guardian of the Threshold promises. Barak and his wife can be heard lamenting their wretchedness. The Empress utters a scream of anguish, and then says clearly and slowly, 'I—will—not.'

The fountain vanishes. For a moment there is silence, and then from the Empress a clear shadow can be seen stretching across the floor. Slowly, the Emperor rises and moves down the steps towards his wife. 'When the heart of crystal is shattered with a cry', he sings, 'the unborn children hasten hither like starshine.' And, indeed, the voices of unborn children are now heard, joyously urging their parents to give life to them.

The scene now changes for the last time, and a beautiful landscape appears, rising steeply, with a golden waterfall, above which can be seen the Emperor and Empress. From below, on opposite sides, Barak and his wife approach each other. As she stretches out her arms to him, her shadow falls across the path between them. 'Your shadow leads me to you', sings Barak, and the as yet unborn children of the Dyer and his Wife praise the beauty of their mother's shadow. A golden bridge replaces the shadow, across which Barak and his wife cross to each other and embrace. From above, the Emperor and Empress approach, and all four join in a somewhat militant but jubilant quartet, supported by the chorus of unborn children. After triumphant trombone fanfares, the orchestra and the opera come to a quiet close, and the curtain falls slowly.

In *Die Frau ohne Schatten* Strauss makes use of a huge orchestra which he deploys skilfully and variously. The spirit voices are usually accompanied by a chamber orchestra of *Ariadne* dimensions, while rich, swirling humanity has the full orchestra. The ambiguous character of the Nurse, whose sympathies are inconstant and who has contact with both worlds, is accompanied by solo obbligato instruments. Throughout the opera, Strauss matches the sweep of his librettist's imagination with an astonishingly wide range of instrumental colour. Speculation as to whether the composer intellectually understood the implications of Hofmannsthal's libretto is pointless in the face of the music's real contribution to and illumination of the meaning of the text. Hofmannsthal never wrote a more fascinating and complex libretto, and Strauss's score is not only his most lavish but also his most exciting. From the Emperor's ecstatic '*Denn meiner Seele*' in Act I to the beautiful duet for Barak and his wife, '*Mir anvertraut*', in Act III, the opera abounds in typically Straussian melody. And, unlike *Der Rosenkavalier*, it has remarkably few *longueurs* throughout its great length. '*Übermächte sind im Spiel*' (Higher powers are at play), mutters the Nurse when her plans go awry. Strauss and Hofmannsthal never exhibited higher powers than in this work, which is their masterpiece.

EIGHT

Intermezzo

A Bourgeois Comedy with Symphonic Interludes in Two Acts
opus 72

Dramatis personae
Christine Storch   (soprano)
Little Franzl (eight years old), her Son   (speaking part)
Hofkapellmeister Robert Storch, her Husband   (baritone)
Anna, their Chambermaid   (soprano)
Baron Lummer   (tenor)
The Notary   (baritone)
His Wife   (soprano)
Stroh, a Conductor   (tenor)
A Commercial Counsellor   (baritone)   } Robert's Skat
A Legal Counseller   (baritone)   } Partners
An Opera Singer   (bass)
A Young Girl   (soprano)
A Domestic Servant   (speaking part)   } in the service of
The Cook   (speaking part)   } the Storchs

LIBRETTO by the composer

TIME: The present (1924)

PLACE: Grundlsee and Vienna

FIRST PERFORMED at the Sächsische Staatstheater, Dresden, 4 November 1923, with Lotte Lehmann (Christine Storch), Josef Correck (Robert Storch), Theo Strack (Baron Lummer), Hanns Lange (Stroh), Liesel von Schuch (Anna) and Ludwig Ermold (Commercial Counsellor), conducted by Fritz Busch.

I

ON 1 December 1919, less than two months after the première of *Die Frau ohne Schatten* in Vienna, Strauss officially became joint Director, with the conductor Franz Schalk, of the Vienna State Opera, a post he was to hold for the next five years. He was required to spend five months of each year in Vienna, conducting performances and planning repertoire, and he performed these duties most assiduously, also inaugurating in 1920 the Vienna Festival (*Wiener Festwochen*), an annual spring event which is still held in Vienna. He made his début as Director by conducting Wagner's *Lohengrin* on 1 January 1920, and during his first season conducted performances of Beethoven's *Fidelio*, Wagner's *Tristan und Isolde*, and Mozart's *Die Zauberflöte*, as well as his own *Ariadne auf Naxos* and *Der Rosenkavalier*. He had at his disposal a superb company of singers, among them Maria Jeritza, Lotte Lehmann, Elisabeth Schumann, Selma Kurz, Richard Tauber, Leo Slezak, Alfred Piccaver and Richard Mayr, and he made the best possible use of them.

Although the Viennese in due course began to complain that he was using his position to put on his own operas, Strauss was responsible for a number of remarkable productions in Vienna of other composers' works: Weber's *Die Freischütz* with Lotte Lehmann, Elisabeth Schumann and Michael Bohnen; *Carmen* with Jeritza in the title-role and Lehmann as Micaela; *Tannhäuser* with Slezak and Lehmann. He staged the more intimate operas, such as *Così fan tutte* and Rossini's *Il barbiere di Siviglia*, in the delightful Redoutensaal or ballroom in the Hofburg, a custom which continued until quite recently.

Strauss was free, of course, to accept engagements as a conductor when he was not occupied in Vienna, and during his five-year tenure with the Staatsoper he visited South America in 1920 and 1923, conducting his own operas and also concerts with the Vienna Philharmonic Orchestra. In 1922 he visited London for the first time since the war, and in the same year made his second visit to the United States, acting as accompanist to the soprano Elisabeth Schumann at her recitals—it was widely rumoured at the time that he was having an affair with her—and conducting his own works with the Philadelphia and the New York Philharmonic Orchestras.

The only major composition completed by Strauss between 1919 and 1923 was the ballet, *Schlagobers* (the title is Viennese for 'whipped cream'), which he began in 1921 and finished the following year. After *Die Frau ohne Schatten*, he and Hofmannsthal had corresponded about future opera projects without having been able to agree upon their next subject. In 1923 they began to discuss seriously the possibility of an opera about Helen of Troy, which in due course became *Die Aegyptische Helena*, but by this time Strauss had completed the composition of another opera without

Hofmannsthal, indeed without any other collaborator, for the compoer
this time wrote his own libretto. This was *Intermezzo*.

II

IT was in 1916, while they were both at work on the second version of
Ariadne auf Naxos, that Strauss had suggested to Hofmannsthal a modern
subject for an opera. In May of that year, he wrote:

> As for a new opera, I have the following two things in mind: either an
> entirely modern, absolutely realistic domestic and character comedy
> of the kind I have outlined to you before, when you referred me to
> Bahr—or some amusing piece of love and intrigue, somewhere half-way
> between Schnitzler's *Liebelei* which, of course, is too sickly and boring,
> and Hackländer's *Geheimer Agent* or Scribe's *Le Verre d'Eau*—a type of
> intrigue for which I've always had a special predilection.

Hofmannsthal's response was immediate, and brutally frank. 'My dear
Dr. Strauss', he wrote, 'I could not help having a good laugh over your
letter. The things you propose to me are to my taste truly horrid, and
might put one off being a librettist for the rest of one's life.' The Bahr
whom he had already recommended to Strauss was the Viennese critic
and dramatist, Hermann Bahr (1863–1934), who had written a popular
comedy, *Das Konzert*, which Strauss admired. Bahr and Strauss met in
Salzburg in August, 1916, and Strauss outlined his idea for a modern
domestic opera, to be based on the following incident which had occurred
in Berlin thirteen years earlier.

Josef Stransky, the conductor of an Italian opera company which was
performing in Berlin in 1903, was having a drink one evening at the Hotel
Bristol with the impresario Edgar Strakosch and the company's leading
tenor, Emilio de Marchi (who had been the first Cavaradossi in *Tosca*, in
1900), when they were approached by a young woman who recognized
Marchi, and who cheekily asked if she could have a free ticket to the
opera. Marchi referred her to the conductor, Stransky, whose name he
apparently mispronounced as 'Straussky'. The conductor promised the
young woman a ticket, flirted lightly with her, and then forgot about it.
Deciding to send him a reminder about the free ticket, the young woman
attempted to look up the address of 'Straussky' in the telephone directory,
but could find only Hofkapellmeister Richard Strauss. She thereupon sent
Strauss a note which arrived in his absence and was opened by his wife
Pauline: 'Dear Sweetheart, do bring me the ticket. Your faithful Mitzi.
My address is Mitzi Mücke, Lüneberger Strasse 5.' By the time Strauss
arrived home from a short holiday on the Isle of Wight after an English

concert tour, Pauline had already consulted a solicitor about their divorce. For days the composer had to endure his wife's stridently delivered accusations until a friend of his managed to get to the truth of the matter. Even then, it proved difficult to convince Pauline that she had been entirely mistaken.

This was the incident around which Strauss wanted to create his domestic opera. Hermann Bahr agreed to collaborate with him, and drafted a synopsis, but Strauss found it unsatisfactory and asked Bahr to rewrite it. In order to have a clearer idea of the kind of thing the composer wanted, Bahr requested him to jot down his suggestions for the actual scenes to be included. When Strauss had done this, and shown Bahr what he had written, the playwright thought it excellent and advised Strauss to go ahead and write the entire libretto himself. This Strauss did, during a week's stay at a sanatorium in Munich in the summer of 1917, incorporating into the plot another real-life incident concerning Pauline and a young confidence trickster who had attempted to borrow money from her.

The composition of the opera, which began its life as *Das eheliche Glück* (Wedded Bliss), but which eventually became *Intermezzo*, occupied Strauss at various times during the next five years. From his villa at Garmisch, the composer wrote to Hofmannsthal in June 1918: 'The composition of my little domestic opera is making excellent progress. The whole thing is very well planned, and its structure and music will no doubt make up for what the piece lacks in poetic power. I'm getting on with it for the time being, until—I hope very soon—I get a new Hofmannsthal.'

Intermezzo was finally completed in August 1923, during one of Strauss's visits to Buenos Aires. By this time his relations with the Vienna Opera, of which he was still joint Director, were becoming strained, so he arranged for the opera to be staged in Dresden under the baton of the excellent Fritz Busch. At Strauss's suggestion, Busch engaged Lotte Lehmann to create the role of Christine, the character based on Pauline Strauss, and the opera was given its première in Dresden, not in the Opera House but in the smaller, more intimate drama theatre, on 4 November 1924, as part of the celebrations for the composer's sixtieth birthday.

Due largely to Lotte Lehmann, whose portrayal of Christine was said by many to have endowed that character with much more sympathy than it was entitled to, *Intermezzo* was sufficiently successful in Dresden for it to be taken up by other German opera companies. It was staged in Hamburg in December, and in Berlin in the following March. In April, it was performed in Austria, at Graz, but it did not reach Vienna until two years later.

Intermezzo has never proved popular outside the German-speaking countries, though it is still to be encountered in Munich and, occasionally,

Vienna. It was first performed in New York in 1963, and in Great Britain in 1965 at the Edinburgh Festival. In 1974 *Intermezzo* was seen in England for the first time when it was staged at Glyndebourne.

III

IN his 1942 reminiscences, Strauss had only this to say of *Intermezzo*:

> The leap into the world of romantic fairy-tales and the over-stimulation of my imagination by the difficult subject of *Die Frau ohne Schatten* aroused anew in me the desire to write a modern, completely realistic opera, which I had long secretly entertained, and during a week spent in Dr. Krecke's sanatorium I wrote *Intermezzo*, after I had told Hermann Bahr the story and had asked him to make a libretto of it for me. Bahr made a draft but eventually declared: 'There's only one person who can handle this story, and that's you.' And so it was done. The harmless little story elicted from Max Reinhardt this praise: *Intermezzo*, he said, was so good that he could produce it as a play without altering a line. The first performance in Dresden coincided with my dismissal from Vienna.

In a preface to the published score of *Intermezzo*, which he wrote at Garmisch in June 1924, Strauss described the method he had adopted in the composition of the opera. He had always paid the greatest possible attention to natural diction and pace of dialogue with, he thought, increasing success from opera to opera. There could be no doubt, he considered, that orchestral polyphony, no matter how subdued its tones or how softly the orchestra played, spelt death to the spoken word on the stage, but he wished somehow to combine speech, recitative both unaccompanied and accompanied, and arioso or melody into one artistic entity. His concern was with the audibility of the text. 'Anybody who knows my more recent opera scores well', he wrote,

> will have to admit that, provided the singer pronounces the words clearly, and the dynamic markings in the score are strictly observed, the words of the text must be clearly understood by the listener, except in a few passages where these words may permissibly be drowned by the orchestra as it plays with increasing intensity for the purpose of pointing a necessary climax. No praise pleases me more than when, after I have conducted *Elektra*, somebody says to me: 'Tonight I understood every word.' If this is not the case, you may safely assume that the orchestral score was not played in the manner exactly prescribed by me.

Strauss explained that there were no arias in *Intermezzo*, and that the opera was composed throughout as prose dialogue. He urged conductors of the work to pay the greatest attention to the gradual transitions from the spoken word to the sung and half-spoken word, and to those subtle turns in the conversation where the prose is poised between *recitativo secco* and *recitativo accompagnato*, finally reaching its climax in a lyrical outpouring. (Such moments are, in fact, rare in *Intermezzo*, whose lyricism is, for the most part, restricted to the orchestra.) He reminded producers that there was no place for the prima donna in this opera whose actor-singers had to represent genuine human beings, and that the casting should reflect the need for a light, conversational tone as well as musical and physical aptitude for the characters to be portrayed. He ended with the assertion that 'by turning its back upon the popular love-and-murder interest of the usual opera libretto, and by taking its subject-matter perhaps too exclusively from real life, this new work blazes a path for musical and dramatic composition which others after me may perhaps negotiate with more talent and better fortune.'

IV

DESCRIBED by Strauss as a bourgeois comedy with symphonic interludes, *Intermezzo* is in two acts, with eight short scenes in Act I and five in Act II. Though its plot is unashamedly autobiographical and its characters are all derived from people in real life, the composer has for the most part used fictitious names. He himself has become Robert Storch, and Pauline is Christine. Their son Franz, however, at the age of eight, appears under his real name as 'Der kleine Franzl'. Stransky is now Stroh. The business man Willy Levin and the bass Paul Knüpfer (a famous Baron Ochs in *Der Rosenkavalier*) who were present when Mitzi Mücke first made herself known to Stransky are identified by profession in the opera, but not by name, and Mitzi is referred to as Mieze Meier. The action takes place partly at the Austrian ski resort of Grundlsee on Lake Grundlsee in the province of Styria, and partly in Vienna.

Without orchestral preamble, the curtain rises on the first scene of Act I, the composer's dressing-room in the family villa in Grundlsee. It is seven in the morning, and Robert Storch (baritone) is packing to go on a journey. Open suitcases are strewn about the room in great disorder and, while Robert attempts to finish his packing, his wife Christine (soprano) fusses over him inordinately, complaining of the servants, of Robert's frequent absences to conduct concerts in Vienna and elsewhere, of the fact that he gets in her way when he is at home, of her unhappy plight in having to look after the house with inadequate help, and of virtually everything else that comes into her mind. Though he occasionally comments on her bad temper, Robert's manner is in general phlegmatic, which only serves to increase his wife's irritation. He has occasion to remind her that her bullying manner has lost them household help in the past, and is likely to do so again. He points out that she has no need to supervise the domestic staff so closely, and that they can well afford to engage additional staff to relieve her of any strain. Christine brushes these reasonable suggestions aside, for she prefers to remain both martyr and tyrant.

Momentarily tiring of complaining about her maid, Anna, and the other servants, Christine begins instead to make disparaging references to her husband's family which, in her view, is considerably less distinguished than her own. The following short extract will give a taste of this married couple's conversational exchanges:

Christine: Well, fancy my having the nerve to compare your relations with my distinguished family.
Robert (tapping his head):   Distinction lies in the mind.
Christine: Hurry up with your packing, you plebeian.
Robert: Look, why don't you go back to bed, instead of taking your early morning bad temper out on me, and shouting about the same old boring things when I'm trying to concentrate and make certain that I've packed everything!
Christine: I'm looking after all that.
Robert: No, you're just disturbing Anna and me.
Christine: Have you got your muffler?
Robert: I think—(checking)—yes, I have.
Christine: Shoe-horn? Gloves? Travelling cap?
Robert: Anna has never yet forgotten anything.
Christine (in a tone of triumphant sarcasm):   Except the keys of all six suitcases when we went to Campiglio!
Robert: Now leave me in peace—I'm going to have breakfast.
He exits.

Christine occupies herself in giving unnecessary instructions to Anna, the maid (soprano), until Robert re-enters, when she promptly resumes her battle of words with him. He maintains a reasonably amiable tone and an air of bemused tolerance until she refuses his request that she write to him while he is away. 'Well then, to the devil with you', he shouts as he leaves. 'Keep your letters, you unbearable cross-patch, you. Goodbye!'

When Anna tells her that the master is waving to her from his sleigh, Christine hides behind the curtains, asking herself, aloud, why he has to travel so much. To the maid's comment that the master seems not to like to stay in one place too long, she replies, 'Yes, I suspect he has a streak of

Jewish blood in him.' At this point, the orchestra quotes from Schumann's First Symphony (rather oddly, since Schumann was not Jewish). While Anna combs her hair for her, Christine gives instructions to their eight-year-old son, dismisses a tax-collector, deals with the parlourmaid and the cook, complains on the telephone to the local fruiterer, and makes a confidante of Anna, to whom she confesses that what irritates her most about her husband is his eternal kindness and thoughtfulness. Why, she asks, does he not occasionally lose his temper and behave brutally, as a real husband should?

A neighbouring housewife telephones to invite her to go tobogan-ning, and Christine accepts. As she begins to consider which dress to wear, the lights dim and the scene is changed while the orchestra takes up several of the fragmentary themes heard in Christine and Robert's con-versational exchanges, working up to a feverish climax.

Throughout this first scene, as throughout most of the opera, the singers are required to perform in a style which restricts them to recitative-like conversation, with no opportunity for sustained lyrical or dramatic flights. In conversing with her neighbour on the telephone, and occasion-ally in dealing with the domestics, Christine resorts to the spoken word, which is punctuated by orchestral phrases. Beneath the conversation, Strauss introduces in the orchestra the various themes that are heard again in the orchestral interludes in which the principal musical interest of *Intermezzo* lies.

At the climax of this first orchestral interlude, motifs associated with Christine give way to downward glissandi on the violins, graphically describing the sledge run which, when the lights come up again, is revealed as the second scene, with sledges rushing down a snow-filled slope, one after the other. Christine is heard to call *'Bahnfrei'* (Make way) before she appears in her sledge at the top of the run. A young man on skis attempts to cross at the bottom of the run, and is knocked over by Christine's sledge, which has come down far too close behind the previous one. Her immediate bad-tempered reaction alters when he introduces himself as Baron Lummer, the son of a family her parents had known in Linz. She invites the young Baron (tenor) to visit her, and the scene changes again. This time the orchestral interlude eases its way into a waltz, begun on solo piano and developed by the strings.

The second scene had lasted no longer than three minutes. The third, even shorter, takes place at the inn in Grundlsee, where a ball is in progress. To a waltz background, Christine and the Baron, who have been dancing, take time out to converse, and Christine professes concern over the Baron's migraine, promising him that, the following day, she will take over the supervision of his holiday in Grundlsee. As they join the dance again the scene changes, the orchestra continuing the waltz during the scene-change, and then gradually dwindling, themes becoming wispier and instruments falling silent, until suddenly the solo piano interrupts with three abrupt chords and the curtain rises on the fourth scene, a furnished room in the house of the Storch family's notary in Grundlsee.

This fourth scene is the shortest of all, barely two and a half minutes, in which Christine, accompanied by her parlour maid, Therese, inspects the room which she intends to rent for the Baron. She gossips away to the notary's wife (soprano) as she does so, describing the young Baron's requirements, his occasional migraine headaches, and something of his family history. As she leaves, again the orchestra takes over, contributing this time a lyrically flowing interlude in Strauss's best *Rosenkavalier* style. Indeed, a criticism of *Intermezzo* might well be that in it Strauss has reverted to the manner of *Der Rosenkavalier*, both in the orchestra and in the vocal parlando by which the plot, such as it is, is advanced; the difference being that inspiration is now intermittent and that the waltzes, for instance, are consequently rather tired-sounding and unspontaneous by comparison with those of the earlier opera.

The fifth scene, a more reasonable twenty minutes in length and somewhat more lyrical in style than the preceding two scenes, takes place in the dining-room of the Storch villa. Christine sits at a table, reading by the light of a lamp the letter she has almost finished writing to her husband. The passages she reads aloud from the letter are spoken, though her comments upon them are sung. She has told Robert of the twenty-two-year-old Baron whose company she has been enjoying in walks and on the ski slopes, and she has also informed her husband that she has promised his help to the Baron, whose family does not appreciate the young man's intellectual pursuits. Perhaps feeling slightly guilty, she reassures herself that she can hardly be expected to sit at home and mope when her husband is absent. If Robert objects, she will simply have to show him who is master of the house.

Christine's musings are interrupted, first by the Cook, who manages to displease her, and then by the arrival of Baron Lummer whose aid she enlists in checking the household accounts. It soon becomes clear that the Baron has something on his mind. He talks of the difficulty he is experiencing in getting started on a career, and hints that he would like to ask a huge favour of Christine. She pays him scant attention, at first reading a newspaper and then talking proudly of her husband's virtues, to the Baron's discomfort. Assuring him that her husband will certainly find a way of helping him, Christine suggests that perhaps it is time he left. She makes a rendezvous with him for the following day, and the Baron departs without having managed to ask his favour.

Left alone, Christine suddenly feels lonely. Her mood is that of the Marschallin at the end of Act I of *Der Rosenkavalier*, though for a less valid reason than the Marschallin had for her sadness. As the curtain falls, the orchestra sustains the wistful mood Christine has established, in the most lyrical and affecting of *Intermezzo*'s interludes.

The sixth scene, a short one of less than five minutes, finds the Baron in his room at the Notary's house, lying on his bed smoking a cigarette and complaining to himself of the attentions of Frau Storch. He has found his evenings with her rather tedious, he is amused that she believes in his migraines, but he objects to her attempts to encourage him to pursue his studies more assiduously. He cynically considers making a declaration of love to her, but fears that, if he did, she would be perfectly capable of answering him with a hymn of praise for her wretched husband.

The Baron's thoughts are interrupted by the arrival of Resi (soprano), a young girl dressed for skiing. He has clearly been spending time in her company, but hurriedly gets rid of her now for fear that the Notary's wife may see her and inform his patroness. Alone again, he begins to write a note to Christine, which he plans to slip into her hand while they are out walking. 'Most honoured and gracious lady', he begins, 'you were so friendly to me today that I did not dare tell you in words. . . .' He is still writing as the curtain falls.

During the next fifty or so bars of orchestral comment, the scene changes back to the dining-room of the Storch villa where, when the curtain rises again, Christine is discovered with the Baron's letter in her hand. Through the window it is seen to be snowing heavily. Christine is in a state of agitation, for she has just read the Baron's request which is for a loan of a thousand marks. She realizes that she has been foolish to encourage his attentions, and she is distressed that he can have been so foolish as to think she would lend him money.

The Baron suddenly enters. Christine sends him out of the room immediately, shouting at him to wipe his feet first, and when he re-enters she informs him that there can be no question of her acceding to his request. They can remain friends, and her husband will do what he can to help the Baron with his studies, but, as her father used always to tell her, lending money can destroy even the closest friendship.

The Baron is foolish enough to protest that he would pay it back, with interest, but Christine is adamant. She suggests that he give lessons to earn the money he needs, but, when he replies that he could not possibly do this and study as well, she observes drily that she has no further advice for him.

At this moment, a maid enters with a letter addressed to 'Hofkapell-meister Robert Storch'. Tearing it open, Christine is horrified to read its brief message: 'My dearest, do let me have another two tickets for the opera tomorrow. Afterwards—in the bar, as usual. Your Mieze Maier.'

Christine has apparently heard of Mieze Maier, for she exclaims, 'A prostitute!' She leaps to the worst possible conclusion, dismisses the Baron, and immediately drafts a telegram which she gives to the maid to take to the post office: 'You know Mieze Maier. Your infidelity proven. We are parted forever.' She orders the startled maid to pack everything for their immediate departure.

This has been another brief, five-minute scene. After an agitated orchestral interlude, the first act ends with an eighth, and almost equally short scene, in little Franzl's bedroom. His mother, in tears, tells the child that his father has behaved wickedly, and that Franzl will never see him again. The little boy stoutly defends his father, while his mother collapses by his bed attempting sadly to comfort both the child and herself. The orchestra takes up her mood in all seriousness, bringing Act I to an end which would be more affecting if one were able to feel much sympathy for the impossible Christine.

The first act having risen gradually from a plateau of conversational exchanges to a peak of lyrcial and dramatic climax, the second act begins at somewhere near the same peak, before descending to a more relaxed lower level, thus giving the opera a symmetrical aesthetic form which is not immediately indicated by its profusion of short scenes.

Act II opens in Vienna, in the living room of a Commercial Counsellor's house, in which four men are playing the card game of skat, a game popular in Austria and Germany. Before the rise of the curtain, the orchestra has set the mood of the lively game, a solo piano onomatapoeically conveying the shuffling of cards. The players are the Commercial Counsellor himself (baritone), a Legal Counsellor (baritone), an Opera Singer (bass), and a Conductor named Stroh (tenor). As they play, they gossip about their absent partner, Storch, and about his wife. The Commercial Counsellor describes Christine as a monster, but Stroh, the Conductor, defends her, asserting that she is really a good-natured person beneath her fierce exterior, and that she has her husband's interests at heart.

When Storch enters, he joins the game immediately, and there is some banter about how pleasant it is to play cards with no possibility of interruption by women. The Legal Counsellor politely enquires after the health of Frau Storch, and Robert replies that she is well, that he has received a letter from her that morning, and that she is enjoying the company of a new young friend with whom she goes walking, skiing and skating. The Commercial Counsellor, who has obviously suffered Christine's quick temper on more than one occasion, makes a slighting remark about her, at which Robert leaps to his wife's defence, after a fashion. 'She is good for me', he explains. 'I need someone of lively temperament around me.' His arioso in praise of Christine is shorter than hers in praise of him in Act I, but no less ardent in tone.

While Robert is in the process of describing Christine as a really gentle and shy creature who has the prickliness of a hedgehog only on the outside, a maid brings in a telegram addressed to him. When he has read it, Robert is completely bewildered. He tells his friends that it is a message from his wife, to which the Commercial Counsellor replies, 'A prick from the hedgehog?' A speechless Robert asks Stroh to read the telegram aloud, for he cannot comprehend it. Stroh reads: 'You know Mieze Maier. Your infidelity proven. We are parted forever.'

'So you know her too?' asks Stroh, to which Robert can only reply, 'Who is she?' 'Oh, one of those—you know—tra la la' Stroh answers airily, and makes it clear he does not believe Robert's repeated protestations that he has never met the lady. Robert, bewildered and concerned, leaves the skat party precipitately, and as soon as he has gone the gossip and the play recommence, Stroh expressing his surprise that Storch, too, knows Mieze Maier.

The music of this scene has been, if possible, even more loosely conversational in style than the first act, with occasional fleeting references in the orchestra to operas by other composers: references so fleeting that listeners to *Intermezzo* are likely to notice them only if they are following the performance with a score.

The second scene of Act II takes place in Grundlsee, in the office of the Storchs' Notary. Christine arrives to set the divorce proceedings in motion, and is exasperated to find that the Notary (baritone) assumes the co-respondent to be the young Baron who is lodging in his house. The Notary, in turn, is surprised to discover that Christine's intention is to take action against her husband. As a friend of Robert's, he declines to handle the case. He tells Christine that he does not consider the letter to Storch which she has shown him to be solid evidence of infidelity, at which Christine flounces out of the room to look for another solicitor.

The orchestral interlude this time is a particularly violent one. Presumably it describes the outraged Christine's feelings as she storms out of the Notary's office, but it also presages the mood in which Robert is discovered at the beginning of the third scene, set in the famous Viennese park, the Prater, during a thunderstorm. As the curtain rises, Robert is seen pacing about in bewilderment and despair. Christine has not replied to his telegram, he has no idea what is going on, but he is reluctant to cancel his Vienna engagements and rush back to Grundlsee when he feels

135

sure everything could be straightened out if only he could communicate with his wife.

Suddenly, Stroh appears upon the scene, and rushes up to Storch to explain to him that Mieze Maier's note had been intended for him, Stroh, whom she had always thought was Storch. She had looked his address up in the telephone directory, and found Storch's. Robert is, of course, immensely relieved, but also furious with Stroh whom he accuses of having allowed the young woman to assume that he was the famous Storch instead of the not so famous Stroh. He insists that Stroh visit Christine personally to explain who the confusion arose. A reluctant Stroh considers it expedient to agree to this, and the two men leave quickly, while the orchestra rages on to a fierce climax. Strauss's conversational word-setting in this scene is as masterly as it continues to be throughout the score, his note-values accurately reflecting the rhythms of natural speech, with remarkably few sustained notes except when Robert twice rises to the baritone's high G, in ironic gratitude on the first occasion and in violent anger on the second.

The orchestra's mood changes to reflect the frenzied disarray of the fourth scene, Christine's dressing-room in the Grundlsee villa. Open trunks and travelling cases are strewn about the room in which the maid, Anna, is helping her mistress to pack, suffering a barrage of unfair criticism and comment from Christine as she does so. Christine, it appears, has sent young Baron Lummer to Vienna to interview Mieze Maier, but is now having second thoughts concerning the wisdom of this. When Therese enters with a telegram, the tenth her husband has sent her, Christine is reluctant to open it but, persuaded by Anna, does so, and reads: 'Unfortunate confusion with colleague Stroh who himself will arrive tomorrow with evidence to clear matters. Your innocent, highly delighted Robert.'

Disinclined to believe his message, Christine is still discussing the situation with Anna when Therese enters to announce that Herr Kapellmeister Stroh has arrived and would like to see her. She gives orders that Stroh is to await her in the study, and, as the curtain falls, the orchestra, its mood excited and almost exultant, begins to anticipate a satisfactory outcome of the subsequent interview which takes place off-stage.

This orchestral interlude, the last of the opera's twelve, leads to the fifth scene of Act II which takes place in the dining-room of the villa. Therese announces the Master, who rushes in only to be met coldly by Christine who is clearly not prepared to forgive her husband too quickly for a sin he has not committed. He talks of his three days of torment, while she counters with her distress. He is relieved that the confusion is now all in the past, while she considers he is taking it all too lightly. Soon they are embroiled in furious argument, in the course of which Christine asserts that she does not believe Stroh's story. This is too much for Robert who is incautious enough to expostulate that he had, after all, come back immediately to forgive her for her absurd suspicion and jealousy. Christine retorts that she is sorry she ever married him and suggests that he may as well ask his solicitor friend to go ahead and arrange a divorce. 'Do it yourself', shouts Robert as he rushes out of the room.

A somewhat surprised Christine murmurs that she always knew one day it would end like this. At this moment Baron Lummer enters precipitately, having accomplished his mission in Vienna. The score indicates the beginning of a sixth and final scene with the Baron's entrance, though there is neither scene-change nor orchestral interlude, and the action continues without a pause. Baron Lummer has met Mieze Maier and confirmed that she knows Storch. He is surprised when Christine explains the misunderstanding (in which, apparently, she now believes), and informs him that her husband has returned home. Assuring him that Robert's behaviour has been completely blameless, Christine dismisses the Baron who departs as Robert re-enters.

Robert asks who the young man was whom he had seen leaving, and Christine tells him. He makes it clear that he has already heard from his friend the Notary about her not altogether discreet friendship with the Baron, and he attempts to have a little fun at her expense, but Christine does not have the sense of humour to appreciate this. She confesses, however, that she had found Baron Lummer a sympathetic and agreeable companion until he asked her for a thousand marks. Amused by this, Robert magnanimously offers to help the young man since he had, after all, been kind to Christine.

The Baron was not very satisfactory to argue with. For that, says Christine, you need a partner you know well, and you need common ground, or else there's no fun in it. Reconciliation is near, and eventually Christine admits her love for her husband, asks his forgiveness, and tells him she thinks their marriage perfect. On this tender moment the curtain takes its opportunity to fall, and the opera to end, before the happy couple can begin quarrelling again.

The music has become lyrical, indeed sentimental, in these closing moments, which sound like a somewhat pallid reworking of the more nostalgic parts of *Der Rosenkavalier*. That the work should end on this note is perhaps just as well, for throughout the rest of *Intermezzo* Christine has been depicted as so charmless a shrew that one is surprised to find the marriage of Richard and Pauline Strauss surviving the opera. On the other hand, the sentimentality of the final scene and the occasional tastelessness of other sections of the work have militated against its general acceptance, despite the fact that the celebrated theatrical producer Max Reinhardt assured Strauss that he considered the libretto so excellent a piece that he would be prepared to stage it, without music, as a play.

Fritz Busch, who conducted its première, apparently found *Intermezzo* extremely embarrassing. In his memoirs, published nearly thirty years later, he wrote that, as Strauss grew older, he 'passed ever more indifferently and unemphatically over [sentimental] passages when conducting, as if he were ashamed at having composed them.'

Lotte Lehmann, shrewd observer of the Strauss domestic scene as well as superb creator of the role of Pauline-Christine, wrote:

I should have known better than to make a careless remark in Pauline's presence when, after the first performance, we crowded into the hotel, surrounded by a mass of people who had all been to the opera and were now ogling Pauline and her famous husband with undisguised curiosity. 'This opera', I said, 'is really a marvellous present to you from your husband, isn't it?'

Tensely, everybody waited for her answer. She looked round, cast a quick glance at her husband, then said in a loud, clear voice: 'I don't give a damn.'

Embarrassed silence.

Strauss smiled.

NINE

Die Aegyptische Helena

Opera in Two Acts
opus 75

Dramatis personae
Helena (Helen)   (soprano)
Menelas (Menelaus)   (tenor)
Hermione, their Child   (soprano)
Aithra   (soprano)
Altair   (baritone)
Da-ud, his Son   (tenor)
Two Female Servants   (soprano and mezzo-soprano)
Three Elves   (two sopranos, and one contralto)
The Omniscient Mussel   (contralto)

LIBRETTO by Hugo von Hofmannsthal

TIME: c. 1190 BC (after the Trojan War)

PLACE: Egypt

FIRST PERFORMED at the Sächsische Staatsoper, Dresden, 6 June 1928,
with Elisabeth Rethberg (Helena), Curt Taucher (Menelas), Maria Rajdl
(Aithra), Friedrich Plaschke (Altair) and Helene Jung (The Omniscient
Mussel), conducted by Fritz Busch.

I

'THE first performance [of *Intermezzo*] in Dresden coincided with my dismissal from Vienna', Strauss recalled in his *Recollections and Reflections* many years later. It was, in fact, while Strauss was in Dresden for the rehearsals of *Intermezzo* that an official from the Austrian Ministry of Education arrived from Vienna to inform him that his co-director Franz Schalk had during the summer contrived to negotiate a new contract for himself by the terms of which Schalk would, during Strauss's absences from Vienna, have sole responsibility for making artistic decisions.

Unwilling to agree to this, Strauss immediately resigned. In January 1925, he wrote to Hofmannsthal:

My son tells me about the charming afternoon he spent with you. . . . You understand now why I have turned my back on the Vienna State Opera: the annoyance with that —— Schalk was too much, the means for achieving anything worthwhile too little, and the offer of the Minister—who only wanted me as window-dressing and as a willing drudge for when he gets the post of 'Director-General of the State Opera', said to have already been promised him when he resigns as Minister—unworthy of me.

Strauss went on to inform Hofmannsthal that, rid of the burden of the Vienna State Opera, he was feeling extremely well, had just completed a piano concerto (op. 73), and was gradually getting on with 'Act II of *Helena*'.

Hofmannsthal had first suggested the subject of Helen of Troy to Strauss in February 1922; the following year they had given serious thought to an opera about Helen. Strauss at this time was immersed in *Intermezzo*; but, having completed its composition in Buenos Aires in August 1923, he wrote to Hofmannsthal the following month from Dakar: 'I am on my voyage home, in good health and high spirits . . . I hope to find *Helena* at Garmisch, preferably with entertaining ballet interludes: a few delightful elf or spirit choruses would also be most welcome.'

What Strauss was hoping for, he told his librettist, was 'something delicate, amusing and warm-hearted'. What Hofmannsthal, in his reply, promised was 'two very rich acts of roughly equal length . . . something like that of a Puccini opera'. Hofmannsthal envisaged Maria Jeritza as Helen, and either Karl Oestvig or Richard Tauber as Menelaus. As usual, he was not averse to suggesting what kind of music Strauss should write:

The style must be easy-flowing, on occasion as nearly conversational as the Prelude to *Ariadne*, sometimes coming close to the conversation scene in *Der Rosenkavalier*, but never so heavy as in the opera in

140

Ariadne. There will, however, be plenty of opportunity for duets and trios. These *lyrical passages* will, unless I fail with my libretto, stand out clearly from the effortless and often psychologically subtle conversation. The more lightly, indeed light-heartedly you can handle this, the better it will be. There is, in any case, no German artist who does not become more heavy-handed over whatever he does than he ought to be.

In his next letter, Hofmannsthal encouraged the composer to handle their new opera 'as if it were to be merely an operetta—it's bound to be by Richard Strauss in the end'. However, the libretto he provided was hardly of a kind to inspire music of a light, operetta-like nature, for it proved to be one of Hofmannsthal's more complex creations, combining a tortuous plot with portentous philosophizing and obscure symbolism, and including in its cast of characters one which might well have perplexed a more intellectual musician than Strauss: a talking sea-shell he called *Die Alleswissende Muschel* (The Omniscient Mussel)!

Strauss appears to have coped remarkably well with all this. He informed Hofmannsthal in October that he had begun to sketch the first act, most of which, he thought, would virtually set itself to music. By July of the following year, Act I was completed, but the second act gave more trouble to both composer and librettist, and its composition proceeded at a much slower pace. Strauss continued to work on the opera throughout 1925, between visits to France, Spain and Italy, and 1926, in which year he also visited London to conduct the orchestral accompaniment for a silent film of *Der Rosenkavalier* and to record excerpts from that opera.

It was not until October 1927, that Strauss finally completed the opera which was to be called *Die Aegyptische Helena* (The Egyptian Helen). 'After much hesitation, rejecting, rewriting, altering and all the pleasant birth-pangs, the conclusion has now turned out very beautiful, brilliant, yet simple', he assured Hofmannsthal, adding that he hoped the first performance would be given in Dresden the following June.

Die Aegyptische Helena was given its première in Dresden, conducted by Fritz Busch, but not with the singers whom Hofmannsthal had hoped would be engaged. When Maria Jeritza demanded too high a fee, Strauss wrote to Hofmannsthal:

Since I believe there is no chance now of getting Jeritza, I have definitely decided on [Elisabeth] Rethberg, whose somewhat bourgeois appearance has 'greatly improved' in America. She is not so tall as Madame Jeritza, and will therefore go better with the short [Curt] Taucher as Menelaus . . . She intends to call on me during the next few days so as to convince me personally of her 'sophisticated appearance'.

Hofmannsthal was furious:

> You want me to write something new for you, and yet at the same time you inflict on me what I consider more loathsome than anything else that could happen. It looks as if, although we have known each other for so long, and mean well by each other, you had not the least idea what it is in our collaboration that gives me pleasure and what has the opposite effect. I do not think there is anyone who knows me so little . . . It is not the face of the actress that matters . . . nor does it matter whether Madame Rethberg has now got a better dressmaker and looks 'more sophisticated' (what passes for sophisticated among theatrical people in Germany is in any case something awful), but everything depends on the magic of acting and movement . . . Madame Rethberg may sing like a nightingale, I understand nothing about that. What I do know is that she is worse than mediocre as an actress, and this will ruin Helen, completely ruin her.

Understandably, Strauss was offended by Hofmannsthal's tone. 'Why do you always turn so poisonous the moment artistic questions have to be discussed in a business-like manner and you don't share my opinion?' he asked. 'To accuse me immediately of not understanding you is neither polite nor just. If I may say so, I think I understood you a great deal sooner than many other people. Otherwise I wouldn't have set your libretti to music against the advice of the "most competent" people.'

Before the première, Hofmannsthal and Strauss for a time seemed keen to engage Strauss's beloved Lotte Lehmann for the title-role. 'Lehmann is now right at the top, both in singing and in acting', Strauss wrote to Hofmannsthal, who in turned expressed the view that her voice was 'indeed at present perhaps the most beautiful and least strained in Europe'. But Lehmann, probably annoyed that, having scored so great a success in *Intermezzo*, she had not been considered the only possible interpreter of Helen, was playing hard to get. Strauss attempted to persuade her to sing the role in the first Vienna performances, but was forced to admit to Hofmannsthal that 'Madame Lehmann has perfidiously let me down'.

When *Die Aegyptische Helena* was given its première in Dresden on 6 June 1928, Elisabeth Rethberg sang Helen, and Curt Taucher was the Menelaus. The conductor was Fritz Busch. Five days later, on 11 June, Strauss himself conducted the opera in Vienna with his and Hofmannsthal's first choice, Maria Jeritza, in the title-role. It was Jeritza, too, who sang Helen in New York in the Metropolitan Opera production which followed in November. However, neither in these cities nor in Berlin, where it was staged in October, did *Die Aegyptische Helena* meet with

Die Aegyptische Helena

success, the general opinion being that the work was ponderous and lacking in inspiration. 'These sumptuous harmonies', wrote the critic of the *New York Herald Tribune* after the Metropolitan première,

that richly fibred counterpoint woven by Strauss's glowing orchestra, have neither salience nor life. Hollow and unkindled, they depress us by the emptiness of their rhetoric, the triteness of their musical speech. The power and pungency of the greater Strauss of former days are missing from this splendidly, vacuous score. At best he can only borrow from himself, at worst he can but remember his inferiors. . . .

(The producer of the Dresden première was Otto Erhardt, who thirty years later told the present writer that he had undertaken the task with reluctance since he thought the opera mediocre, and that Pauline Strauss had made such a nuisance of herself by her frequent interference at rehearsals that he, Erhardt, at one point screamed in desperation the final words of Herod from *Salome*: '*Man tötet dieses Weib!*' [Kill that woman].)

In 1933, for its production at the Salzburg Festival, Strauss agreed to a few changes to the opera, and composed some new music for it, at the instigation of the conductor Clemens Krauss and the producer Lothar Wallerstein. Further changes, authorized by Strauss, were made by Krauss and the producer Rudolf Hartmann for Munich in 1940.

II

HOFMANNSTHAL thought that his libretto for *Die Aegyptische Helena* was the best he had done. 'In its construction', he wrote to a friend a few months after the Dresden première, 'it meets the requirements for being performed on an operatic stage, in its rhythm it tends towards song, and aria-like parts alternate with declamatory passages, which Strauss handles with such power.' Although Strauss's music shows no significant falling-off of his powers, the new opera, in its return to a more sumptuous style after the domestic *Intermezzo*, cannot avoid sounding as though its composer were marking time rather than setting out in a new direction.

If, however, *Die Aegyptische Helena* is finally an unsatisfactory piece, the blame rests primarily with Hofmannsthal's dense and complex libretto. Although he would have denied the charge, Hofmannsthal's principal failing as a librettist is that he was never willing to leave enough for the music to do. It is no compliment to say of his libretti that they are fine enough to be performed as plays without music. The ideal librettist is the poet whose words provide indications for the composer, but do not inhibit his imagination by doing too much of the work for him in advance. Hofmannsthal's plot for *Die Aegyptische Helena* is too confused, and his

143

dramaturgy already too self-contained for Strauss's imagination to be more than intermittently inspired by it.

One does not need any great knowledge of Greek mythology to understand the world of the opera. Helen of Troy, wife of Menelaus and daughter of Leda and the god Zeus, was abducted by Paris. This, according to Homer, led to the Trojan War. Another version of the story, however, is told by Euripides in his play, *Helen*, in which Paris abducts from Troy not Helen but a phantom created in her likeness by the goddess Hera, in order to cause war between the Greeks and the Trojans. The real Helen, kidnapped by Hermes, remains in Egypt throughout the war, but is finally reunited with Menelaus. Hofmannsthal's plot uses the Euripides version of events as its background.

The opera begins with Strauss setting forth turbulently in the orchestra a cluster of themes representing Helen, her husband Menelaus (his German spelling is 'Menelas') and Troy. When the curtain rises the music becomes calmer and a dance-melody emerges.

The first act of the opera takes place on a small island off the coast of Egypt, in a hall of the palace of Poseidon, the sea-god. It is evening, and a supper table is laid for two. Poseidon's lover, an Egyptian princess and enchantress named Aithra (soprano), sits on a throne awaiting Poseidon, and wondering why he has not returned as she has prepared a splendid meal for him. Apart from serving maids, Aithra's only companion is a huge sea-shell. This is the All-Knowing Mussel which, in addition to being omniscient, also has the gift of human speech with a contralto timbre.

The Mussel assures Aithra that Poseidon's love for her is as strong as ever, but the princess becomes agitated when it adds that Poseidon is at present with the Ethiopians. Aithra's maid-servant (soprano) wants to bring her a phial of lotus juice to calm her, but Aithra refuses. The Mussel now begins to describe a ship at sea. A man, the only person on board who is not asleep, awakens one of the sleepers to whom he hands over the helm, and then goes below to a sleeping woman, the most beautiful woman in the world. He bends over her as though about to kiss her, but then suddenly produces a dagger. 'Aithra', the Mussel exclaims urgently, 'Do something to help, for the man on the ship is killing his wife!'

Aithra asks who these people are, and the Mussel replies that the woman is Helen of Troy and the man her husband, Menelaus. Aithra immediately uses her magical powers to conjure up a violent storm which she directs to attack the ship at sea. The Mussel continues to describe the scene. The storm has now reached the ship, the masts snap, those on board are thrown to and fro, and the ship founders. The man and his wife are in the sea, swimming. He is supporting her. At the Mussel's behest, Aithra now calms the waves. The next picture transmitted by the Omniscient Mussel is of Menelaus striding to the shore with Helen in his arms, as the foaming waves part for him.

Helen and Menelaus have come ashore on Aithra's island. Aithra sends her maidservant with a torch to light the way to the palace for them, and then asks herself if it can be true that she is about to receive the famous Helen of Troy, the most beautiful woman in the world but also the most dangerous. She slowly withdraws into an adjoining room where she can still be seen.

The orchestra pauses, and for a moment the hall of the palace remains empty. Then the maidservant rushes in, carrying a torch and followed by a handsome man clenching a sword in his teeth and dragging after him an extremely beautiful woman whose long golden hair flows loosely around her shoulders. The maidservant leaves, and the woman, Helen, goes up to a mirror and begins to arrange her hair. Menelaus (tenor) peers about him, places his sword on the stool next to the Mussel, and murmurs 'Where am I? What place is this?'

Helen (soprano), immediately in control of the situation, observes that they are in a splendid hall, with two thrones, a welcoming fire and a table laid for two. Clearly a king and queen are expected. Will Menelaus sit and eat with her? Menelaus, who is still determined to kill the wife who has been unfaithful to him, refuses, even when Helen in '*Bei jener Nacht*' (With that night), a solo passage which rises somewhat above the workaday musical level of the rest of the scene, tries to tempt him with a goblet of wine, and later a fig from which she has taken a bite.

Menelaus threatens Helen with the weapon he had used to cut the throat of her lover, Paris, warning her that he intends to bring up their daughter in ignorance of her mother's shame. 'Forget what has happened, and kiss me' is Helen's only reply. In a duet, they both invoke unearthly powers. She prays for aid from the dark forces below, while he addresses the gods above. Her desire is to be restored to the arms of Menelaus: his is for the courage to kill her. Their prayers nevertheless end in unison, and soprano and tenor rise together to a final high C.

Menelaus is about to kill Helen. His hand is stayed only momentarily by her extreme beauty, when Aithra decides to intervene. Summoning a host of *Nachtelfen*, elves of the night, she bids them conjure up the noise of battle to distract Menelaus. A three-part chorus of elves now simulates the clamour of the battle-field, and announces that Paris has arrived to fight. 'Have the dead come here to be killed again?' cries a distraught Menelaus as he rushes off to do battle.

Helena staggers towards Aithra's throne and collapses upon it. Aithra now appears, and explains that Helen is in the palace of Poseidon and that

145

she, Aithra, wishes to protect her from the frightful man who may at any moment return. 'Oh, how I hate him', she exclaims. But 'Oh, how I love him', Helen replies. 'Troy is in the past, and now I belong to him.'

Helen's wet clothes are dried by Aithra's magical glance, and the lustrous shine of her hair is restored by the enchantress's soothing hands. Soon Helen and Aithra are singing a typically Straussian duet about the superior strength of two women who trust each other. Aithra gives Helen a potion to drink which will restore her lost innocence to her, and erase all memory of recent events. As Helen sways, overcome with sleep, the Mussel warns of the imminent return of Menelaus, the voices of the elves can be heard nearby, and Aithra orders her serving-maids to take Helen to her bedroom, and clothe her sleeping form in Aithra's loveliest blue gown.

As the maids take Helen to the adjoining room, Menelaus rushes in, clutching his sword, and Aithra quickly conceals herself behind the curtains. Menelaus reveals that he is distraught because he believes he has just found Helen with Paris and has slain them both. Aithra now emerges, graciously welcoming Menelaus as her guest. After persuading him to partake of her all-purpose remedy, the lotus juice, she requests that he speak quietly so as not to disturb his wife who is asleep in the next room, tired after a long journey.

Menelaus finds her words confusing, but Aithra eventually persuades him that, on the day nine years past when Paris abducted Helen, the gods were secretly watching over Menelaus, and substituted a phantom Helen who was borne away by Paris. The real Helen, meanwhile, was hidden in a remote place, the castle of Aithra's father on the slopes of the Atlas mountains. For years, Helen has been in a state of magically induced slumber, dreaming that she lies in the arms of her husband. The woman who today has been defying the threats of Menelaus is that shadow-Helen, but Aithra is now about to restore the real Helen to her husband. Menelaus comments to himself that enchantresses who live on lonely islands have been known to show images of the dead to visitors, but Aithra insists that he prepare himself to see Helen. At a sign from her, the hall of the palace darkens, lit now only by a bright stream of light from the adjoining room. Curtains part to reveal the sleeping Helen, lying on a couch in a gown of shimmering blue.

The orchestra's mood is solemn as Helen slowly opens her eyes, while Aithra's unseen elves murmur encouragingly in the background, and an enraptured Menelaus, hardly daring to look at her, sings of his eternal longing for his beloved wife. While Helen is awakening, Aithra repeats the information about his wife's lengthy sojourn in the Atlas mountains which she has already imparted to Menelaus. 'Am I not still the wife you once desired?', Helen shyly asks her husband, and Aithra quietly but triumphantly points out to him that there is nothing of the siren about this chaste creature. An ensemble builds up in which husband and wife timidly approach each other, while comment is contributed sympathetically by Aithra and somewhat flippantly by her elves over whom the enchantress would appear to have but imperfect control.

Aithra offers to have a ship made ready to take Helen and Menelaus back to Sparta, but Helen is startled by this suggestion. Fearing the past, she prefers to remain with Menelaus in her newly found and enchanted present, far from people who know her, in a place where no one has heard of Troy and its war. Aithra agrees to build for them a pavilion by an oasis at the foot of the Atlas mountains, to which she will magically transport husband and wife. In an aside to Helen, she mentions that she will provide her with certain necessities, among them a phial of the lotus juice, a few drops of which it would be expedient to add to her or her husband's drink occasionally, to prevent unwanted memories returning.

The newly reunited Helen and Menelaus lovingly enter together the adjacent sleeping chamber, and Aithra makes a sign to her serving-maid to extinguish the lights. The elves are now openly sniggering, until Aithra stamps her foot and orders them to be silent. When all is still, and even the maid-servant has fallen asleep, the orchestra brings Act I to a serene close and the curtain slowly falls.

When the curtain rises again on Act II, without orchestral preamble, the scene revealed is a tented pavilion opening on to a palm grove with a view of the Atlas mountains in the background. On the left is the entrance to the pavilion's inner room in which can be seen a richly ornamented chest. As she takes from the chest a golden mirror with whose aid she entwines ropes of pearls into her hair, Helen sings a rapturous aria, '*Zweite Braut-nacht*' (Second wedding night) in which she recalls the night she has just passed with her husband, and the bliss of their reunion. These are the finest pages of Strauss's score, perhaps the only pages in which he re-captures something of the matter as distinct from the manner of his earlier style. Most of the first act of *Die Aegyptische Helena* has sounded like *Die Frau ohne Schatten* at a distinctly lower level of inspiration. In '*Zweite Brautnacht*', however, Strauss not only regains his former mastery but also anticipates the exalted mood of the *Vier letzte Lieder* (Four Last Songs) with which he would end his career twenty years later.

Menelaus, who has been sleeping on a cushion at Helen's feet, now awakens in some confusion. He remembers the events of the previous night, and the rage with which he had struck down the woman whom he had thought was Helen, but he wonders at the nature of the drug which had calmed him so quickly and at the miracle by which his wife has been restored to him. This reminds Helen to offer him another dose of the lotus juice.

While she searches for it in the chest, she accidentally knocks Menelaus's sword from its sheath. As it falls to the floor, Menelaus snatches it up. Reminded of his use of it the previous night, he warns Helen, of whose reality he is by no means completely convinced, to flee from him lest he find his anger rising again within him. Helen realizes that Aithra's magic potion has its limitations. Flinging it back into the chest, she resolves to win her husband's trust back by her own efforts.

Suddenly, a group of horsemen can be heard approaching the oasis, and Helen calls to Menelaus to protect her as a number of desert warriors in chain mail appear and take up positions in the grove around the pavilion. They are followed by messengers who rush in and throw themselves at Helen's feet. Finally, a regal personage with raven-black hair enters, flanked by standard bearers. He is Altair, Prince of the Mountains (baritone). He kneels before Helen, touches first the ground and then his forehead in homage to her, and then rises, in response to a gracious gesture from Helen. At his behest, two black slaves come forward and spread a gold embroidered carpet at Helen's feet. Helen, smiling, sits on the chest which, with its gold fittings, resembles a throne, while Menelaus, his sword drawn, stands behind her. Helen graciously indicates to Altair that he may step upon the carpet. He does so, kneeling again on the edge of it. She now has Menelaus sit beside her on her improvised throne, and then bids Altair speak.

Altair informs Helen that he has been commanded by the three queens Aithra, Morgana and Salome, to whom he owes allegiance, to offer his land to her. Again, he prostrates himself before Helen. Slaves now approach, bearing caskets full of gifts, three veiled maidens throw themselves at Helen's feet, and then retreat to be replaced by a group of slim youths, among whom is Da-ud, son of Altair. Helen has only to command, says Altair, and the blood of these youths will be shed joyfully for a single glance from her eyes.

The youths confirm this by shouting that they are ready to die for Helen, and Da-ud (tenor), stepping forward, declares that it would be right to die for her sake, since she is the most beautiful woman in the world. The conductor of the opera's première, Fritz Busch, thought Da-ud's brief solo a cheap, mawkish piece, and said so, to which Strauss replied that one needed at least one such aria in every opera, in order to appeal to the public. But Da-ud's impassioned outburst, a mere eighteen bars long, is hardly likely to make much of an effect. It has about it something of the manner of Jokanaan's prophetic utterances in *Salome*. (Strauss initially wanted to make Da-ud a *travesti* role with a mezzo-soprano voice, but was persuaded by Hofmannsthal to write the role for the tenor voice, with mezzo-soprano as an optional choice.)

Menelaus has been staring at the handsome Da-ud. In his still confused condition, he half imagines the youth to be Paris, whom he has apparently forgotten that he has already killed. He looks about wildly for his sword, while Helen attempts to sooth him and Altair comments that the goddess's favourite seems unnecessarily surly. However, to ingratiate himself with the divine Helen, Altair is prepared to organize a hunt in honour of Menelaus, to whom he offers his son Da-ud as a hunting companion. 'The prey, I hope, will be worthy of the hunter', he adds, throwing at Helen a wild glance that is not lost on Menelaus who, glaring at Da-ud, repeats Altair's words to himself.

Altair leaves, and Menelaus asks himself what can be happening to him. This youth, this beautiful woman, this country, all are strange to him. Is this an adventure or a vivid dream? He goes to the inner room to dress for the hunt, and Da-ud takes the opportunity to tell Helen that it is he, Da-ud, who must ride beside her, not her companion. Ignoring Helen's advice to him that he should stay away from the fire or he will melt like wax, he fervently declares his love and devotion. He kneels before her, then suddenly leaps up and departs. Helen turns away, laughing.

Menelaus emerges from the inner room, dressed for the hunt but not yet armed. As Helen hands him his helmet, he reminds her that once before he had gone hunting, and returned to find his wife had gone. He addresses Helen as '*reizende Nymphe*' (charming nymph) and asks her name, confessing that he had been bewildered the previous evening and had failed to hear it clearly. He picks up his sword which Helen tries to wrest from his grasp. She tells him it is a dreadful weapon to hunt gazelles with, but Menelaus will not be parted from it. This sword, he warns her, is all that remains to him, and he forbids her to touch it.

Helen realizes that there is a long road to be travelled before she can reinstate herself in the eyes of her husband. Menelaus leaves for the hunt, with a parting comment that when one goes hunting one never knows whether one will find one's wife unchanged on one's return, and Helen, watching him go, wonders how to return from the path along which magic arts have carried her. Aithra's lotus juice, she tells herself, was both too strong and not strong enough for the heart of Menelaus.

One of the three slave girls now reveals herself to Helen as Aithra. While the other two begin to rummage in the chest, Aithra explains that she and her two servants have hastened to her to prevent a calamity. One of the girls had carelessly included a second phial of magic potion in the casket, a quite different potion which, when taken, gives one something quite dreadful: total recollection of the past. Helen exclaims that this is precisely what she needs, for Aithra's lotus juice has given her only a living death, a phantom existence. Menelaus, she explains to Aithra, had taken

149

her for a strange woman provided by Aithra for a night's amusement, and had considered that, in making love to her, he had betrayed the real Helen whom he thought dead. Only if Menelaus has his memory restored to him can there be any hope of real happiness and trust for them both.

Helen snatches the draught of recollection, despite Aithra's protests, and commands the serving maids to prepare a strong measure of it for Menelaus to drink. As they are doing so, Altair suddenly returns and begins to pay court to Helen, promising her a superb banquet, which he says may prove dangerous for her companion, Menelaus, but will be a glorious experience for her. At this point, pastiche oriental music is heard in the grove outside, as though to substantiate his claim.

Aithra's two serving-maids (soprano and mezzo-soprano) have been watching the hunt, which they now describe. The falcon has captured a gazelle, and both the brave hunters, Menelaus and Da-ud, are galloping towards the prey. Altair tells Helen that she is the most beautiful prey, but that, unlike his sons, he does not intend to pine to death in the desert for her sake. He knows a better way to proceed. Helen tries to cool his ardour, while Aithra laughs quietly to herself. As Helen retreats before Altair's confident approach, the maid-servants, still watching the hunt, exclaim that one of the hunters, Menelaus, is lifting his sword against the other, Da-ud. They describe Da-ud's attempt at flight, Menelaus's pursuit, and Da-ud's death. Unmoved, Da-ud's father merely remarks that he has plenty of arrows in his quiver and plenty of other sons in his tent. He can think of nothing but that night's banquet and his hoped-for conquest of Helen.

Da-ud's body is solemnly brought in by negro bearers. Menelaus approaches it, as if in a trance, horrified at having killed the youth. Meanwhile, despite Aithra's warnings that the time is not propitious, Helen bids the maidservants prepare the potion of recollection. While brilliantly arrayed guests of indeterminate sex gather outside for Altair's feast, Helen announces the commencement of her own feast. Neither Altair's oddly menacing eunuch guests nor Aithra's well-intended protests can prevent her offering the potion to Menelaus. He willingly takes it, convinced that it is poison and that through death he will be reunited with the real Helen. Sounds of distant thunder can be heard as both Helen and Menelaus drink from the goblet.

Menelaus's first impulse, when his memory is restored, is to lift his sword against his faithless wife whom he now recognizes standing before him. But Helen no longer fears death, and in any case Aithra's timely intervention, announcing the immediate arrival of their child, Hermione, prevents Menelaus from carrying out his purpose. He throws his sword aside, gazing now on Helen with love. Aithra comments that grief and infidelity were necessary stages in their progress to a mature relationship. She, Menelaus and Helen combine to express their feelings in a trio which is somewhat more characterful than the music for the solo utterances of Helen and Menelaus in this scene.

Altair now bursts in with his followers, threatening Helen with rape and Menelaus with imprisonment, but Aithra suddenly reveals her identity, invoking the aid of Poseidon and summoning up armed warriors. Recognizing the great queen to whom he owes obedience, Altair humbles himself before her, and the opera ends as Helen and Menelaus, with their child Hermione, prepare to ride off on splendidly apparelled horses provided by Aithra.

It is difficult not to feel that *Die Aegyptische Helena* is a work defeated both by Hofmannsthal's obtuse libretto and by Strauss's lack of real musical invention, a lack which becomes more obvious as the opera progresses. That the composer was reverting to an earlier style need not have mattered, had he proved capable of still composing imaginatively within that style. But even the music for Menelaus, a role which Strauss composed with the great Richard Tauber in mind, is as lifeless as his writing for the tenor voice so frequently could be. Fortunately, both composer and librettist were to find their best form again in their next, and final collaboration.

TEN

Arabella

Lyrical Comedy in Three Acts
opus 79

Dramatis personae

Count Waldner, Retired Cavalry Officer   (bass)
Adelaide, his Wife   (mezzo-soprano)
Arabella   (soprano) ⎫
Zdenka   (soprano) ⎭ their Daughters
Mandryka   (baritone)
Matteo, an Officer   (tenor)
Count Elemer   (tenor) ⎫
Count Dominik   (baritone) ⎬ Suitors of Arabella
Count Lamoral   (bass) ⎭
Fiakermilli   (coloratura soprano)
A Fortune-Teller   (soprano)

LIBRETTO by Hugo von Hofmannsthal

TIME: 1860

PLACE: Vienna

FIRST PERFORMED at the Sächsische Staatsoper, Dresden, 1 July 1933, with Viorica Ursuleac (Arabella), Alfred Jerger (Mandryka), Margit Bokor (Zdenka), Martin Kremer (Matteo) and Friedrich Plaschke (Count Waldner), conducted by Clemens Krauss.

Alexander Young (Matteo), Joan Carlyle (Zdenka) and Dietrich Fischer-Dieskau (Mandryka) in *Arabella*, Covent Garden, 1965

(above) Joseph Ward (Schneidebart), David Ward (Morosus) and Barbara Holt (Aminta) in *Die schweigsame Frau* at Covent Garden in 1961

(below) scene from the première of *Friedenstag*, Munich, 1938

I

IT was in 1928 that *Die Aegyptische Helena* was unsuccessfully offered to the public. For the genesis of *Arabella,* the next opera by Strauss and Hofmannsthal, one has to go back to September 1922, when Strauss, while composing *Intermezzo,* mentioned in a letter to Hofmannsthal that he felt like doing another *Rosenkavalier.* Or perhaps one should go much further back, to 1909, the year in which Hofmannsthal wrote a short story, 'Lucidor', whose plot he incorporated nearly twenty years later into that of the *Rosenkavalier*-like new work upon which he and Strauss eventually embarked.

It was not until *Die Aegyptische Helena* was nearing completion that either of the collaborators took the 'new Rosenkavalier' possibility any further. Then, in September 1927, Strauss mentioned that within a week he would have finished the full score of *Helena.* 'But now I have no work', he complained,

> completely cleaned out! So please, write some poetry. It may even be a 'second *Rosenkavalier*' if you can't think of anything better.
> If the worst comes to the worst, a little stop-gap job—a one-act piece—to keep my hand in. Oil to prevent the imagination from rusting up.

The suggestion that he might produce 'a stop-gap job' was, of course, considered highly offensive by Hofmannsthal. 'I cannot just *dash something off* for you', he replied to Strauss. 'The day when I could do this would be accursed, and your work would not prosper.' It is also likely that, unlike Strauss, he preferred to see one project safely launched before embarking upon another: he was, at this stage, rather concerned about the casting of the première of *Die Aegyptische Helena.* However, he gave some thought to Strauss's request, and two days later wrote again to the composer, mentioning *Der Fiaker als Graf* (The Cabby as Count), a comedy which he had begun to write two years previously. He had sketched out a three-act scenario, and then abandoned the subject. But

> last night it occurred to me that this comedy might perhaps be done for music, with the text in a light vein, largely in telegram style.
> The first act—as far as I recollect—will do. The second will be particularly suitable: it takes place in a ballroom, and offers enchanting possibilities. The third act I can no longer remember very clearly. Now yesterday it occurred to me for the first time that the whole thing had a touch of *Rosenkavalier* about it, a most attractive woman as the central figure, surrounded by men, mostly young ones, a few episodes, too—no sort of outward likeness or similarity to *Rosenkavalier,* but an innate affinity.

Hofmannsthal promised to dig out his notes, and give serious thought again to the subject. Six weeks later, he had come to the conclusion that *Der Fiaker als Graf* was, by itself, 'too flimsy for an opera'. He now intended to combine it with elements from 'another projected comedy' to produce the libretto of a three-act comic opera ('indeed almost an operetta') which, he assured Strauss, would not only be kindred to *Der Rosenkavalier*, but would not fall short of *Die Fledermaus* in gaiety.

The new elements in Hofmannsthal's libretto came, in fact, not from a projected comedy but from 'Lucidor', a long story or novella he had written nearly twenty years earlier. On 16 December 1927, he and Strauss met, and Hofmannsthal read a synopsis of his libretto to the composer. On this occasion, he must have given Strauss the impression that a man named Mandryka, in love with the heroine, Arabella, would be the opera's central character, for two days later Strauss expressed certain misgivings:

So far as I can pass any considered judgement after no more than a cursory acquaintance with your draft, it seems to me that you are again making the mistake that led you, as the loving author, to overestimate the theatrical effect of Ochs von Lerchenau. However well this figure is equipped by the poet, and however much it is bound to interest us artists, we are not the public! And strangely enough, to that public Ochs is not only a matter of indifference, uninteresting or boring, but to the Italian audience downright repulsive and distasteful in the extreme. The character which . . . ensured final victory for *Der Rosenkavalier* is the Marschallin: her meditations about time, the passage about the clocks, the parting—and this is what seems to be to be lacking in the new subject. Your Croatian (even if enacted by a guest *Pagliacci* baritone [*sic*] such as Chaliapin) wouldn't draw a hundred people into the theatre . . .

Hofmannsthal accepted Strauss's criticism calmly. He had, he assured the composer, always intended the central figure to be a woman, and indeed had already given his notes the provisional title, '*Arabella oder der Fiakerball*' (Arabella, or the Cabbies' Ball). Strauss, impatient to start work on the new opera, had found in the Vienna Hofbibliothek four volumes of South Slav folk-songs which he was studying. 'I am meanwhile doing exercises in Croatian costume', he informed Hofmannsthal shortly before Christmas.

By the end of April 1928, Hofmannsthal had finished the first act of his libretto, which he sent to Strauss at Karlsbad, where the composer was taking the waters. 'It is not without some anxiety that I am sending something so important as the first act of our comic opera to Karlsbad of all places', he wrote to Strauss. 'I remember that the cure makes you nervous and irritable. Please, if you feel that way, it would be better not to look at the act, for over such a gay and attractive piece we must not have a repetition of what I shall never be able to forget: how you let me send you *Ariadne* at the very moment when the effort to stop smoking had set you at odds with everything for several weeks!'

Strauss was apparently taking the cure in his stride, for he replied from Karlsbad early in May that he found the first act, on the whole, splendid. His only criticism concerned the character of Arabella herself, whom he thought rather vaguely outlined, and the ending of the act. 'To my mind', he wrote, 'it would have to end definitely with a solo voice, an aria, a lyrical outpouring from Arabella. The present curtain is quite pretty, but not effective enough for an opera. Cosima Wagner once told me: "The main thing is the curtains".'

After the première of *Die Aegyptische Helena* at the end of June, composer and librettist were able to devote almost their entire attention to *Arabella*. By the end of the year, the libretto had been completed, Hofmannsthal having patiently revised it in the light of Strauss's comments. 'I find we understand each other better every year', Strauss had written. 'A pity such good, continuous progress towards perfection must come to an end some day, and that others must start again from the beginning.' He can hardly have foreseen just how soon that end would be for Hofmannsthal.

Work on *Arabella* progressed slowly, for both Strauss and Hofmannsthal were ill in the early part of 1929: first Hofmannsthal with gastric influenza which dragged on for weeks, and then Strauss, who on his recovery went to Italy to recuperate, and back to Karlsbad again for the thermal cure. Strauss had not begun to compose any of the music, for he was awaiting a final, definitive draft of the libretto from Hofmannsthal. He had asked for more lyrical interludes. 'The aria, after all,' he reminded his librettist, 'is the soul of opera. And there's a marked lack of that. *Separate numbers with recitatives in between*. That's what opera was, is, and should remain.' It is heartening to find the composer returning to first principles, after the meandering formlessness of *Die Aegyptische Helena*.

The end of the great Strauss-Hofmannsthal partnership came with brutal suddenness. On 10 July, the librettist sent a final revision of Act I to the composer, and on the evening of 14 July Strauss responded by telegram: FIRST ACT EXCELLENT. HEARTFELT THANKS AND CONGRATULATIONS. The telegram was delivered on the morning of 15 July, but Hofmannsthal never opened it. It was the day of the funeral of his son Franz who had killed himself two days earlier. As he was dressing to attend the funeral, Hofmannsthal suffered a stroke, and died within minutes.

Shocked by his collaborator's death, Strauss asked Pauline and their son Franz to represent him at Hofmannsthal's funeral. To the librettist's widow, he wrote: 'This genius, this great poet, this sensitive collaborator, this kind friend, this unique talent! No musician ever found such a helper and supporter, and no one will ever replace him either for me or for the world of music!'

Strauss decided to proceed with the composition of *Arabella* as a tribute to Hofmannsthal, using the text exactly as it stood, although the second and third acts had not been given their final revision by the librettist. It took Strauss more than three years to finish the opera, in between attending to various other tasks and engagements. At the Munich Festival in the summer of 1929 he conducted two Mozart operas, *Le nozze di Figaro* and *Così fan tutte*, and Wagner's *Tristan und Isolde*. In the autumn he worked on a new composition, *Austria*, a setting for male chorus and orchestra of a poem by Anton Wildgans. Dedicating the work to the city of Vienna, he conducted its first performance there in January 1930.

By the end of 1929 Strauss had almost completed Act I of *Arabella* when, at the instigation of the Viennese conductor Clemens Krauss, he was invited by the producer Lothar Wallerstein to revise Mozart's *Idomeneo*, an opera at that time erroneously considered to be a work, which though interesting, could not possibly be staged for modern audiences in the form in which Mozart had left it. Strauss spent most of 1930 on this project, rearranging numbers, composing new recitatives, and adding an interlude in Act II and a new finale to the opera. He conducted his version of *Idomeneo* at the Vienna Staatsoper in April 1931, with no more than moderate success.

In the latter half of 1931, Strauss resumed work on *Arabella*, concentrating his energies completely upon the opera from the end of 1931. He noted in the full score that Act I was completed at Garmisch on 6 March 1932, Act II on 6 June, and Act III on 12 October. The work was dedicated 'To my friends Alfred Reucker and Fritz Busch'. Reucker was the Intendant at the Dresden Opera where Busch, who had conducted the premières of Strauss's most recent two operas there, was still the Musical Director. It was arranged that *Arabella* would be given its première at Dresden in the summer of 1933.

By the summer of 1933, however, even the determinedly non-political Strauss can hardly have failed to notice the changes that had taken place in Germany. In January, the German president, Hindenburg, had appointed Adolf Hitler, leader of the National Socialist Party, as Chancellor. Within weeks, using the burning of the Reichstag, the German parliament, as their pretext, the National Socialists had established a one-party rule. The country's widespread anti-semitism was now given official sanction, and

Jews, their sympathizers, and indeed all who did not enthusiastically and vociferously support the new regime, were dismissed from all positions of responsibility. The conductor Otto Klemperer and the producer Max Reinhardt lost their posts in Berlin. In Dresden, Reucker, who was Jewish, and Busch, who was not, were dismissed, and both men became refugees.

Strauss attempted to insist that *Arabella* be conducted by Busch and produced by Reucker, and threatened to withdraw his score unless they were reinstated. However, the Dresden Opera held him to the terms of his contract, and Strauss gave in, stipulating only that he must personally approve the artists to be engaged. In the event, *Arabella* was conducted at Dresden by Clemens Krauss, with the conductor's *inamorata*, Viorica Ursuleac, in the title-role. (She subsequently became Krauss's second wife.) Strauss would have preferred his favourite Lotte Lehmann with whose warm, beautiful voice in mind he had composed the role. He found it expedient, however, to accept Viorica Ursuleac, especially when Lehmann, who lived in Vienna but in the first half of 1933 was touring in the United States, made it clear that she would not sing again in Germany while the Nazis were in power.

The replacement producer in Dresden was Josef Gielen; the leading male role, Mandryka, was sung by the popular Viennese baritone Alfred Jerger. The première on 1 July was only moderately successful: the opera was politely received, but enthusiasm was not forthcoming until the Vienna première on 21 October, with Lotte Lehmann at last as Arabella. Lehmann sang the first performance in Vienna under tragic circumstances, her mother having died the same morning; Strauss came on to the stage to express his gratitude to her. Viorica Ursuleac sang the title-role in Berlin under Furtwängler, and before the end of the year there were productions in Olomouc (in Czech) and Stockholm (in Swedish). The following year, *Arabella* was staged in Basle, Monte Carlo (in French), Buenos Aires (conducted by Fritz Busch, who had been forced to leave Germany), Amsterdam (conducted by Strauss himself), Budapest (in Hungarian) and in London at Covent Garden, where it was produced by Otto Erhardt and conducted by Clemens Krauss with a cast that included most of the singers from the Dresden première, among them Ursuleac, Jerger, Margit Bokor and Martin Kremer. The opera was unenthusiastically received, the consensus of opinion suggesting it to be a poor imitation of *Der Rosenkavalier*.

Arabella achieved a degree of popularity only in the post-war years when an enchanting young Swiss soprano, Lisa Della Casa, made the role her own until her retirement from the stage in 1974, and the German baritone Dietrich Fischer-Dieskau proved to be the ideal Mandryka. The opera was first staged in America at the Metropolitan Opera, New York, in 1955, when it was sung in English translation by a cast headed by Eleanor Steber (Arabella), Hilde Gueden (Zdenka) and George London (Mandryka), and conducted by Rudolf Kempe. In 1960, at the Music Academy of Santa Barbara, California, the opera was given its American West Coast première in a production by Vienna's first Arabella, Lotte Lehmann.

II

THE opera is set in Vienna in the year 1860, its entire action taking place in the course of one day, Shrove Tuesday. It begins in the morning at the hotel where Count Waldner, a retired cavalry officer, and his family live, continues at the Cabbie's Ball that evening, and ends later that night back at the Waldners' hotel. (More than one old Viennese hotel has been identified as the original of the one in which Hofmannsthal placed the Waldners, among them the Munsch and the Erzherzog Karl. The present writer's choice is the Hotel König von Ungarn, in the Schulerstrasse near the Stefansplatz.)

There is no prelude. A descending figure is heard in the woodwind section of the orchestra, and the curtain rises immediately on the living-room of the hotel suite occupied by the Waldners. Count Waldner's wife, Adelaide (mezzo-soprano), is discovered sitting at a table with a fortune-teller (soprano), and one realizes that the orchestra is indulging in an onomatopoeiac rendering of the shuffling of cards which the fortune-teller is attempting to read. At another table is Zdenka (soprano), the younger of the Waldner's two daughters, putting a pile of bills in order. Though she is a girl in her late teens, Zdenka is dressed as an adolescent boy, for a reason which is revealed early in the ensuing scene.

A knock at the door is answered by Zdenka. When the caller proves to be one of their creditors, Zdenka announces that father is out and mother suffering from a bad headache. Accepting the bill, Zdenka adds it to the mounting pile. Meanwhile, Frau Waldner is being told by the woman who is reading her cards that a fortune is eventually on its way. The fortune-teller can see Count Waldner gambling and losing large sums, but she can also discern in the cards a rich stranger who has been summoned from afar by letter. Adelaide assumes this to be a rich suitor for her elder daughter, Arabella, but the fortune-teller warns her that someone will come between Arabella and the rich gentleman, and suddenly asks if Frau Waldner has a second daughter. Adelaide tells the fortune-teller in confidence that Zdenko, as he is called, is really a girl, Zdenka. She and her husband have dressed her as a boy because they are not well enough off to launch two girls in Viennese society in keeping with what they consider to be their social position. Since Zdenka adores her elder sister, she would certainly not attempt to cause dissension between her and a rich husband. The fortune-teller insists, however, that the cards never lie. Adelaide invites her to come into the adjoining room where they can continue their reading of the cards without interruption.

Left alone, Zdenka, who has already had to receive another bill while the two older women were talking, now confesses to herself her fear that, in order to escape their creditors, her parents might decide to leave Vienna. This would mean her never seeing again a young officer named Matteo with whom she is desperately in love. Since Matteo thinks she is a young man, Zdenka is unable to reveal her affection for him, and in any case Matteo is in love with Arabella who, though she once seemed fond of him, has since grown bored with the young officer. The best that Zdenka can hope for is that Arabella's affection for Matteo might be rekindled. She would be willing to sacrifice herself for this, and would live the rest of her life dressed as a man so long as Matteo was happy with Arabella.

Strauss's music in these opening pages, and throughout *Arabella*, has a light Viennese charm which makes it much more immediately accessible than the heavier and more turgid orchestral world of *Die Aegyptische Helena*. As usual, motifs which will be associated with various characters, events and situations are woven into the orchestral fabric. In the first few minutes of the opera, various motifs and themes representing not only the three characters already encountered but also Matteo, Arabella, Mandryka, and the concept of a 'right man' (*Der Richtige*) for Arabella, are juxtaposed with the highest degree of skill, and all within a context in which the rhythmic lilt of the Viennese waltz is never far distant.

Matteo (tenor) now arrives, and Zdenka has the difficult task of concealing her own feelings for him while at the same time assuring him that Arabella still loves him, and promising to deliver to him another letter from her sister. Poor Matteo cannot understand why Arabella's behaviour when they meet should be so cold, since her letters to him are so affectionate. (The letters, of which Arabella is ignorant, are of course being written by Zdenka.) Unless he can have Arabella's love Matteo is determined to ask for a transfer to Galicia. If he cannot forget Arabella there, he will shoot himself.

He rushes out, leaving Zdenka distraught at the realization that she will never see Matteo again unless she persuades Arabella to return his love. At this moment, her sister Arabella (soprano) enters, dismissing, in a few gentle phrases, the female companion who has accompanied her on her walk on the Ring (the boulevard which encircles the inner city of Vienna). Seeing a bouquet of roses which Matteo has left for her, Arabella asks if these flowers had been bought by a hussar. When Zdenka tells her they are

159

from Matteo, she tosses them aside. There are also presents for Arabella from her trio of noble admirers, the Counts Elemer, Dominik and Lamoral, of whom she is fond without taking any of them seriously.

When Zdenka begins passionately to plead Matteo's cause, Arabella shrewdly asks her sister if she is in love with him. She thinks it is high time that Zdenka was allowed to appear as her real, female self. Zdenka replies that she would rather remain a boy to the end of her days than a woman like Arabella, proud, coquettish and cold in her behaviour to Matteo. '*Er ist der Richtige nicht für mich*' (He isn't the right man for me), Arabella tells her sister earnestly. This is the start of the first extended lyrical episode in the opera, a solo which turns into a duet, '*Aber der Richtige*' (But the right man) (Ex. 16), as Arabella sings of her conviction that, one day, the right

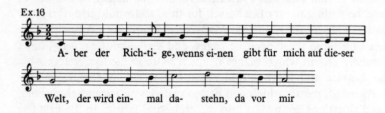

Ex.16

A- ber der Rich-ti- ge, wenns ei-nen gibt für mich auf die-ser
Welt, der wird ein- mal da- stehn, da vor mir

man will appear, and she will instinctively know, without any doubt, that they are meant for each other. Zdenka's voice, confused, unhappy, but sympathetic and loving to her sister, joins Arabella's. This flowing duet for the two sopranos, with its typically long and winding Straussian vocal line, and its air of sensuous yearning for a future happiness, is based on a simple south Slavonic folk-tune which Strauss included as a footnote in his short score.

At the conclusion of the duet, the jingling of sleigh bells is heard, announcing the arrival of Count Elemer who has come to take Arabella for a drive. The carnival season will reach its climax that evening with a ball at which Arabella feels she must make up her mind whom she will marry. Perhaps it will have to be Elemer. At this, Zdenka has a sudden vision of Matteo's suicide, and imagines herself kssing for the first time his ice-cold lips. Then everything will be over for her.

Arabella, who has been looking out of the window, now reveals what was in her mind when she had asked earlier if the roses had been brought by a hussar. She had noticed, as she left the hotel that morning, a tall stranger in a fur travelling-cloak, either a Hungarian or Wallachian, with his servant, a hussar, standing behind him. The stranger had gazed at her

intently. Flowers from him today, says Arabella, would have meant more
to her than anything else. Her tone has been light and conversational until
the words *'der hat mich angeschaut . . .'* (he gazed at me), when her vocal
line expands lyrically and a greater warmth and intensity steal into the
orchestra. This foreigner, it seems, could well be the right man for
Arabella.

The rhythm of the polonaise now heralds the entrance of Elemer (tenor)
with whom Arabella flirts lightly, agreeing to go for a drive with him half
an hour later, as long as her 'brother', Zdenko, is allowed to accompany
them, a condition to which Arabella's besotted suitor reluctantly agrees.
As Elemer departs, Zdenka comes back into the room and Arabella
suddenly calls her attention to the foreigner—*'Mein Fremder'* (my
stranger) she calls him—who has again taken up his post in the street
outside. But, to her disappointment, after looking up as though seeking
her window the attractive stranger walks on. The two young women go to
their rooms to dress for the sleigh ride with Count Elemer, as Adelaide
enters the room with her husband, Count Waldner (bass).

Waldner, who has been losing money at cards and is unable to pay any
of his debts, explains to his wife that he had sent a photograph of Arabella
to an old army colleague, a rich eccentric from Croatia called Mandryka
who had once had the streets of Vienna strewn with three thousand
bushels of salt in the middle of summer because his beloved wanted to go
for a sleigh-ride. Waldner conveys this information to his wife in a lively
arietta, *'Da war ein gewisser Mandryka'* (There was a certain Mandryka), to
which a ripe flavouring is added by his Austrian dialect.

Waldner's hope was that Mandryka might take it into his head to come
to Vienna and marry Arabella, thus rescuing the Waldner family from
poverty. But there has been no reply from Mandryka, only more final
demands from various creditors. Adelaide is, in any case, not happy at the
prospect of Arabella marrying a man her father's age. She proposes,
instead, that the family should leave Vienna to live with their wealthy aunt
in one of her castles in the country. Zdenka would have to continue her
male impersonation, but the fortune-teller has prophesied a rich match for
Arabella. Meanwhile, there is no money left, and Adelaide has already
pawned her last piece of jewellery.

His wife retires to her room, and Waldner orders a brandy, only to be
snubbed by the waiter who has orders not to extend any further credit to
the occupiers of Suite no. 8. When the waiter returns to announce a visitor
named Mandryka, Waldner is naturally overjoyed. The man who enters,
however, is clearly too young to be Waldner's friend from his old regi-
ment. He is no more than thirty-five, powerfully built, but with a certain
elegance. He produces the letter which Waldner had sent, apologizing for

the blood-stains on it, caused by an old bear which, he says, charged him when he went hunting. (The orchestra tersely describes this encounter.) He explains that he is now the only living Mandryka, nephew of Waldner's old colleague who is now dead (a reverent comment from the woodwind), and that he had opened the letter intended for his uncle and been struck by the photograph of Waldner's daughter. If she is still not spoken for, he has come to ask for her hand in marriage. His servant, Welko, produces the photograph, and confirms that it is the young lady who resides in the hotel. Clearly, Mandryka is the attractive foreigner whom Arabella had noticed gazing up at her window.

The music has taken on a more solemn tone with the arrival of Mandryka (baritone) whose utterances, especially on the subject of Arabella, have a kind of moral earnestness which is emphasized by the halo of sustained woodwind chords surrounding them. In the andante arioso, '*Wenn aber das die Folge wär' gewesen*' (But supposing this had been the consequence), with its sprightlier concluding section in which he informs Waldner that he is the owner of forests and villages in Croatia, a far distant province of the Empire by the banks of the Danube, with four thousand serfs dependent on him, Mandryka has no difficulty in persuading Arabella's father to part with his daughter, especially after he has described the powerful effect upon him of Arabella's photograph. For twelve weeks he had lain in bed with crushed ribs from the embrace of the old bear, twelve weeks in which his stewards, farm hands and foresters wondered what ailed him, not understanding that what ailed him was love. He had sold off one of his forests to finance a journey to Vienna to win the hand of Arabella.

Mandryka, now in an expansive and generous mood, extends his wallet to his future father-in-law with the words, '*Teschek, bedien' dich!*' (Please, help yourself). Waldner has no hestitation in doing so. He then offers to introduce Mandryka immediately to his wife and their daughter Arabella. Mandryka, however, considers his first meeting with his future bride to be something sacred, and not to be rushed into unceremoniously. He will take rooms in the hotel, and await a future invitation. His tone is indeed reverent as he explains, *Das ist ein Fall von andrer Art*' (That is a different kind of occasion), and then descends to a more matter-of-fact level as he takes his leave of Waldner.

Left alone, Waldner can hardly believe his good fortune. '*Teschek, bedien' dich!*', he repeats delightedly, trying out various inflections, as he contemplates the banknotes he has extracted from Mandryka's wallet. He departs, no doubt to lose his newly acquired wealth in a card game, as Zdenka enters, in despair at the thought that she may well be about to see Matteo for the last time. Almost on cue, Matteo now slips quietly into the room to ask if his young friend has a letter from Arabella for him. Caught off guard, Zdenka hastily improvises, assuring Matteo that Arabella will give him the promised letter that evening at the Cabbies' Ball. Matteo leaves quickly, and a moment later Arabella enters, dressed for the sleigh-ride with Elemer. She sends Zdenka off to dress, and then soliloquizes in a long aria, which is preceded by a solo viola introduction ('*Mein Elemer! Das hat so einen sonderbaren Klang . . .*': My Elemer! What a strange sound that has . . .) in which she considers her rival suitors, and then finds her thoughts turning again to the stranger who, though she has not met him, fascinates her so mysteriously. She attempts to put him out of her mind by telling herself that he is probably a married man, and forces herself to end her aria gaily in anticipation of that evening's Ball, of which she will be the acknowledged Queen. Zdenka enters, ready to go out, and the sisters leave as a lively waltz rhythm mounts to its climax in the orchestra.

Act II takes place that evening at the Cabbies' Ball, held in a hotel in Vienna. Again without orchestral preamble, the curtain rises on the scene, the foyer of a ball-room, with a staircase leading to a balcony which overlooks the ball-room itself. Mandryka and Waldner are watching Arabella and her mother descend the staircase, and Mandryka exclaims at the angelic loveliness of Arabella. Her parents obviously have spoken to Arabella of Mandryka; if she did not realize then that he and her exotic stranger were one and the same person, she certainly does now. Waldner introduces both mother and daughter to Mandryka, and then he and his wife leave Arabella and Mandryka together.

What ensues is a long duet scene in which Mandryka and Arabella, with shyness on her side and passionate intensity on his, explore each other's personalities. By the end of the duet they have implicitly declared their love for each other, and Arabella is certain that she has met '*der Richtige*', the right man for her. Before their conversation can get under way, however, they are interrupted twice, first by Dominik (baritone) and then by Elemer, both of whom want Arabella to dance with them. She puts them off till later, and concentrates her attention upon Mandryka who, in a passage whose very moving quality is due as much to Hofmannsthal's unexpected verbal directness and simplicity as to Strauss's touching vocal line and sensitive scoring, tells Arabella that he once had a wife, a sweet and beautiful creature, who died after they had been married for only two years.

Mandryka's tone becomes more urgent, almost vehement, as he attempts now to find words to express his love for Arabella. He is interrupted by the third of Arabella's trio of noble admirers, Lamoral (bass), whom she dismisses almost absent-mindedly. The love duet continues, a string of tender, delicately winding Straussian melodies, as Mandryka sings of his estate, and of the clear waters of the Danube which flows past his house. He describes to Arabella a charming custom in his village by which the betrothal of lovers is marked. The maid draws a glass of water from the well and offers it to her beloved as a token that they are betrothed in the eyes of God and man.

The final section of their duet, '*Und du wirst mein Gebieter sein*' (And you shall be my lord) (Ex. 17), based on another south Slavonic folk-tune,

Ex.17 Andante mosso

Und du wirst mein Ge-bie-ter sein, und ich dir un- ter-tan-

in which the voices of Arabella and Mandryka blend in symbolic union, is perhaps the most beautiful part of their scene together. As the duet ends, Arabella asks Mandryka to allow her to stay awhile at the ball, alone. She would like to dance, and to bid farewell to the years of her girlhood, just for an hour. Mandryka is reluctant to leave the ball while she remains, but promises to keep away from her for the rest of the evening.

A crowd of dancers now enters, among whom is a gaudily attired young woman who presents a bouquet to Arabella, naming her Queen of the Ball. She is Fiakermilli, the cabmen's mascot (coloratura soprano). She is also one of Strauss and Hofmannsthal's least happy creations. Her florid coloratura solo, '*Die Wiener Herrn*' (The Viennese gentlemen), with its jodelling cadenza and its hectic top C's and D's, is, however, soon over, and Arabella goes off into the ball-room on the arm of Dominik.

While Mandryka pays compliments to his future mother-in-law, Zdenka (who, of course, is dressed in male evening attire) has a difficult time with Matteo who is miserable at being ignored by Arabella. Mandryka invites the Waldners, indeed the entire gathering, to a lavish supper, and is soon gaily ordering huge quantities of food, champagne and flowers. Arabella says a tender farewell in turn to her three Counts, Dominik, Elemer and Lamoral, making it clear to each of them that they are meeting for the last time.

As Arabella goes off into the ball-room with Lamoral for a final waltz, Matteo and Zdenka continue with their discussion, and Zdenka gives Matteo a letter which she says is from Arabella. Matteo is reluctant to take it, fearing it may contain a word of final dismissal, but Zdenka insists that he open it. He does so, to find no letter but only a key. It is, says Zdenka, the key to Arabella's room at the hotel. Matteo is to go there now, and wait in her room for Arabella, who will be with him in a quarter of an hour. A bewildered but excited Matteo leaves quickly.

Unfortunately, this conversation has been overheard by Mandryka who orders his servant Welko to call Matteo back. But it is too late: Matteo has wasted no time in making his exit from the ball. Mandryka's supper guests are now assembling, but when a servant comes in with a note for him from Arabella, which tells him that she has gone home, and promises that from tomorrow she will be his, Mandryka fears the worst, and gets drunk very quickly, exhorting his guests to do likewise. He flirts with Fiakermilli, and when Arabella's mother asks if he knows where her daughter is, he answers her brusquely.

Adelaide calls her husband away from one of his card games to deal with what is rapidly becoming an extremely awkward situation. Unable to understand why Mandryka should be behaving so oafishly, Waldner decides that he should accompany them, and Waldner's card-playing friends, to their hotel to find Arabella. As he leaves with the Waldners, Mandryka announces to those remaining at the ball that they should consider themselves his guests. 'Hurrah!' reply Fiakermilli and the other guests, as the curtain quickly descends.

The latter half of Act II has been musically somewhat threadbare, a very poor attempt to imitate the frenetic liveliness of Act II of that other Strauss's *Die Fledermaus*, but the composer makes amends with the extended orchestral Prelude to Act III. (In a version first performed in Munich in 1939 to celebrate Strauss's seventy-fifth birthday, these last bars of Act II are omitted, and the orchestra continues without a pause into the Act III Prelude. However, in the opinion of the present writer, the original version in three separate acts is to be preferred on grounds of formal structure).

Like the Prelude to *Der Rosenkavalier* more than twenty years earlier, the Prelude to Act III of *Arabella* is intended as a description of the sexual act. This, one must assume, is now taking place in what the gullible (for operatic purposes) Matteo thinks is Arabella's room. As one will discover later, 'Zdenko' has rushed back to the hotel, thrown off 'his' male formal evening wear and transformed 'himself' into Zdenka to await Matteo in the dark. Matteo, we are to assume, manages to have sexual intercourse in a darkened bedroom with Zdenka, under the impression that his partner is Arabella. The orchestra graphically depicts their passion and its eventual subsidence.

When a respectable state of orchestral detumescence has been reached, the curtain rises. The scene is the lobby of the Waldner's hotel. It is night, and the lobby is illuminated by oil-lamps. A staircase leads to the first floor on which the doors of several rooms can be seen. Emerging from one of the rooms, Matteo is about to descend the stairs when a ring at the outer door causes him to conceal himself. A porter crosses the lobby to open the front door, and a moment later Arabella enters, wearing her ball gown which is covered by a cloak. At the foot of the stairs she pauses, and sitting in a rocking-chair she sings a simple, though somewhat high-lying song in which she imagines driving through forests and rolling fields in a carriage with Mandryka, and being introduced to the workers on his estate.

Matteo, convinced that he had left her in her room only a few minutes earlier, is astonished to see a fully dressed Arabella at the foot of the stairs. She is equally surprised to find him there late at night, and asks him if he is staying at the hotel. He in turn asks if she is going out so late, to which she replies that she has just come home from the ball.

A conversation at cross-purposes ensues, Matteo's insinuations being met by Arabella with incomprehension, while her comparative aloofness is wounding and perplexing to him. When Matteo thanks her for what she has just given him, Arabella replies, 'Thanks for what? Whatever was between us is all over.' His attempts to make her acknowledge their love-making upstairs are beginning to irritate her, and in turn what he calls her appalling virtuosity of behaviour now angers him. 'We were in the dark', he reminds her in desperation, 'and I couldn't see your eyes. Give me just one glance now to seal everything for the last time, and you are free for ever.'

While Arabella has been attempting to pass Matteo on the stairs, the door-bell has rung again, and now her parents, her father's gambling associates, Mandryka and his two servants all enter the lobby. Mandryka, seeing Arabella in conversation with Matteo, whom he recognizes as *'der Verfluchte mit dem Schlüssel'* (that accursed creature with the key), assumes the worst, and orders his servants to pack, as they are going home by the first train. He will not listen to Arabella's assurances that she has done nothing wrong, and when she calls on Matteo to confirm that their behaviour has been in no way unseemly, that young officer's manly silence seems a further accusation.

By now, tempers and voices have been raised, and a crowd of hotel residents, awakened by the commotion, has begun to assemble in the upstairs corridor to observe the goings-on. Waldner challenges Mandryka to a duel, then remembers that he has pawned his pistols. Mandryka urges Arabella to confess that Matteo is her lover, and when she swears she is speaking the truth, he tells her in anguished tones that he himself saw 'the boy' give Matteo the key to her room. 'What boy?' asks Arabella. 'The boy, your footman, whom you sent', he replies. Arabella realizes he must be referring to Zdenka, but has not time to consider the implications of this, for

Mandryka now asks her, brutally, 'Do you wish to marry that man, with whom you have had so sweet a rendezvous no more than ten minutes after we became engaged?'

The musical dialogue in which this scene has been conducted represents both Strauss and Hofmannsthal at their best. The music now ceases, as Arabella speaks her dignified reply to Mandryka: 'I have no answer to make, Herr von Mandryka, to your question.' Mandryka's next words, too, are spoken. They are a request to Welko to awaken the nearest swordsmith and produce two swords, and also to have a doctor standing by, for he proposes to fight a duel with Matteo in the adjacent winter garden.

Suddenly Zdenka's voice is heard calling, 'Papa! Mama!', and the music begins again as Zdenka, wearing only a woman's negligé, comes running down the stairs to kneel at the feet of her father. Strauss's style becomes more lyrically expansive from here to the end of the opera, while still managing to encompass the swift unravelling of plot which is now necessary. Zdenka confesses all, and Matteo, embarrassed to discover that he has been making love to his friend Zdenko, can only murmur in his state of sexual confusion, '*O, du mein Freund, du meine Freundin!*', of which an unkind but not inaccurate translation would be 'Oh, my friend, oh, my girl friend!'

Mandryka attempts to apologize to Arabella, who is at that moment more concerned with comforting her sister. He then takes command of the situation, presenting Matteo to Waldner as a suitable husband for Zdenka.

Relieved at what seems to him to be a happy conclusion to the evening's excitement, Waldner goes off with his companions to resume his game of cards, Matteo says a tender goodnight to his newly found love, and Adelaide then takes Zdenka upstairs. Left alone with Mandryka, Arabella merely asks his servant, Welko, to bring to her room a glass of pure cold water from the hotel's well. She goes upstairs without any further word to Mandryka. He soliloquizes in remorse, and Welko is seen to take the glass of water to Arabella's room.

A moment later, Arabella appears at the head of the staircase, holding the glass of water. She has remembered the village custom which Mandryka had described to her earlier in the evening, and, as she slowly descends the staircase, with the words '*Das war sehr gut, Mandryka, dass Sie noch nicht fortgegangen sind*' (It is good, Mandryka, that you have not yet gone) she begins the great solo finale of the opera, one of Strauss's most beautiful arias for soprano, and indeed one of the most affecting moments in all opera. 'This final, long, aria-like speech of Arabella's is indescribably beautiful, and makes the opera's ending an ever new and gripping experience to me', wrote Lotte Lehmann years later. 'Everything dissolves in harmonious and sensuous melody.'

At the foot of the stairs Arabella offers Mandryka the glass of water. He drinks, then hurls the glass to the floor. They declare their love for each other. 'And you will stay just as you are?', asks Mandryka. *'Ich kann nicht anders werden, nimm mich wie ich bin'* (I cannot be anything else, take me as I am), cries Arabella as the curtain falls.

After *Die Frau ohne Schatten*, the operas of Strauss are uneven in quality. Unlike Verdi, Strauss was not a composer who simply got better as he got older. But two of the operas he wrote after *Die Frau* are, in their way, as fine as any of his earlier works for the stage, and *Arabella*, even though a few pages of its score are competent rather than inspired, is certainly one of them. Some of its shortcomings are due to the fact that Hofmannsthal had not revised the second and third acts of his libretto before he died. It is more than likely that Strauss would have been as assiduous as he usually was in his desire to get the words absolutely right before beginning to compose. He chose, however, as a form of tribute to Hofmannsthal, to set the text precisely as his colleague had left it. As it happens, the actual words of the libretto could hardly have been improved upon, for on this occasion the domestic nature of the subject did not allow Hofmannsthal to indulge in any of his occasional flights of arcane rhetoric. The structure of Act II and Act III does, however, leave something to be desired.

The final shape of *Arabella* might well have proved to be more satisfactory, but Hofmannsthal's newly acquired simplicity of diction and Strauss's rediscovered wealth of melody and felicitous orchestration combine to make their last collaboration one of their most successful in artistic terms, and by no means their least popular. The popularity of *Arabella* with audiences has, indeed, increased over the years, as familiarity with its typically Viennese blend of gaiety and sentiment has bred affection. It is an opera with much of the charm of *Der Rosenkavalier* but few of the earlier work's occasional *longueurs*. The use of folk-song in Mandryka's music brings the work close to operetta, as does the amusing if unsubtle characterization of such minor characters as the Waldner parents, to say nothing of the dreadful Fiakermilli. Strauss's music for Arabella and Mandryka is often radiant, and throughout the opera the transparent delicacy, variety of colour and euphonious warmth of the composer's scoring are a continual delight. Although its eponymous heroine probably takes second place in audiences' affections to the wise and mature Marschallin of *Der Rosenkavalier*, *Arabella* is nevertheless one of the most attractive of Strauss's operas, and possibly the most entertaining.

ELEVEN

Die schweigsame Frau

Comic Opera in Three Acts
opus 80

Dramatis personae
Sir Morosus   (bass)
His Housekeeper   (contralto)
The Barber   (baritone)
Henry Morosus   (tenor)
Aminta, his Wife   (soprano)
Isotta   (soprano)
Carlotta   (mezzo-soprano)   }   Members of a
Morbio   (baritone)   Theatrical Troupe
Vanuzzi   (bass)
Farfallo   (bass)

LIBRETTO by Stefan Zweig, after the play *Epicœne or The Silent Woman*
by Ben Jonson

TIME: Around 1780

PLACE: A room in Sir Morosus's house in a suburb of London

FIRST PERFORMED at the Sächsische Staatsoper, Dresden, 24 June
1935, with Maria Cebotari (Aminta), Friedrich Plaschke (Sir Morosus),
Matthieu Ahlersmeyer (The Barber), Martin Kremer (Henry Morosus)
and Erna Sack (Isotta), conducted by Karl Böhm.

I

IT was in 1931, while he was still at work on *Arabella* more than two years after Hofmannsthal's death, that Strauss first met the distinguished novelist and biographer, Stefan Zweig. During the summer, Strauss had asked a friend, the publisher Anton Kippenburg, to find out if Zweig, who was one of Kippenburg's authors, would be interested in providing him with an opera libretto. Zweig wrote to the composer in October, enclosing as a gift a privately printed Mozart letter (apparently one of the slightly obscene ones Mozart used to write to his Augsburg cousin Maria Anna Thekla Mozart), and asking if he might visit Strauss to discuss a musical project with him.

Strauss replied, thanking Zweig for the delightful gift, but could not refrain from adding that he owned an original Mozart letter, one 'so inoffensive that it could be read openly even in a Mozart Club'. He invited Zweig to visit him at his villa in Garmisch, and confessed that what he would most like to receive 'from the creator of *Das Lamm des Armen*, *Volpone*, and the magnificent *Fouché* 'would be a libretto about a type of woman whom Strauss had not yet been given an opportunity to put in any of his operas: 'the woman adventurer, the *grande dame* as a spy'. Hofmannsthal, Strauss told Zweig, had considered spy dramas unacceptable, but, he continued, 'I am old-fashioned enough to be fascinated by Augustin Scribe's *Ein Glas Wasser* [*Le Verre d'Eau*] and Victorien Sardou's *Letzter Brief* [whose French title is *Les Pattes de Mouche*].'

This, however, was distinctly not the kind of thing that Stefan Zweig had in mind at all. When the two men met, not at Garmisch, but on 20 November in Munich (where Strauss was to conduct *Elektra* that evening), at 11 a.m. at the Hotel Vier Jahreszeiten [Four Seasons], Zweig outlined two much more intellectually respectable proposals. The one which Zweig himself thought the more significant and important was a kind of pantomime for dancing, which he had already described rather dauntingly in a letter to Strauss as 'a work, clear in its outlines, universally understandable, playable on every stage in the world, in all languages, before any audience highbrow and lowbrow, at the same time challenging the man of music to his highest accomplishment—a work which comprises all contrasts of the arts, from the tragic to the light-hearted, from the Apollonian to the Dionysian, timeless, a work in which a man and a musician like yourself can attain the epitome of his life's task.'

Strauss strongly preferred Zweig's other suggestion, for an opera to be based on the comedy *Epicœne, or The Silent Woman*, by the English Elizabethan and Jacobean playwright and poet, Ben Jonson. Strauss had already seen and enjoyed Zweig's adaptation of Jonson's *Volpone* for the German-language theatre, and he responded immediately and favourably to the idea of composing an opera on *The Silent Woman Die schweigsame Frau*). As Zweig wrote later, in his autobiography, *The World of Yesterday*,

It was a pleasant surprise to see how quickly, how clear-sightedly Strauss responded to my suggestions. I had not suspected in him so alert an understanding of art, so astounding a knowledge of dramaturgy. While the nature of the material was being explained to him he was already shaping it dramatically and adjusting it astonishingly to the limits of his own abilities, of which he was uncannily cognizant.

According to Zweig, Strauss, who was now in his late sixties, admitted at their first meeting that his musical inspiration no longer possessed its pristine power. He also told Zweig that, as an art form, opera was dead. Wagner had been so gigantic a peak that no composer could possibly rise higher. 'But', Strauss had added, with a broad Bavarian grin, 'I solved the problem by making a detour around it.'

In the spring of 1932, Strauss wrote to remind Zweig of the project they had discussed in Munich and to ask how work on it was progressing. In June, Zweig sent the composer a synopsis of the plot and some finished scenes of Act I of the libretto which at this stage was entitled 'Sir Morosus', after its leading character. Strauss responded with delight: 'It is enchanting—a born comic opera—a comedy equal to the best of its kind—more suitable for music than even *Figaro* and *The Barber of Seville*.' He urged Zweig to complete the first act as soon as possible, as he was keen to start composing. However, Strauss had first to complete *Arabella*, to which he devoted as much of the summer as possible, though he had also to conduct performances of Beethoven's *Fidelio* at the Salzburg Festival.

Zweig was able to let Strauss have a completed first act of 'Sir Morosus' in mid-October. When the composer confessed he was unable to decide whether to opt for *recitativo secco* or spoken dialogue between the musical numbers, adding that the diatonic and harmonic Mozartian simplicity of *recitativo secco* was not really his cup of tea, Zweig offered some useful advice. 'I consider prose dialogue for the less important passages to be the most natural form', he wrote,

yet I feel that music should not be *wholly* eliminated from prose dialogue but should be sprinkled over it from time to time with an ironic, illustrative spark—otherwise the entry of each instrument will sound like the beginning of an aria. I am thinking of short, pointed, sometimes jingly interferences of the music in the spoken dialogue. The audience should at all times be aware of the orchestra's presence—but merely calling, teasing, chatting during the spoken passages on the stage, and only afterwards dominating the scene again fully and in

171

earnest. I have in mind dashes of colour from individual instruments, and imagine a delightful effect of such discreet, witty illustrations.

Zweig's libretto was completed in mid-January 1933, and, according to its author, Strauss did not require a single line of it to be changed. 'There developed between us', Zweig wrote in his autobiography, 'the most cordial relations imaginable; he came to our house, and I would visit him at Garmisch where, with his long, thin fingers, he played for me on the piano little by little, from his sketch, the whole opera.'

It was taken for granted by both Strauss and Zweig that they were beginning a partnership which would continue. Indeed, the composer had already approved a suggestion from the librettist for a second opera. However, two weeks after Zweig had sent Strauss the finished libretto of *Die schweigsame Frau*, Hitler came to power in Germany. At first, both men attempted to ignore the political situation. 'Politics pass, the arts live on, hence we should strive for that which is permanent and leave propaganda to those who find it fulfilling and satisfying', Zweig wrote smugly to Strauss in April. But already their work was being affected. Strauss and Zweig lived not very far from each other and from the German-Austrian border, but Strauss was in Germany and Zweig in Austria: Hitler imposed a prohibitive tax of 1000 marks for crossing the border between the two countries. The purpose of the tax was to ruin the Austrian economy by preventing German tourists from entering the country, but it also acted as a symbolic warning to German composer and Austrian-Jewish librettist that their ways might soon be parted.

Meanwhile, after the première of *Arabella* in Dresden on 1 July, Strauss was able to concentrate on the composition of *Die schweigsame Frau*. On 14 August, his new version of *Die Aegyptische Helena* with its largely revised Act II was conducted by Clemens Krauss at the Salzburg Festival, though with no greater success than the opera had achieved at its Dresden première five years earlier.

Strauss could not ignore the political situation for long. He was clearly not interested in any of the large questions raised by the fact that his country was now a National Socialist dictatorship, but he was certainly interested in the state of his own career and its emoluments, and to the extent that his earnings were likely to be affected by political events this interest extended to the state of affairs in Germany. A number of distinguished musicians, Gentiles as well as Jews, were leaving the country, some to take up residence in Austria, and others, perhaps the more far-sighted ones, to live in England or America. This was not a course of action which Strauss ever considered.

Apparently not even the rabid anti-Semitism of the Nazis affected the deeply self-obsessed composer, although by this time he had acquired a Jewish daughter-in-law and, subsequently, half-Jewish grandchildren. In this context, an account, given more than thirty-five years later by Otto Klemperer, the famous German-Jewish conductor who emigrated to the United States in 1933, of a visit paid by Klemperer and his wife (the soprano Johanna Geissler) to the Strausses in Garmisch in the summer of 1932 is revealing of the attitudes of both Strauss and his wife, and shows the bad-tempered Pauline for once in a favourable light:

> Strauss and his wife were there, and the Jewish daughter-in-law, *née* Grab, from Prague, but not the son . . . Anyway, we drank tea and naturally the talk turned to the theme of that day, the Nazis, who were obviously coming to power. Strauss said, 'But tell me, what will happen to the German theatres and opera houses if the Jews leave?' Frau Strauss turned to me. 'Herr Doktor, if the Nazis give you any trouble, just you come to me. I'll show those gentlemen who's who.' Strauss looked at her in surprise. 'That would be just the right moment to stand up for a Jew!' The shamelessness was so naked one couldn't be angry. I said nothing and later we left. I didn't see him again until after the war. . . .
>
> But then the whole of Strauss's development was highly unsympathetic. I mean, that he accepted the Nazis with such unconcern. Why didn't he leave? He was Richard Strauss, famous throughout the whole world, and if he had left Germany, then people would have realized that the outlook there was black. But no, he stayed. And why? Because in Germany there were fifty-six opera houses and in America only two— New York and San Francisco. He said it himself. 'That would have reduced my income.' . . .

Not only did Strauss not leave Germany, he appeared to have no qualms about the political respectability of the new regime. In May 1933, he conducted the Berlin Philharmonic Orchestra after storm-troopers had threatened that 'everything in the hall will be smashed to pieces' if the Jewish Bruno Walter conducted. In the summer Strauss conducted *Parsifal* at Bayreuth, having offered himself when he heard that the anti-Fascist Toscanini had withdrawn from the engagement. Later in the year, Strauss accepted the presidency of the *Reichsmusikkammer*, a state bureau set up by Goebbels to direct German musical life. Toscanini's comment on Strauss's behaviour was: 'To Strauss the composer, I take off my hat. To Strauss the man, I put it on again.'

Strauss's view was both selfish and simplistic. He had been a German composer first in the days of the old dukedoms, then under the Kaiser, and later in the Weimar Republic. He was now a German composer under the Nazis. Should the country in due course become a Marxist regime, he would still remain a German composer. As he wrote to Zweig in April 1933, 'I am doing fine. Again I am busily at work, just as I was a week after the outbreak of the Great War.'

In May, while he was in Berlin to supervise rehearsals of a revival of *Intermezzo*, Strauss took the opportunity of discussing with Goebbels the embarrassing matter of his current librettist's racial origin. Having earlier confused Stefan Zweig with Arnold Zweig, a German Jewish novelist (unrelated to the Austrian Stefan) who was an advocate of both socialism and Zionism, Goebbels assured Strauss that no objection would be raised to his collaboration with Stefan Zweig.

By November 1933, Strauss had completed *Die schweigsame Frau* in short score. He worked on the orchestration of the opera throughout most of the following year, presumably pausing in June to allow the musical world to pay homage to him on his seventieth birthday. On that day, 11 June, at an official ceremony at the *Reichsmusikkammer*, he was presented with two silver-framed photographs, one of Hitler, inscribed 'To the great German composer, with sincere homage', and one of Goebbels, inscribed 'To the great tonal master in grateful homage'. On 20 October 1934, Strauss finally completed the full score of *Die Schweigsame Frau*, though not the overture which he composed later (on 17 January 1935) on themes from the opera and which he described as a potpourri.

The opera's future was threatened when, one day in July, Goebbels walked unannounced into the Villa Wahnfried, the Wagner family residence in Bayreuth where Strauss (who was conducting *Parsifal* again in Bayreuth) was staying. Goebbels had come to announce that he had changed his mind. The collaboration of Germany's greatest composer with a Jewish librettist would be an embarrassment to the government. Strauss assured the Minister of Propaganda that he had no wish to embarrass Hitler, and was prepared to withdraw *Die schweigsame Frau* completely. Goebbels decided to leave the final decision to Hitler who read Zweig's libretto and could find nothing in it to which he could legitimately object. The opera was, after all, set in England, and appeared to make fun of the English. There was nothing remotely anti-German about it. Hitler gave his blessing to the undertaking.

Strauss wrote to Zweig, who was in London doing research for a book on Mary, Queen of Scots, to inform him that there was now no objection to *Die schweigsame Frau* being given its première in Dresden in the summer of 1935. At his earlier meeting with Goebbels in Berlin, Strauss has been naïve enough to request that, as a favour to him, the anti-Jewish propaganda be toned down somewhat, but was forced to confess to Zweig that 'all efforts to relax the stipulation against Jews here are frustrated by the answer: impossible as long as the outside world continues its lying propaganda against Hitler.'

Strauss and Zweig were already corresponding about two possible future projects for operas, but Strauss thought it necessary to warn his colleague that,

> for strategic reasons it might be wise, in case we should again collaborate on one or more works, not to say a word to anyone. If anyone asks me, I say 'I am not working on anything now, I have no libretto.' In a few years, when all projects are finished, the world probably will look different.'

When Strauss made the more specific suggestion that, if he and Zweig wrote more operas, they should do so in secret and put them into a safe 'that will be opened when we both consider the time propitious', Zweig replied to the composer with a candid rebuke and a generous counter-proposal:

> Sometimes I have the feeling that you are not quite aware—and this honours you—of the historical greatness of your position. . . . One day your letters, your decisions, will belong to all mankind, like those of Wagner and Brahms. For this reason it seems inappropriate to me that something in your life, in your art, should be done in secrecy. . . . I am aware of the difficulties that would confront a new work if I were to write the text; it would be considered a provocation. . . . I will be happy, however, to assist with advice anybody who might work for you, to sketch things out for him—without compensation, without boasting about it, simply for the pleasure of serving your great art and in order to show my appreciation of the fact that you took *Die Schweigsame Frau* and created from it a work of art for the world. I will co-operate with anybody whom you care to name, without credit or reward.

Strauss, however, preferred his own method:

> Your beautiful letter saddened me deeply. If you abandon me, too, I'll have to lead the life of an ailing, unemployed retired person from now on. Believe me, there is no other poet who could write a usable libretto for me, even if you generously and unselfishly were to 'co-operate'. My warmest thanks for your magnanimous offer. I have repeatedly told Minister Goebbels and also Goering that I have been searching for a librettist for fifty years. Dozens of texts were sent to me, I negotiated with all the German writers (Gerhart Hauptmann, Bahr, Wolzogen, and so on). To find *Salome* was a stroke of luck, and *Elektra* introduced

175

me to the incomparable Hofmannsthal, but after his death I thought I would have to resign myself forever. Then by chance (is that the right word?) I found you. And I will not give you up simply because we happen to have an anti-Semitic government now. I am confident this government would place no obstacles in the way of a second Zweig opera and would not feel challenged by it, if I were to discuss it with Dr. Goebbels who is very cordial with me. But why raise at this time unnecessary questions that will have taken care of themselves in two or three years? So I am sticking by my request: do a few more beautiful libretti for me (I will *never* find another writer), and we will keep the matter confidential until we both think the time right to come out with it. This is not undignified, but wise.

Early in June, Strauss travelled to Dresden to attend rehearsals of *Die schweigsame Frau*. To Zweig he wrote enthusiastically of Josef Gielen's production, of the conducting of Karl Böhm, and of the young sopraon, Maria Cebotari, whom he thought 'charming, and just made for' the title-role. He was confident of the quality of the work itself. 'You can rest assured', he told Zweig, 'that this opera is a bull's-eye, even if it has to wait until the twenty-first century.'

Two days before the première, Strauss was having an afternoon game of skat in his hotel with three friends, the artist Leonhard Fanto, the tenor Tino Pattiera, and Friedrich von Schuch, the Dresden Opera's business manager (and son of Ernst von Schuch who had conducted the premières of *Feuersnot*, *Salome*, *Elektra* and *Der Rosen Kavalier*). In the middle of the game Strauss suddenly announced that he would like to see a proof of the handbill for the performance. Obviously, he had been warned by someone that his collaborator's name would not be found on it. After some delay, Schuch nervously produced a proof of the handbill, from which Strauss saw immediately that it contained no mention of Stefan Zweig. He went red in the face with anger, and exclaimed that, unless Zweig's name appeared, and in type as large as Hofmannsthal's had been on the *Rosenkavalier* handbill, he would leave Dresden immediately. Paul Adolph, the Intendant of the Opera House, took responsibility for adding Zweig's name to the handbill, an action which led to his dismissal. As a consequence of Strauss's insistence that full credit be given to his Jewish librettist, neither Hitler nor Goebbels attended the première of *Die schweigsame Frau*. The reason given at the time was that their flight to Dresden had been prevented by bad weather.

The première took place on 24 June, and was a great success. The opera was enjoyed not only by the audience but also by most of the music critics, and even in the Nazi newspapers Zweig's libretto was praised equally with

Strauss's music. Three further performances were given, and then suddenly, in the middle of July, the opera was officially banned throughout Germany and its composer found himself no longer so highly regarded by the Nazi hierarchy.

This had come about because the secret police had intercepted a letter Strauss had written on 17 June and had posted from Dresden to Zweig who was then in Switzerland. Strauss's letter was in reply to one from Zweig, written on 15 June, in which the librettist set out clearly the reasons why future collaboration between them would not be possible. Zweig had, after all, been careful to say or do nothing that might jeopardize Strauss's standing with the authorities, or indeed the composer's safety. But inevitably Zweig felt a sense of solidarity with other Jews who were being persecuted by the Nazis, and now that Strauss was President of the *Reichsmusikkammer* the librettist considered that he was being put in the position of seeming to be collaborating with a representative of the Nazis. In his letter to Strauss, Zweig referred to the two occasions when Strauss as a conductor had stepped in to replace Bruno Walter in Berlin and Arturo Toscanini in Bayreuth, occasions which had led to strong criticism of Strauss in the foreign press, and about which strauss felt extremely sensitive.

Strauss's sensitivity, however, was a one-way affair. His reply to Zweig, written from Dresden on 17 June, a week before the *Schweigsame Frau* première, though it infuriated the Nazis was nevertheless extraordinarily insensitive in its attitude to Zweig's situation. 'Dear Herr Zweig', wrote Strauss,

Your letter of the 15th is driving me to distraction! This Jewish egoism! It's enough to make one an anti-Semite! This racial pride, this feeling of solidarity! Do you think that I have ever been guided, in any of my actions, by the thought that I am German? (Perhaps, *qui le sait?*) Do you believe that Mozart consciously composed as an Aryan? I recognize only two types of human being: the talented and the untalented. For me, the populace exists only from the moment it becomes an audience. Whether they are Chinese, Bavarians, New Zealanders or Berliners, it's all the same to me, so long as they've paid the full price of admission. . . . Who has told you that I have become so deeply involved in politics? Is it because I conducted a concert in place of Bruno Walter? I did that for the sake of the orchestra. Because I substituted for that other non-Aryan Toscanini? That I did for the sake of Bayreuth. It has nothing to do with politics. How the gutter press presents it is none of my affair, nor should you worry about it. Because I pose as President of the *Reichsmusikkammer*? I do it to bring about good and to prevent greater disasters! Simply because I know my artistic duty. I would have taken on this tiresome honorary office under any government. But neither Kaiser Wilhelm nor Herr Rathenau [the Jewish Minister of Foreign Affairs in the days of the Weimar Republic] asked me to. So be good, forget Herr Moses and the other apostles for a couple of weeks, and keep on working at your two one-acters [these were eventually to become the operas *Friedenstag* and *Capriccio*]. The performance here is going to be splendid. Everyone is tremendously excited! Should I therefore stop working with you? Never, on any account!

Strauss's letter, addressed to Zweig at the Hotel Bellerive in Zürich, was intercepted by the Gestapo in Dresden, Strauss having been incautious enough to have posted it in his hotel's letter-box. The Governor of Saxony, one Martin Mutschmann, sent a copy of the letter to Hitler, accompanied by the following note:

My Führer!
The enclosed copy of a letter from Herr Dr. Strauss to the Jew Stefan Zweig fell into the hands of the Gestapo of Saxony. It is forwarded for your information.
I should like to add that the world première of *Die schweigsame Frau* took place before a full house, which included five hundred invited guests. The second performance was so sparsely attended that the management distributed complimentary tickets. The third performance was cancelled, ostensibly due to the illness of the principal soprano.
Heil, respectfully,
Martin Mutschmann

On 6 July, Strauss was visited by Otto von Keudell, an emissary of the Secretary of State Walter Funkl, and ordered to announce that he was resigning from the Presidency of the *Reichsmusikkammer* on grounds of ill health. Strauss agreed to resign, but in a memorandum in his notebooks dated 10 July, he summarized his interview with the official, and commented upon the situation:

On 6 July, Ministerial Counsellor Keudell, acting on behalf of State Secretary Funkl, called on me and demanded that I resign as President of the *Reichsmusikkammer* for reasons of 'ill health'. I did so at once.
Herr Keudell pointed several times to a copy of a personal letter to my friend and, until now, collaborator Stefan Zweig, marked in red ink. Although *the full name of the sender* appeared on the envelope, the letter had apparently been opened by the State Police of Saxony.

. . . I was not aware that I, the President of the *Reichsmusikkammer*, was under the direct surveillance of the State Police, and that I, after a lifetime of creating eminent works 'recognized throughout the world', was not considered a 'good German' and above criticism. Nevertheless, the unheard-of has occurred: Herr Minister Goebbels has dismissed me without even asking for an explanation of my confiscated letter to Zweig, which, to unauthorized readers not aware of the background, or of its connection with an intricate correspondence concerned with purely artistic questions, is bound to be completely misunderstood.

The beginning of the letter about Zweig's Jewish stubbornness and his (understandable) feeling of solidarity with his persecuted tribal brethren contained my obvious answer that Teutonic composers have never considered whether their compositions were sufficiently German and Aryan. Ever since Bach we have simply composed whatever our talents have allowed us to, and we are Aryans and Germans without having to be aware of it. This can hardly be construed as treason, but is loyal service to the fatherland, even though my libretto, like Mozart's, was written by a non-Aryan [Lorenzo da Ponte]. About the passage most heavily marked in red, I may be in disagreement with Dr. Goebbels who, as a statesman, naturally has to judge people differently. The passage says that, for me—and it's a personal view, expressed in a personal letter—the 'people' start when they become an 'audience'. That is, people begin with the upper two million, the educated audience that pays for its tickets in full, not those who for 15 to 30 pfennigs listen to *Die Meistersinger* or *Tristan*, causing great financial loss to the theatres and requiring ever larger subsidies from the government if those theatres are to fulfil truly higher cultural goals. Hence, this passage also concerns a purely artistic question, not a question of *my* purse, as it was evidently maliciously interpreted. . . .

Now let us examine the price I had to pay for not keeping my distance, from the beginning, from the National Socialist movement. It all began when, to do a favour to the [Berlin] Philharmonic Orchestra and at the urging of Kopsch [a Berlin jurist, composer and conductor] and Rasch [music editor of the Nazi *Völkischer Beobachter*, an early member of the Storm Troopers, and a friend of Strauss], I substituted in the last subscription concert for Bruno Walter who had been driven out. I gave my fee of 1,500 marks to the orchestra. That started a storm directed against me by the foreign, but particularly the Jewish Viennese press, which did more damage to me in the eyes of all decent people than the German government can ever compensate me for. I was condemned as a servile, self-seeking anti-Semite, whereas in truth I have always stressed at every opportunity to everyone of importance

179

here (much to my disadvantage) that I consider the Streicher-Goebbels Jew-baiting a disgrace to German honon :, and evidence of weakness, the basest weapon of untalented and lazy mediocrity against superior intelligence and greater talent. I openly acknowledge here that I have received so much support, so much selfless friendship, so much generous help and intellectual stimulus from Jews that it would be a crime not to acknowledge it all with gratitude.

It is true that I have had adversaries in the Jewish press. On the other hand, I would call it, compared with the enmity displayed towards my highly disparate opposite Gustav Mahler, almost friendly. But my worst and most malicious enemies were 'Aryans'. I need mention only the names of Perfall, Oscar Merz (of the *Münchener Neueste Nachrichten*), Theodor Goering (*Der Sammler*), Felix Mottl, Franz Schalk, Weingartner, and the whole Party press: the *Völkischer Beobachter* and the rest.

Despite what the Governor of Saxony said in his note to Hitler, there appear to have been four performances of *Die schweigsame Frau* in Dresden before the ban was imposed. The opera was then staged in Austria, at Graz, where it was conducted by Karl Rankl in February, 1936. The following month, it was performed in Fascist (but not at that time officially anti-Semitic) Italy, in Italian translation, in Rome and later in Milan. A production in Zürich followed in May, and in 1937 Georg Szell conducted the opera in Prague. A proposed Nazi-financed performance at Covent Garden by the Dresden company, which Sir Thomas Beecham attempted to organize, fell through, and Beecham's subsequent plan to stage the opera at Covent Garden in 1938 with Maria Cebotari (who had sung the title-role at the Dresden première), the American tenor Charles Kullman (as Henry), Alexander Sved (the Barber) and Josef Manowarda (Sir Morosus), was also not realized. There had been several embarrassing incidents at Covent Garden, following Hitler's invasion of Austria, when singers such as Lotte Lehmann, Richard Tauber, Rose Pauly, Kerstin Thorborg and Herbert Janssen had appeared in the same casts as a number of rabid Nazi performers who had been extremely unpleasant to them. The likely mix of Nazis and non-Nazis in any Covent Garden cast of *Die schweigsame Frau* kept the opera off the stage of the Royal Opera House until well after the end of World War II.

Die schweigsame Frau re-surfaced in Germany in 1946, when it was conducted by Joseph Keilberth in the smaller auditorium of the Dresden Opera House. In a letter of thanks to Keilberth, Strauss wrote: 'Now, after ten years, the honourable Sir Morosus has been liberated from the concentration camp of the *Reichstheaterkammer*, and has returned to his native town, where twelve years ago I had a lot of trouble to get the name of the librettist on to the programme.'

Strauss might have chosen his words more carefully. By this time, Stefan Zweig had died, not in a concentration camp, but by his own hand. He and his wife had moved to England shortly before the German annexation of Austria in 1938, and then on to the United States and Brazil. In Germany, his books were burned. Zweig and his wife Elisabeth killed themselves in Brazil on 23 February 1942. Zweig was sixty.

The first American performance of the opera was given by the New York City Opera in English in 1958, as *The Silent Woman*. Hilde Gueden and Hans Hotter were the leading singers in a Salzburg production in 1959, and *The Silent Woman* finally reached Covent Garden, in English, in 1961. It has never become one of the more popular of Strauss's operas.

II

STRAUSS'S self-justificatory notebook entry of 10 July 1935, was, of course, not intended for immediate publication. Nor was the essay he had written a week earlier, dated 3 July 1935, which was also entered in his notebooks, and which was discovered only after his death. Headed 'The History of *Die schweigsame Frau*', it read as follows:

Hugo von Hofmannsthal, attacked and maligned by the press and the profession for thirty years, is dead. He was a faithful genius, and I obstinately stuck with him. Now, after his premature death, he is finally recognized as 'my true poet'. I must resign myself to admitting that my period of creating operas has come to a close. *Salome* by Oscar Wilde, which the Viennese lyric poet Anton Lindner recognized as a covert opera text, was an exception. Hofmannsthal alone was the writer who, in addition to his poetic creativity and his dramatic talent, had the sensitivity to offer a composer theatrical themes in a form suitable for composition. He was able to write a libretto that was at once effective on the stage, met high literary standards, and could be set to music. I flirted and negotiated with the best German poets, repeatedly with Gerhart Hauptmann; also with d'Annunzio. But in fifty years I found only the wonderful Hofmannsthal. He was resourceful in inventing musical themes. Although hardly 'musical', he, like Goethe, had clear-sighted musical intuitions, and an astonishing flair for knowing what subjects were suitable for my requirements.

After *Intermezzo*, where I copied, as it were, with some dramaturgical finesse two tragicomic episodes of my family life, and poured some music over the product, my 'poetical potency' was definitely exhausted. When I had just about given up hope of ever finding a librettist again, I was visited by Anton Kippenberg of the publishing firm of Insel, who was on his way to see Stefan Zweig in Salzburg. Earlier, in Vienna, I had seen Ben Jonson's *Volpone* and the amusing comedy *Das Lamm des Armen*. Casually I said to Kippenberg, 'Why don't you ask Zweig' (whom I did not know in person) 'whether he has an opera subject for me?' That was in the winter of 1931–32. Presently I got a letter from Zweig saying he did in fact have some thoughts but until now had not been bold enough to present them to me. We made an appointment in Munich, where Zweig told me about an interesting subject for a ballet—but it ranged just about from Prometheus to Nijinsky, and was too much for me at sixty-eight. After that, he suggested, shyly, the Ben Jonson subject, and I knew at once that this was my comic opera and grabbed it. In the summer, in Salzburg, he presented me with the idea for the entire play which, in its blend of noble lyric poetry and farce, constitutes an entirely new genre of *opera buffa*. In the autumn the text was done. Except for a minor cut in Act II (Morosus–Aminta) I was able to set it to music, lock, stock and barrel, without the slightest further change. None of my earlier operas was so easy to compose, or gave me such light-hearted pleasure. Then came the Third Reich, and with it his expulsion from the new Kultur state.

Everybody who read Zweig's text was enthusiastic about the witty, poetic and truly dramatic book. The opera had already been accepted in Dresden when the anti-Semitic bombshell burst in Bayreuth, as a result of an attack by someone by the name of Will Vesper, writing in *Freiheitskampf*.

In the morning after my first performance of *Parsifal*, Minister Dr. Goebbels (after having uttered to Winifred Wagner the fateful words, 'Little monk, you are on a difficult mission'*) entered my room in 'Wahnfried'. I received him, saying it was perhaps significant that in the house of the 'great martyr' I too, the smaller man, had to suffer my martyrdom. I told him that I did not wish to embarrass Adolf Hitler and himself by performing my opera, and that I was willing to withdraw *Die schweigsame Frau* altogether and to forgo all showings at home and abroad. Goebbels said later that this talk had 'deeply impressed' him—perhaps because I told him openly that the whole affair was a 'huge disgrace'. In parting, we agreed to submit the score to the Führer for a final decision. Before that, Goebbels had commented that he was

---

* Words spoken to Martin Luther by Georg von Frundsberg, head of Charles V's army, in 1521.

able to muzzle the press but would not be able to prevent the throwing of a stink bomb on the opening night.

In the afternoon I returned to Garmisch. Next day, Goebbels telephoned, saying that he had carefully considered my 'case', had also talked with Hitler, and that he wanted me to submit the libretto. Goebbels added that, if the book was unobjectionable (other than being written by an uncomfortably talented Jew), he hoped that there would be no difficulties with the world première in Dresden.

And so it was. The work by itself won the victory, although Hitler and Goebbels did not attend the Dresden performance—either on purpose or, as was announced, prevented from flying by a storm in Hamburg.

State Commissioner Hinkel then gave a good, warm talk at the City Hall. It is a sad time when an artist of my rank has to ask a brat of a minister what he may set to music and what he may have performed. I, too, belong to the nation of 'servants and waiters'. I almost envy my friend Stefan Zweig, persecuted for his race, who now definitely refuses to work with me in public or in secret because, he says, he does not want to have any 'special privileges' in the Third Reich. To be honest, I don't understand this Jewish solidarity, and regret that the artist in Zweig cannot rise above political fashions. If we do not preserve artistic freedom ourselves, how can we expect it from soap-box orators in taverns?

With *Die schweigsame Frau* my life's work definitely seems to have come to an end. Otherwise I might have been able to create other works not entirely without merit. It is regrettable.

That Strauss was unheroic, selfish and insensitive to suffering that was not his own, these are human failings at which the prudent will refrain from casting the first stone. But what is one to think of the excessive venality which led the composer, only some days after confiding those comments to his private notebooks, to write an obsequious letter to Hitler? In it, Strauss rehearses (and tactfully rephrases) the arguments he had already set forth, complains that he was not given a chance to explain the background to his intercepted letter to Zweig, and ends thus:

My Führer! My whole life belongs to German music and to an indefatigable effort to elevate German culture. I have never been active politically, nor even expressed myself in politics. Therefore I believe that I will find understanding from you, the great architect of German social life, particularly when, with deep emotion and with deep respect, I assure you that even after my dismissal as President of the

Reichsmusikkammer I will devote the few years still granted to me only to the purest and most ideal goals.

Confident of your high sense of justice, I beg of you, my Führer, most humbly to receive me for a personal discussion, to give me the opportunity to justify myself in person, as I take farewell of my activity in the *Reichsmusikkammer*.

I remain, most honoured Herr Reichskanzler, with the expression of my highest esteem.

Can one envisage Mozart, Beethoven or Verdi—or indeed any great composer other than Wagner—writing such a letter? Hitler did not reply to it.

In his memoirs, Zweig had this to say of the *Schweigsame Frau* affair:

In January 1933, when Hitler came into power, the piano score of our opera *Die schweigsame Frau* was as good as finished, and the first act practically orchestrated. A few weeks later, a strict order was issued to German theatres not to produce any works by non-Aryans or even any in which a Jew had merely participated. This comprehensive ban reached even to the dead, and to the indignation of music lovers everywhere the statue of Mendelssohn, in front of the Gewandhaus in Leipzig, was removed. For me this order seemed to seal the fate of our opera. It went without saying that Richard Strauss would abandon further work on it and begin another with someone else. Instead, he wrote me letter after letter asking what had got into me; quite the contrary, he said, for, as he was already orchestrating it, he wanted me to work on the text of his next opera. He would not think of letting anybody forbid his collaboration with me, and I have to admit that he kept faith with me throughout this whole affair as long as it was possible for him to do so. To be sure, he simultaneously took steps which I liked less: he approached the men in power, met frequently with Hitler, Goering and Goebbels, and, at a time when even Furtwängler was still in mutiny, allowed himself to be made president of the Nazi Chamber of Music.

Strauss's open participation was of tremendous importance to the National Socialists at that moment. For, annoyingly enough, not only the best writers but also the most important musicians as well had openly snubbed them, and the few who held with them, or came over to the reservation, were unknown to the wide public. To have the most famous musician of Germany align himself with them at so embarrassing a moment meant, in its mere decorative aspect, an immeasurable gain to Goebbels and Hitler. Hitler, who had, as Strauss told me, during his Viennese vagabond years scraped up enough money to travel

(above) Ashley Putnam (Danae) and Mary Jane Johnson (Xanthe) in *Die Liebe der Danae* at the Santa Fé Opera, 1982

(above) James Hoback (Mercury),
Victor Braun (Jupiter) and Carolyne
James (Leda) in *Die Liebe der Danaë*
Santa Fé Opera, 1982

(left) Ryland Davies (Flamand) and
Elisabeth Söderström (the Countess)
in *Capriccio*, at Glyndebourne in 197

to Graz to attend the [Austrian] première of *Salome*, was honouring him demonstratively; at all festive evenings at Berchtesgaden, besides Wagner, Strauss songs were sung almost exclusively. Strauss's co-operation, however, was much more purposeful. Despite his art-egoism, which he always acknowledged openly and coolly, he was inwardly indifferent whatever the regime. He had served the German Kaiser as a conductor and had arranged military marches for him, later he had served the Emperor of Austria as court-conductor in Vienna, and had been *persona gratissima* in the Austrian and German republics. To be particularly co-operative with the National Socialists was further-more of vital interest to him, because in the National Socialist sense he was very much in the red. His son had married a Jewess and thus he feared that his grandchildren whom he loved above everything else would be excluded as scum from the schools; his new opera was tainted through me, and his earlier operas through the half-Jew Hugo von Hofmannsthal; his publisher was a Jew. Therefore it seemed to him more and more imperative to create some support and security for himself, and he did it most perseveringly. He conducted wherever the new masters wanted him to, he set a hymn to music for the Olympic games, at the same time writing me with little enthusiasm in his shockingly frank letters about his commission. In truth, in the *sacro egoismo* of the artist he cared only about one thing: to keep his work alive, and above all for a production of the new opera which lay particularly close to his heart.

III

EPICŒNE, or *The Silent Woman*, first performed in 1609, is the second of the four great plays of Ben Jonson's maturity: the others are *Volpone* (1606), *The Alchemist* (1610), and *Bartholomew Fair* (1614). The plot of *Epicœne* concerns an old miser, Morose, who cannot stand noise of any kind, and who even plans to marry a dumb wife. His nephew, whom he intends thus to disinherit, tricks the old man into marriage with a desir-ably demure young woman, who, after the ceremony, turns into a voci-ferous shrew who belabours her husband mercilessly. (This might be the situation of *Intermezzo* all over again, or even of the Strauss marriage.) Morose in desperation offers his nephew a generous allowance and his inheritance if he will take this extremely unsilent woman off his hands. The nephew complies immediately by removing Epicœne's wig, revealing the bride to be a boy whom he, the nephew, had carefully trained and engaged for the purpose of tricking Morose.

185

Jonson's play is set in London at the time of its performance in the early seventeenth century. Zweig's adaptation, a very free one, moves the action forward more than a century and a half to around 1780, and does not saddle 'Sir Morosus', as he is now called, with a boy-bride, but with a real woman, who turns out to be already married to the nephew. Jonson's title, *Epicœne*, being no longer appropriate, the opera used instead the play's sub-title, 'The Silent Woman'.

If the plot of *Die schweigsame Frau* seems very similar to that of Donizetti's *Don Pasquale*, there is every reason why it should. Jonson's *Epicœne* was used as the basis of an opera, *Angiolina, ossia il matrimonio per susurro*, by Salieri in 1800, and also (with the female impersonation aspect removed) by Pavesi in 1810 for *Ser Marcantonius*, an opera whose libretto was written by Angelo Anelli. Anelli's text was made use of in 1843 by Giovanni Ruffini as the basis of his libretto of *Don Pasquale* for Donizetti.

IV

STRAUSS'S Overture, or Potpourri as he called it, is a slight but tuneful and, of course, brilliantly scored piece utilizing a number of themes which, in the opera, will be associated with various characters and events. It efficiently serves its purpose to set the mood and pace of the comedy which is to follow.

The curtain rises on the living-room of Sir Morosus's house in London, decorated in such a manner as to make it clear that it is the home of a retired seaman. Apart from the nautical decorations, the other unusual feature of the room is that its doors are covered with curtains of thick material to keep out noise. It is morning, and the Housekeeper (contralto), an elderly woman, is tidying up, when there is a knock at the door which she opens to admit the Barber. (In the list of characters, she is described simply as the Housekeeper and he as the Barber. However, she addresses him as Herr Schneidebart—Mr Cutbeard, which is his name in Jonson's play—and her name is later revealed to be the Widow Zimmerlein).

The Barber (baritone) wants only to get on with his task of shaving Sir Morosus, but the loquacious Housekeeper prattles on, attempting to persuade the Barber to recommend to Morosus that he marry her. The Barber makes it clear that this is the last thing he would advise Morosus to do, and a noisy quarrel ensues, which awakens Morosus who comes storming into the room to add his insults to those of the Barber. The Housekeeper is chased out, and the Barber begins to shave his client.

It is obvious right from the beginning of the opera that Strauss has chosen to compose a deliberate pastiche of Rossinian *opera buffa*, with clearly defined separate numbers and ensembles, but with spoken dialogue in place of Rossini's *recitativo secco*. One recalls the letter of admiration Strauss had written as a young man to Verdi, after the appearance of the great Italian master's final opera, *Falstaff*. There is in *Die schweigsame Frau* at least an attempt to achieve something of the form and the spirit of *Falstaff*, for there is something of Verdi's Shakespearean knight about Sir Morosus, just as there is a touch of Rossini's barber, Figaro, in Strauss's Schneidebart.

As he shaves Morosus, the Barber suggests to the old man that he should look for a nice, quiet young wife—'*eine schweigsame Frau*'—and get rid of his gossipy old housekeeper. While Morosus fulminates against the noise of the London taverns, 'befouling the night with their accursed din', Strauss's orchestra produces fleeting references to a string of operas, among them *Faust, Die Zauberflöte, Die Meistersinger* and *Der Freischütz*. The old man's complaint about the church bells at night is uttered as an ill-natured parody of 'Oranges and lemons, say the bells of St. Clemens'.

The contributions of Morosus to this dialogue are sung, but the Barber occasionally use speech, under which the orchestra provides a light commentary very much along the lines that Zweig had suggested to Strauss. Sir Morosus's dream of domestic bliss is expressed in an affecting arietta, whose mood, however, Morosus cannot sustain for long. He is of the opinion that a silent woman will be no easier to discover than an ocean without salt or a ship without rats, but the Barber sings a cheerful little song, described in the score as a canzona, '*Mädchen nur, die nichts erfahren*' (Only girls of no experience), in which he encourages Morosus to believe that a quiet, submissive young woman might be found who would be prepared to marry him. The canzona ends as a duet, with Morosus continuing to insist that he is too old to marry.

A noisy altercation is suddenly heard outside the door, between the Housekeeper and a visitor who insists on seeing Morosus. Finally, the visitor manages to force his way into the room (very like Baron Ochs in Act I of *Der Rosenkavalier*). He turns out to be Henry (tenor), Morosus's long-absent nephew who had 'dropped-out' of the University of Pavia some time previously. Overjoyed to see him, Morosus immediately invites him to stay. He will no longer need a wife to look after him now that his nephew, whom he will make his heir, has returned. Henry, somewhat embarrassed, begins to explain that he is not alone, and that his troupe is waiting downstairs. Morosus understands him to mean troops, a private army, and the orchestra launches into a rather stately comical march to accompany the entrance of what turns out to be a troupe of Italian opera singers.

Henry's company consists of three other men and three women, as well as a full opera chorus. He introduces the principal singers to his uncle:

Aminta (soprano) who is also Henry's wife, Isotta (soprano), Carlotta (mezzo-soprano), Cesare Vanuzzi (bass) who is a favourite of the Pope, Carlo Morbio (baritone) celebrated for his Orfeo, and Giuseppe Farfallo (bass) the favourite of Bologna. Henry has brought them to England to fulfil an engagement to perform in a season of Italian opera at the Haymarket Theatre in London. The shamelessly anachronistic operatic references in the orchestra at this point include 'La donna è mobile' from Verdi's Rigoletto and 'Mir anvertraut' from Strauss's own Die Frau ohne Schatten.

In disgust, Morosus hastily disinherits his nephew, insults the opera singers, and, after ordering the Barber to find him a pliable and silent young woman to marry the very next day, storms out of the room. Henry and Aminta are distressed, and the rest of the company highly indignant. But the Barber defends his old client, telling Henry and his company that they must make allowances for him. Morosus, he says, is the kindest creature imaginable. He finds noise intolerable because he was once blown sky-high with the powder-magazine of his ship. It was a miracle that he survived to be fished from the sea, but his ear-drums were completely shattered, since when he can abide no noise save that which he himself makes.

The Barber advises Henry not to turn his back on his uncle and, more importantly, his uncle's fortune of sixty or seventy thousand pounds. Aminta offers to return to Italy so as not to stand in the way of Henry's reconciliation with his uncle, but Henry will not hear of this. The duet for Aminta and Henry is tender, and almost Mozartean in its lightness and grace, though not in the quality of its melody. In the ensemble which follows, the singers of Henry's troupe combine to express their loyalty to one another.

Wondering where he is going to find a wife for Morosus within twenty-four hours, the barber asks if one of the women in the company would be willing to marry the old man and stay quiet for ever, for the sake of a fortune? The possibility of a silent life is rejected by Isotta and Carlotta in brief solo arias. Suddenly the Barber has an idea. The company, disguised as priest, notary, and witnesses, will assist at a mock wedding ceremony, with Aminta as the demure bride who, immediately after the marriage, will turn into a shrew. An allegro finale, launched by Henry, becomes an ensemble to which all contribute, with a concluding stretta in the best tradition of Italian opera buffa.

Act II takes place in the same room of Morosus's house, on the afternoon of the next day. The Barber has apparently moved quickly, for when the curtain rises Morosus is discovered in silver silk breeches, being helped by his Housekeeper to dress in grand ceremonial attire. He is excited about the forthcoming wedding, while she attempts to dissuade him from what, having been listening at the keyhole when the plot was being hatched, she knows to be a disastrous course of action for Morosus who, however, refuses to listen to her. 'Off with you, scum', he shouts as he contemplates his appearance in a mirror. There is a knock at the door, and the Barber enters, also ceremonially attired 'like a match-maker'.

A tranquil minuet has preceded the rise of the curtain, and its tempo and temper persist through most of the old Housekeeper's scene with Morosus, until he loses his temper with her. The entrance of the Barber restores the musical pace to a good-humoured *moderato*, as Morosus is told that not one, but three of the quietest, most silent girls in the county are waiting outside. 'You can choose, as Paris did between the goddesses', the Barber assures him, adding that he has already obtained the consent of parents or guardians of all three girls, as well as the services of a parson and a notary. In an amiable but melodically arid canzona (*'Nur das Eine lasst Euch bitten'*: Let me entreat you this one thing), the Barber advises Morosus to treat the applicants gently, for they are all shy young maidens of refined manners.

To a version of the odd little march which had introduced the troupe of singers in Act I, the Barber now ushers three young women into the room. With their altered coiffures and costumes, none is easily recognizable. Carlotta, disguised as a country wench in gaudy stockings and a straw hat, affects a broad accent; Isotta, her manner that of a genteel wallflower, is somewhat affectedly attired; while Aminta is quite plainly dressed as a poor town girl. The first two candidates are quickly turned down by Morosus: Carlotta is clearly too coarse for him, and Isotta too loquacious in boasting of her intellectual attainments. In a gentle, delicately scored arietta (*'Ach, Herr, dass ich es offen sag'*: Ah, sir, if I may speak openly), in which she confesses that her favourite pursuit is to sit quietly, sewing, Aminta wins the old man's heart immediately. He proposes marriage to her and is shyly accepted, at which the two unsuccessful young ladies flounce out of the room in high dudgeon. The Barber is sent off to fetch the parson and the notary.

Left alone with Aminta, or Timida as she now calls herself, Morosus pours out his heart to her in a solemn but dull aria with occasional contributions from Aminta who already begins to feel sorry for the old man but who manages to suppress her sympathy for the sake of the cause. The Barber now returns, with Vanuzzi who is disguised as a Priest, Morbio who is dressed in the costume of a Notary, and the Housekeeper, all of whom enter while the orchestra plays a transcription of a lively piece from the Fitzwilliam Virginal Book, a collection compiled shortly after 1609, and the most important source of English keyboard music in the late

Renaissance. Strauss had turned to this collection of instrumental pieces from the time of Ben Jonson, ignoring the fact that in the opera the period of the action had been changed from the play's 1609 to 1780. The piece in question is an anonymous Alman (or *allemande*), No. XIV. (From a footnote in the score, it seems clear that Strauss imagined 'Anon' to be the name of an English composer.)

The mock marriage of Morosus and Timida (at least once in the score she is addressed as 'Timidia'), witnessed by the Barber and the House-keeper, is solemnized, the Notary making his speech with the aid of another piece from the Fitzwilliam Virginal Book, an Alman by Martin Peerson, No. XC. A beautiful sextet, slow in tempo, builds up after the ceremony, in which Morosus sings of his bliss at being married to such an angel, and the angel's light soprano soars lyrically to the E above high C.

Suddenly the tranquil atmosphere is shattered by a dreadful tumult outside, and there bursts into the room a horde of noisy seamen carrying drums, bagpipes and various other instruments. They are the chorus of Henry's opera troupe, led by Farfallo in the role of a drunken sailor, but they announce themselves as old naval colleagues of Morosus come to serenade their former Admiral on his wedding-day. The crowd is soon augmented by a chorus of neighbours (among them nephew Henry) who have arrived to investigate the racket. They all make such a row that, by the time they are finally persuaded by the Barber to leave, Morosus is close to collapse.

Although she now feels ashamed of herself for having agreed to dupe her husband's uncle, Aminta has to play her part in the cruel charade. It is not long before she is venting her fury upon Morosus with a top C, demanding obedience from him, insisting on some young and cheerful company being invited to the house, and listing her other requirements which include a coach and three horses, jewellery, servants, and ceaseless music. Taking a dislike to the room's furnishings, she tears the curtains down, and knocks several of Morosus's nautical mementos to the floor.

At the height of her tantrum, Henry appears, and poor Morosus offers his nephew his entire fortune if only he will somehow get rid of this termagant. Henry orders Aminta out of the room, promises that he will have the marriage annulled the next day, and sends his exhausted uncle off to bed. Morosus goes into his bedroom, his last word a drowsy '*schlafen*' (to sleep), growled on his deepest note, a low C. Henry now calls Aminta back into the living-room, and the act ends with a tender duet for the loving couple, punctuated by occasional sleepy murmurs of gratitude or fear from Morosus's bedroom. Strauss is still not at his most inventive melodically, but the duet is richly scored, and the ending of the act is highly effective with Aminta's *'Dank'* (Thanks) on her high D flat, echoed by a *'Dank'* four octaves below from Morosus, next door.

A flurrying *fugato* orchestral introduction to Act III depicts the goings-on in the Morosus household next morning. When the curtain rises, a number of workmen (members of the opera company in disguise, of course) are to be seen hammering nails into walls and moving furniture about. Aminta is directing the proceedings: a servant brings in a parrot in a cage, and she orders it to be placed by Morosus's bedroom door. The parrot's cries of *'Kora Kakadu'* (Cora Cockatoo) are noted in the score, though without pitch or note-values, against an accompaniment of strident discords in the orchestra's wind and brass sections.

The housekeeper attempts to persuade her new mistress to lessen the noise, but in vain. She exits in despair, followed soon by the workmen, as Henry and Farfallo now enter, dressed as music-teacher and accompanist, and Aminta is given a singing-lesson, accompanied at the cembalo by Farfallo, but also by Strauss's orchestra. (Zweig presumably had *Il barbiere di Siviglia* in mind at this point.) The solo that Aminta sings is announced by Henry to be 'the aria from Monteverdi's *L'incoronazione di Poppea'*, although in fact it is the opening section of *'Sento un certo'*, a duet from that opera, of which Strauss has taken only the words and the opening musical phrase.

The Monteverdi 'aria' soon turns into pure Strauss, an amusing piece of coloratura pastiche which takes Aminta up to a sustained top E. Her singing-teacher has joined her in the final section of the aria, and the noise brings Morosus out of his bedroom, begging them to cease. This merely has the effect of encouraging Aminta and Henry to embark upon a duet, for which Strauss has plundered the opera *Eteocle e Polinice*, composed by Giovanni Legrenzi in 1675. Legrenzi's *'Dolce amor'* is, of course, simply the starting point for more Zerbinetta-like coloratura, and the duet turns into a quartet when Morosus and the Housekeeper, who has returned, add their complaining voices. In the final bars, the cockatoo joins in as well.

(In his vocal score, Strauss included a footnote to the effect that, if the opera company performing *Die schweigsame Frau* does not have at its disposal two first-class coloratura sopranos for Aminta and Isotta, and thus allots the role of Aminta to a *'jugendlich-dramatisch'* [young dramatic] soprano, these two Italian arias can be sung by Isotta, who would arrive with Henry and Farfallo. The 'singing lesson' would then become a 'concert' with Aminta as audience. This footnote did not find its way into the full score).

The Barber enters to inform Morosus that the Lord Chief Justice, accompanied by two notaries 'of the Upper Chamber', will shortly arrive. Henry and Farfallo leave discreetly, for they will have roles to play in the ensuing scene, Farfallo as one of the notaries and Henry as an important witness. At the request of Morosus, the Barber attempts, in an elegant exchange with 'Timida' above an accompanying minuet, to bribe her to leave Morosus, but she professes herself highly satisfied with her marriage, and refuses to be bought off. The Housekeeper now announces the Lord Chief Justice, and takes Morosus off to dress properly for the occasion. Vanuzzi enters in the costume of the Lord Chief Justice, accompanied by Farfallo and Morbio as notaries. Strauss chose another piece from the Fitzwilliam Virginal Book to accompany Vanuzzi's appearance, an 'In Nomine' by Doctor John Bull (no. XXXVII), which he gives to bassoons, horns and trombones. The conspirators relax in a noisy quintet, resuming their grave official manner when Morosus returns in ceremonial dress, followed by his Housekeeper.

With frequent recourse to comical Latin, the petition for annulment of the marriage is heard. Carlotta and Isotta in their Act II disguises are brought in to give evidence, but it is not until Henry, hidden behind a beard, is called, and admits to having had carnal knowledge of Lady Morosus, that Morosus apepars to have won his case. Henry is allowed a graceful aria in which he urges Lady Morosus to acknowledge their love. One of the Notaries raises an objection: there is nothing in the marriage contract to say that the bride must be *virgo intacta*. A huge ensemble develops, in the middle of which Morosus in desperation covers his head with cushions, for he can bear the din no longer.

At a sign from the Barber, the noise begins to subside. When the singing has ceased, and even the orchestra has fallen silent, Aminta and Henry remove their disguises and kneel before Morosus. The finale of the opera begins as a hesitant solo clarinet, and then a bassoon, introduce Henry's tender expression of affection for his uncle. Aminta, too, reassures the old man, and the entire plot is explained to him. At first furious, Morosus finally bursts into laughter, and compliments Henry and his troupe on their performances. In a spirit of *Falstaff*-like reconciliation, he orders wine for the assembled company, and tells them they can make as much noise as they like. When one has endured a 'silent wife', one can endure anything.

The members of the opera company sing their farewells to Morosus, with quotations from the roles they have been playing for him, and make their exits. Left alone with Henry and Aminta, Morosus sips a glass of wine, and remarks how beautiful music is, especially when it is over, and how wonderful a wife is, especially when she is someone else's. He lights a pipe, leans back in an arm-chair, clasps the hands of the young couple, and sighs contentedly as the curtain slowly—and quietly—descends.

Die schweigsame Frau is a not unattractive work, and there is something charming about Strauss's apparent desire to compose a kind of tribute to Italian *opera buffa*. But he has not the melodic fecundity of the most successful practitioners of that genre, and in consequence *Die schweigsame Frau* seems anaemic when compared with works such as *Don Pasquale* and *Il barbiere di Siviglia* with which it would like to have more in common than it has. A Teutonic heaviness of humour and an inability to move on quickly are attributes which distinguish Strauss from Donizetti, Rossini and the Verdi of *Falstaff*. Strauss's sparkle is only on the surface, beneath which there lurks a certain turgidity. Nor does Zweig's libretto exactly abound in lightness and wit. Strauss ought perhaps to have reflected upon the fact that Mozart's comedies, which he would so dearly love to have been able to emulate, had the inestimable advantage of an *Italian* Jewish librettist.

TWELVE

Friedenstag

Opera in One Act
opus 81

Dramatis personae
Commandant of the Besieged Town   (baritone)
Maria, his Wife   (soprano)
Cavalry Sergeant   (bass)
Rifleman   (tenor)
Corporal   (baritone)
Musketeer   (bass)   } of the Besieging Army
Bugler   (bass)
Officer   (baritone)
Front-line Officer   (baritone)
A Piedmontese   (tenor)
The Holsteiner, Commandant of the Besieging Army   (bass)
The Mayor   (tenor)
The Preacher   (baritone)   } of the Besieged Town
A Woman of the People   (soprano)

LIBRETTO by Joseph Gregor, based on a synopsis by Stefan Zweig

TIME: 24 October 1648

PLACE: The citadel of a besieged town, at the end of the Thirty Years' War

FIRST PERFORMED at the National Theater, Munich, 24 July 1938, with Hans Hotter (Commandant), Viorica Ursuleac (Maria), Georg Hann (Cavalry Sergeant), Julius Patzak (Rifleman), Ludwig Weber (The Holsteiner), Peter Anders (A Piedmontese), Karl Ostertag (The Mayor) and Georg Wieter (Corporal), conducted by Clemens Krauss.

I

WHILE *Die schweigsame Frau* was being written, Strauss and Zweig were already thinking about subjects for future operas. Various ideas were discussed, but the one which was eventually to lead to Strauss's next opera (though not with Zweig as librettist) emerged in a letter which the librettist wrote to his composer on 21 August 1934. Zweig's suggestion was for a one-act work which would combine three elements: 'the tragic, the heroic and the humane, ending in a hymn to international conciliation and to the grace of creativeness'. Zweig then went on to explain in detail the plot of the proposed work, which would be set in a besieged town at the end of the Thirty Years' War. It is the plot of *Friedenstag*, whose working title at this stage was *24 Oktober 1648*. Zweig made it clear that he would not mind in the slightest if Strauss were to pass his synopsis on to someone else who would then write the libretto, 'to save you any wretched political bother'.

Strauss liked Zweig's idea, but thought that, as it stood, it was perhaps too plain and in need of adornment. He suggested adding a love affair 'between the wife of the fortress commander . . . and one of the commander's lieutenants'. Rather more politely than Hofmannsthal would have done, Zweig rejected the love affair which he thought 'a bit too operatic in the unfortunate sense of the word'. He confessed that he always felt uncomfortable 'where men representing heroes burst into an amorous aria'. But Strauss did not give up easily. 'You are undoubtedly right', he told Zweig,

and the material as you describe it is certainly purer and greater, but please don't forget I have to compose it, and it has to express feelings which kindle emotional music in me. The motives of despair, heroism, weakness, hatred, reconciliation and so on do not, I'm afraid, inspire enough music in me that truly goes to the heart. It's true, my suggestions were operatic, but where does the kitsch end and the opera begin?

In due course, Zweig won that particular battle. He then began to recommend politically acceptable, i.e. Aryan, librettists to Strauss, and suggested at least three writers before Strauss grudgingly agreed to accept Zweig's friend, Joseph Gregor, an Austrian whose *History of the Theatre* was much admired by the composer. Zweig and Gregor were used to showing each other their work in draft, and Zweig agreed to keep in close contact with Gregor during the actual writing of the *Friedenstag* libretto. Strauss met Gregor in a hotel at Berchtesgaden on 7 July 1935, to discuss *Friedenstag* and other possible projects. Later in July, Gregor stayed at the Strauss villa at Garmisch where the two men worked on the libretti of both

Friedenstag and another subject which in due course became the opera *Daphne*.

Gregor wrote the *Friedenstag* libretto in the summer, and Zweig rewrote the closing scene for his friend in November. By the end of the year, Strauss had been presented with a finished libretto and could begin composing. He was not, however, at all enthusiasticabout the text with which he had been provided. 'Your entire dialogue', he had told Gregor at one stage, 'is still developed on far too literary and untheatrical lines.' He insisted on a complete re-writing, after which 'we must submit it to our friend [Zweig] for the most merciless criticism, and the most fundamental final revision.' To Zweig, in due course, Strauss wrote:

I thank you warmly for the trouble you have taken over *Friedenstag*. Your version is more theatrical and concise than that of our friend Gregor. . . . I have been busy with the composition for the last few weeks, but it still won't be the kind of music I would want to write. The entire material is, after all, rather too commonplace. Soldiers—war— hunger—mediaeval heroism—people all dying together—with the best will in the world, it doesn't really suit me. . . . I would have preferred a little joy in my work for these last years of my life. . . . *Friedenstag* is too wearisome a task. Gregor's verses have no depth. . . .

Strauss completed the opera in short score on 24 January 1936, and by mid-June had finished the orchestration. *Friedenstag* was then set aside while Strauss and Gregor worked on *Daphne*, Strauss's intention being to have the two one-act operas performed together, conducted by Karl Böhm, at a joint première in Dresden. Indeed, he had promised as much to Böhm. It seems, however, that Clemens Krauss, in Munich, was determined to secure the première of *Friedenstag* for himself, with his wife, Viorica Ursuleac, in the leading female role. Krauss clearly exerted pressure on Strauss who capitulated, and indeed dedicated the opera to Krauss and Ursuleac. It was given its première in Munich on 24 July 1938, preceded by a performance of Beethoven's ballet, *Die Geschöpfe des Prometheus* (The Creatures of Prometheus). *Friedenstag* was subsequently performed together with *Daphne*, at the première of the latter piece, in Dresden in October of the same year, under the baton of Karl Böhm, to whom *Daphne* was dedicated.

There were productions of *Friedenstag* in Graz in October, in Berlin and Vienna the following year, 1939, and in Venice in 1940, after which the opera seems to have been dropped from the repertory of German theatres. This is hardly surprising in view of the fact that its libretto, essentially the brain-child of Stefan Zweig, is a plea for tolerance and an indictment of war. Of course, Zweig's name was not mentioned anywhere in connection with the opera. On all programmes, posters, and in the printed score, the work was described as 'Oper in einem Aufzug [opera in one act] von Joseph Gregor: Musik von Richard Strauss'. *Friedenstag* was first performed in the United States of America at the University of Southern California in Los Angeles, in 1957, first heard in Great Britain on BBC Radio in May 1971, and was given in concert performance in Oxford and London in 1985. It has yet to be staged in Great Britain.

II

THE Thirty Years' War (1618–1648) developed from a revolt in Bohemia into a general conflict between Catholic and Protestant Europe. At various times battles were fought throughout central Europe, involving most of the German states, Austria, Bohemia, France, Sweden and Denmark. Germany was almost completely devastated by the war, suffering irreparable losses of wealth, the destruction of many towns, a severe reduction of the population and a vast increase in poverty. The date on which the events in Strauss's opera take place is that on which the Treaties of Westphalia were signed, bringing thirty years of war to an end. As the opera begins, an unnamed German Catholic town is under siege by Protestant forces from Holstein.

After a few bars of a very slow march, the curtain rises on a huge circular room in the town's citadel. Steps lead up to the battlements, and down to the lower rooms and to the street. It is dawn. The tempo of the march quickens, and continues under the conversation of a Cavalry Sergeant (bass) and a Rifleman (tenor) in which the unlikely influence of Kurt Weill (that 'decadent' Jewish composer who had been forced to flee Germany in 1933) can be strongly discerned. In his replies to his superior's questions, the Rifleman paints a dismal picture of the ravaged and desolate countryside and the misery of its inhabitants. '*Wie soll das enden?*' (How will it all end?), he wonders. The Sergeant bids him think of their dedicated Commandant who has been at his desk the entire night, poring over maps, still planning to achieve victory over the besieging forces.

As the soldiers begin to awaken, a young Italian (tenor) from Piedmont who had made his way through the enemy lines to bring a letter from the Kaiser to the Commandant, begins to sing a song of his homeland, of peace and of love. This brings ironic comments from the soldiers, some of whom are too young ever to have known peace. Suddenly the sound of an approaching mob is heard. It is the townsfolk who, made desperate by hunger, are marching on the citadel. As the outer gates are stormed, an officer announces that a deputation headed by the Mayor has entered.

The music now changes to a grim Funeral March as the bedraggled citizens appear, headed not only by the Mayor (tenor) but also by a Priest (baritone). The Commandant (baritone), a handsome man of about fifty, dressed in black, now appears on the upper level of the citadel, and addresses the mob. They plead with him to surrender the town, before all its citizens starve to death. He refuses, speaking, as befits a soldier, of the Emperor and of duty. He has no sympathy for their plight, and is unmoved by the arguments put forward by the Mayor and the Priest.

When an Officer (baritone) enters to announce that the situation is now hopeless unless the Commandant releases the ammunition which is stored beneath the Citadel, the Commandant refuses. But, as the voice of the crowd swells in urgency and despair, he tells them to disperse and to wait for a sign which he will give at midday. The crowd breaks up, but the orders which the Commandant now gives to his soldiers are to spread out the gunpowder under the fortress, and bring him the fuse with which, at midday, he will destroy the citadel rather than surrender.

Strauss's score has been plodding mundanely along until the Commandant's ballad. 'Zu Magdeburg', which he addresses to the Sergeant, and for which the composer has recourse to the bitter, ironic style of Mahler. The Commandant's staff are given the option of remaining with him and dying, or leaving the citadel immediately. Some are stupidly heroic, others sensibly unheroic. The Piedmontese messenger is dismissed, the others either depart or take up their posts on the battlements, and the stage empties, leaving the sun to shine brightly upon the scene.

The Commandant's wife, Maria (soprano) now appears. She is the only character in the opera to be given a personal name, though she could as easily have been described simply as 'Commandant's Wife', for she is no more than a personification of various attributes. In an extended aria, she notes with surprise that the citadel is apparently deserted, and expresses her anxiety at the unusual behaviour of both solidery and citizens whom she has encountered in the streets. She sings of her husband, whom she loves although she cannot share his professional view of war as something glorious. She contrasts the horrors of war with the joys of peace in the closing section of her aria which goes through the usual Straussian motions to express her passionately held views, though only mechanically in comparison with the great soprano scenes of Strauss's earlier days.

The Commandant now reappears. In the duet which ensues, his wife extracts from him the truth, which is that, rather than surrender to the enemy, he is planning to blow the citadel and its inhabitants sky-high. He extols the virtues of war and of blind obedience to the Kaiser's commands while she expresses her loathing of the senseless brutality of war. Nevertheless, though he begs her to flee and thus save her life, she refuses to leave her husband, declaring that she will die with him. Their duet, musically banal, can end excitingly if the soprano, whose high notes have been sorely tested throughout, has the stamina to maintain her tone to its final bars in which she soars to her top D flat.

The Commandant and his wife remain locked in a loving embrace throughout the ensuing orchestral intermezzo, until the soldiers begin to re-appear, last of all the Sergeant carrying the fuse to ignite the gunpowder which will destroy the citadel. When a distant cannon shot is heard, suggesting that the enemy is about to attack, the Commandant seizes the fuse from the Sergeant, and extinguishes it. It would, after all, be preferable to die fighting. But the expected attack does not materialize. Instead, bells begin to ring out in the town, a sound which most of the inhabitants have never heard before but which they understand to mean peace. This is the most poetic moment in the opera. Though his soldiers report to him that the advancing Holsteiners are dressed not for battle but ceremonially, and that they carry a white flag, the Commandant refuses to believe in peace, his life being dedicated to war. Even when he is informed that the enemy troops have been welcomed into the town joyfully by the citizens, the Commandant declines to accept the situation.

To a march in quick tempo, in which the strains of the Protestant chorale '*Ein feste Burg*' can be discerned in the bass, the Holstein troops enter the citadel, and their leader, described in the score simply as the Holsteiner (bass), calls for the Commandant whom he refers to as a great hero of the war. Though the great hero answers him intemperately, the Holsteiner, unperturbed, announces that peace has been declared by the armistice council in Münster. His news is greeted with joy by Maria as well as by the crowd which has followed the troops into the citadel, but the Commandant continues to maintain a belligerent stance. Refusing to shake the hand of the Holsteiner, he antagonizes the man whom he still regards as his enemy until, at the end of a duet in which the Holsteiner keeps up his conciliatory tone as long as he decently can, the Commandant refers slightingly to the Holsteiner's religion, and draws his sword. The Holsteiner naturally follows suit, and a fight is averted only by the intervention of Maria. In a brief aria which really forms the emotional climax of the opera, she preaches her sermon of peace and reconciliation, imploring her husband not to resort to the sword to solve every problem, but to act reasonably.

Maria's aria, though out of context it might not seem anything other than bombastic, is effective at this point. It is certainly, though most improbably, successful in effecting a change of heart in the Commandant who throws his sword aside, approaches the Holsteiner and embraces him. The citizens of the town as well as soldiers of both armies have been crowding into the citadel, and a great chorus of peace and friendship, begun in the distance by those still outside the citadel, launches the opera's finale. Maria's voice soars above the chorus. A brief duet episode in unison for the Commandant and the Holsteiner finds Strauss at his most four-square and uninspired, but the final C major section of the ensemble, sung by Maria and the entire chorus, brings the opera to a rousing if musically dull conclusion.

It is as easy to respond positively to the intentions of Strauss, Zweig and Gregor in *Friedenstag* as it is difficult to admire the opera itself. Its libretto is naïve and undramatic, and its leading character, the Commandant, positively ridiculous, while its music is for the most part unworthy of Strauss, who seems to be unenthusiastically writing self-pastiche verging, at moments, on self-parody. To write an opera on the subject of the preferability of peace to war is platitudinous: to write so dramatically unconvincing a work almost undermines the worthiness of the undertaking. Strauss and his librettists may have been able to persuade themselves that they had produced something that ran counter to the belligerent spirit of the times, but, as it happens, they played into the hands of the Nazis with *Friedenstag's* message of peace, for at the time of its composition Hitler's claim was that he wanted peace in Europe. Indeed, when it was first staged the opera was acclaimed by Nazi officialdom as a work created in the spirit of National Socialist ethics, which must have deeply embarrassed Strauss.

Friedenstag has its supporters, who appear to hear in it echoes of Beethoven's *Fidelio*, though all that the two works have in common is a perceived similarity of 'message'. But the similarity is more apparent than real. *Fidelio* is about love, courage and freedom, while *Friedenstag* is about something quite different, the senseless horror of war. Also, *Fidelio* is a blazing masterpiece: *Friedenstag* is not. It would be pleasant to be able to praise this elementary diatribe against war for the humanity of its intention. Unfortunately, successful operas are made not from humane intent but from musical and dramatic achievement.

An opera which takes about eighty minutes to perform, *Friedenstag* has some interesting moments at the beginning, with its echoes of Weill, Mahler and (according to some critics) Berg. But, with the exception of a few passages for the soprano role of Maria, in which Strauss momentarily recaptures something of the lyrical splendour which he had last displayed in *Arabella*, the opera is disappointingly lacking in interest. Though a short work, it does not seem so in performance, and is, in fact, too long to be performed on the same evening as its intended companion piece, Strauss's next opera, *Daphne*.

THIRTEEN

Daphne

Bucolic Tragedy in One Act
opus 82

Dramatis personae
Peneios, a Fisherman   (bass)
Gaea, his Wife   (contralto)
Daphne, their Daughter   (soprano)
Leukippos, a Shepherd   (tenor)
Apollo   (tenor)
Four Shepherds   (tenor, baritone, two basses)
Two Maids   (sopranos)

LIBRETTO by Joseph Gregor

TIME: Mythical Antiquity

PLACE: Greece. Outside the hut of Peneios, by the river bearing his name.

FIRST PERFORMED at the Sächsische Staatsoper, Dresden, 15 October 1938, with Margarete Teschemacher (Daphne), Torsten Ralf (Apollo), Helene Jung (Gaea) and Martin Kremer (Leukippos), conducted by Karl Böhm. (On the same evening, after an interval of about one hour, another one-act opera by Strauss was performed. This was *Friedenstag*, receiving its first Dresden performance three months after its Munich première.)

I

WHEN Strauss and Joseph Gregor met in a hotel in Berchtesgaden in July 1935 to discuss opera projects, they decided to proceed immediately with two operas, one of which was *Friedenstag*. The other was *Daphne*, and it was Strauss's intention that the two one-act operas be performed together in Dresden on the same evening. Although he subsequently agreed to allow *Friedenstag* to be staged first in Munich, sharing the programme with a ballet, Strauss still conceived of *Daphne* as a companion piece to the other opera. When *Daphne* finally reached the stage in Dresden, on 15 October 1938, it was as a curtain-raiser to the somewhat shorter *Friedenstag*.

In Greek mythology, Daphne, the daughter of a river-god, was loved by Apollo, from whom she escaped by being transformed into a laurel-tree. The synopsis for an opera about Daphne which Gregor presented to Strauss at their first meeting reads thus:

Daphne. One act of tragedy with dances and choruses—wonderful Grecian landscape. Mankind identified both with nature and with the gods. Old Peneios is at the same time both the river and the singing fisherman who lives by the river. Gaea is both his wife and at the same time the lovely green earth by the Peneios river. Their daughter Daphne is in the deepest state of emotional unawakening.

Daphne's sport with the waves of the Peneios which are choruses of nymphs. Two suitors: Apollo as cowherd, wise, baritone-like, surrounded by his servant-priestesses, and the young, tenorish shepherd, Leukippos. Daphne remains enigmatic, even when on one occasion the cowherd confronts her with lightning.

Leukippos, persecuted by the jealous Apollo, conceives the idea of dressing as a girl. This entirely changes Daphne's attitude to him: she now treats him as one girl would another. Through this deception, he comes to attain his desire. Daphne is now thoroughly upset, and opens her heart to the cowherd.

Apollo reacts, both as god and as man, and slays Leukippos with a thunderstorm. Peneios begs Zeus, during the funeral choruses for Leukippos, to change mankind back into its primeval state. This Zeus agrees to do, and, amidst the play of the water-nymphs and in front of the burning pyre of Leukippos, the tree (Daphne) grows aloft.

Gregor sent a draft of his libretto to Stefan Zweig who commented upon it, improved it, and finally expressed himself delighted with it. It was then forwarded by Gregor to Strauss early in September 1935. Strauss found it disappointing, said so to Gregor, and also to Zweig.

A second version of the libretto was produced by Gregor at the beginning of the following year, and sent to Strauss. It was discussed thoroughly before being rejected by the composer, after which Gregor made a third attempt to produce something along the lines that Strauss wanted. It was in April 1936, that Gregor sent his third version of *Daphne* to the composer, and again the two men met on several occasions, finally hammering out between them a libretto which the composer thought at least tolerable.

Strauss had been commissioned to compose a hymn for the opening of the Olympic Games which were to be held in Berlin in 1936. ('I kill the boredom of the Advent season,' he had written to Zweig in December 1934, 'by composing an Olympic Hymn for the proletarians—I, of all people, who hate and despise sports.') On 1 August 1936, he conducted his Hymn at the opening of the Olympic Games in Berlin, in the presence of the Führer. He began the composition of *Daphne* later in the summer, breaking off to visit London in November where he conducted the Dresden State Opera in a performance of *Ariadne auf Naxos* at Covent Garden. This was part of a ten-day season by the Dresden company, consisting of two performances each of *Don Giovanni*, *Le nozze di Figaro*, *Tristan und Isolde*, and Strauss's *Der Rosenkavalier* (all conducted by Karl Böhm), and a single performance of *Ariadne*. The season opened on 2 November with *Der Rosenkavalier*. Marta Fuchs sang the Marschallin, Strauss sat in a box with Ribbentrop, the German Ambassador, and was called to the stage to acknowledge applause after the second and third acts. He conducted *Ariadne* on 6 November, with Marta Fuchs as Ariadne, Torsten Ralf as Bacchus, and Erna Sack as Zerbinetta. On the previous evening Strauss had attended a concert of the Royal Philharmonic Society at which he was presented with the Gold Medal of the Society, and his tone-poem, *Also sprach Zarathustra*, was conducted by Adrian Boult.

The finale of *Daphne* occupied Strauss's thoughts during the following months. Gregor, who had planned the opera as part of a double-bill with *Friedenstag*, wanted both works to end with a chorus. However, although a choral ending to *Friedenstag* seemed perfectly appropriate, Strauss resisted the idea of ending *Daphne* in the same manner. He consulted the conductor Clemens Krauss, who suggested that the opera should end with the solo voice of Daphne, after her metamorphosis into a tree. 'Now, in the moonlight, but fully visible', wrote Strauss to Gregor in May, 'the miracle of transformation is slowly worked upon her—but with the orchestra alone. . . . Right at the end, when the tree stands there complete, she should sing without words—only as a voice of nature—so, eight more bars of the laurel-tree motif!'

The composition of *Daphne* occupied Strauss throughout 1937, though he also continued to accept conducting engagements. In September he was to have conducted *Der Rosenkavalier* and *Ariadne auf Naxos* at the World

Fair in Paris, but he became ill, and his place was taken by Clemens Krauss. Strauss went to Sicily to convalesce, and it was at Taormina, on Christmas Eve, 1937, that he completed the orchestral score of *Daphne*, which he dedicated to his friend Karl Böhm who was to conduct the opera's first performance.

Strauss remained in Italy until April 1938, and then returned to Garmisch where, in June, he began to compose a third Gregor opera, *Die Liebe der Danae*. The first performance of *Friedenstag* was given in Munich in July, and in Dresden on 15 October the opera was staged again, as part of the double-bill which also included the première of *Daphne*. Böhm conducted *Daphne* persuasively, and Strauss professed himself satisfied, though he thought that Margarete Teschemacher's voice was too heavy for Daphne. For the Berlin production in March of the following year, he insisted that the role be given to the lighter-voiced Maria Cebotari.

After their Dresden performance, the two operas were again performed together, in Graz and Vienna, as well as Berlin. In due course, however, the two works went their separate ways, Strauss letting it be known that his preference was for *Daphne* to be preceded by his *Couperin Suite* performed as a ballet. The first production of *Daphne* in the Americas was in Buenos Aires in 1948, when Erich Kleiber conducted the opera with Rose Bampton in the title-role. New York first heard the work in a concert performance in the Town Hall in 1960, conducted by Thomas Scherman, with Gloria Davy as Daphne. The first stage performances in the United States were given at Santa Fé, New Mexico, in 1964, conducted by John Crosby, with Sylvia Stahlman as Daphne. During the Vienna Festival of 1964, Karl Böhm conducted superbly a production at the Theater an der Wien, with Hilde Gueden in the title-role and James King as Apollo. The opera was not staged in Great Britain until 1987, when it was given by Opera North at the Grand Theatre, Leeds, in English. The conductor was David Lloyd-Jones, and the role of Daphne was sung by Helen Field.

II

THE orchestral introduction to *Daphne* is a gentle pastoral piece composed for a small group of woodwind instruments. As soon as the mood of the opera has been established, the curtain rises on a stony riverbank scene, towards evening as the sun is setting. On the right, the ground rises towards the hut of Peneios, who is both a fisherman and also the river-god himself. Beyond is the river Peneios, and in the background can be seen the towering peak of Mount Olympus. Not far away, shepherds are moving their flocks of sheep, to the accompaniment of shouts, bells and the barking of dogs. Suddenly the primitive notes of an alphorn are heard, and an old shepherd (baritone) appears, greeting a younger one (tenor), and drawing his attention to the alphorn which is calling the shepherds to a feast of Dionysus, an occasion for the mating not only of lovers but also of animals. Two more shepherds (basses) are greeted and, as they all move off, a chorus of shepherds in the distance sings a farewell to the fading day.

It is clear from the first bars of the prelude that *Daphne* is to be a work in complete contrast to *Friedenstag* with which it was intended to be coupled, its mood lyrically autumnal rather than dramatic. Strauss depicts the movements of the flocks of sheep rather noisily for a time in the orchestra, after the curtain has risen, but it is the rustic sound of the huge and ungainly alphorn and the gentle song of the shepherds which predominate.

As the noises of the herds fade, and the shepherds move out of sight, Daphne (soprano), the daughter of Peneios and Gaea, enters. She listens to the song of the shepherds as it dies away in the distance, and then begins to sing, softly, a long and reflective aria in which she implores the fading day to stay awhile so that she can continue to commune with the trees, the flowers and the river, with all of whom she feels so close an affinity. The beauties of nature are hidden from her at night, and the activities of men and cattle, trampling on the grass and tearing at the branches of the trees, are hateful to her. She reproaches her father, Peneios, for having summoned the shepherds to Dionysiac revelling.

Daphne, it will be seen, is a real child of nature, already well on the way to becoming a tree, as befits the daughter of a river-god and an earth-mother. Her long, gently winding cantilena has something in common with the style of the heroine's gentle utterance in *Arabella*, though the delicate texture of Strauss's orchestra in *Daphne* beautifully conjures up the magical radiance of the approaching night, and the beauty of nature, as distinct from the indoor, almost hot-house atmosphere of the earlier opera. '*O wie gerne blieb ich bei dir, mein lieber Baum*' (Oh, how I wish to stay here with you, my beloved tree'), Daphne sings in a flowing melody (Ex. 18) in

Ex.18

which she addresses a large and leafy tree as her brother. Assuring the tree that its voice has more power over her than the songs of mankind, she presses herself affectionately against its trunk at the climax of her aria.

Suddenly the mood of her solo scene is shattered, as the young shepherd Leukippos (tenor), who loves Daphne, leaps out at her playfully from behind the trunk of the tree. The friend of her childhood, when she would listen happily to his songs on the flute, Leukippos has now matured into an ardent young suitor who wants something more from Daphne than companionship. To his consternation, however, Daphne informs him that it was not his tender flute-song that used to delight her, but the voice of the wind in his flute, and that the youthful bloom of his cheeks and the almost feminine sadness in his eyes were to her reflections of the bloom of spring and the tears and sorrows of her own heart.

The lyrical mood of Daphne's solo has been dispersed, and replaced by an accompaniment in the orchestra more akin to the style of *Intermezzo* than to that of *Arabella*. When Leukippos, feeling the power of the god Dionysus rising within him, embraces Daphne passionately, declaring his love for her, she breaks away from him with a cry of virginal distaste for that kind of thing. Leukippos runs off dejectedly, and Daphne realizes with sadness that she has lost for ever the innocent companion of her childhood.

Daphne's mother, Gaea (contralto), now appears, calling her daughter into the hut to prepare for the feast of Dionysus. Gaea, the earth-mother, attempts to explain to Daphne that she is almost ready to ripen to love and thus to fulfil the role the gods have allotted to her. The child-like Daphne, however, merely asks if this means that she will become closer to the trees and the flowers. Gaea had watched Daphne's dismissal of Leukippos, and was troubled by it. When Daphne now refuses to wear the beautiful gown and the jewellery which two maids bring out to her from the hut, preferring to go to the feast, if she must, in her own simple clothes, Gaea solemnly tells herself, using the lowest notes of her contralto range, that the gods will make Daphne return to her place in the scheme of things. Daphne has run into the hut, and Gaea slowly follows her.

Left alone, the two maids (sopranos) apostrophize the rejected clothes and jewellery in a light-hearted and delicately scored duet which is overheard by Leukippos, sulking nearby. He thinks they are mocking him, but the maids inform him that they are magical dream-creatures, able to gratify his every wish. They soon persuade Leukippos to accept the garments and adornments intended for Daphne, assuring him that if he disguises himself by wearing them, and appears to Daphne as a female, a mirror-image of herself, he will win her love.

The maids and Leukippos rush off, laughing joyously, and the music assumes a more solemn tone as Peneios (bass), a grave, dignified man with a long beard, enters with Gaea and the shepherds. The precise status of Peneios is rather confusing. Though a river-god, he is not, or is no longer, one of the company of gods on Mount Olympus. He directs the attention of the shepherds now to the sacred mountain, and to the shimmering crimson cloud hovering around its summit. The sun-god, Phoebus-Apollo, declares Peneios, has not yet vanished from the heights of the mountain. The gods, he prophesies, will shortly return to earth, to the hut of their former brother. His words perturb Gaea and the shepherds. She, the earth-mother, begs Peneios not to challenge the gods, reminding him that joy lies in being at one with the earth in quiet contentment, but Peneios insists that preparations must be made for the gods who will shortly arrive to join their fellow god at his festive table. (It is, perhaps, a trifle strange that Peneios should be thinking of greeting Apollo in particular, at a feast dedicated to Dionysus, but this would appear to be a consequence of Strauss's input into Gregor's libretto.)

When Peneios, Gaea and the shepherds sing of the gods and their laughter, the sound of laughter seems to reverberate from all sides, red flashes of lightning can be seen between the trees, and tumult is heard in the orchestra. The shepherds huddle around Gaea in fear, and when Apollo, dressed as a herdsman, enters carrying a bow and arrow, they scream in terror. The noise subsides as Apollo (tenor) greets Peneios and Gaea, declares his humble status, and explains that he was grazing his herd at the foot of Mount Olympus when the delicious fragrance of roasting meat and the sweet smell of wine drifted across the meadows. His restless herd stampeded and galloped down to the river, where they have now been rounded up and calmed by fellow-herdsmen.

Gaea and the shepherds voice their amusement at the fact that, far from having gods attend his feast, Peneios appears to have attracted only simple herdsmen chasing rampaging beasts. The shepherds drift off, laughing, as Peneios orders Gaea to send Daphne out from the hut to serve their newly arrived guest. Strauss advances the action in this scene by means of a not very inspired recitative, and the shepherds' comments have an air of the choral society about them.

Apollo barely has time to conclude a short soliloquy in which he reproaches himself for behaving in a manner unfitting to his divinity, before Daphne returns, carrying a cup in both hands, and followed by a group of maids. They approach Apollo, the maids bow and withdraw, and Apollo immediately voices his admiration of Daphne's great beauty. When he quotes lines from her aria, it becomes clear that his object in descending from Olympus was to make love to her. Daphne knows this can be no ordinary herdsman, but she is puzzled by him and wonders how he has acquired so intimate a knowledge of her as he appears to display. She pours over his hands water from the cup, takes from him his bow and quiver of arrows and puts them aside, and then places across his shoulders a blue mantle she has been carrying. The mantle billows around the god in majestic folds, and at the same time a strange radiance seems to emanate from him. Apollo explains poetically to Daphne how the golden wheels of his chariot as he sped across the sky had been halted that day by her radiance.

The duet which ensues is the kind of lyrical outpouring which Strauss had made his speciality. It is hardly one of his finest in that genre, but it progresses not unsatisfactorily from climax to climax until Apollo, who, in order not to alarm Daphne, has until now referred to his love as brotherly, suddenly embraces her in a passionate kiss. Daphne, whose thoughts were on a higher, more spiritual plane, is confused. At first she submits to his embrace, which Strauss's orchestra accompanies not with an ecstatic outburst but with warm, though slightly uneasy harmonies. Suddenly, the innocent girl understands the nature of Apollo's passion and struggles free from his embrace.

Offstage the voices of the shepherds can be heard offering their prayers to Dionysus, while Apollo continues to woo the confused and reluctant Daphne. The great feast of Dionysus begins, as a procession of shepherds, headed by Peneios, enters carrying torches, while from behind the hut women emerge, led by Gaea, carrying vases and bowls of fruit. Daphne flees to Gaea's side, while Apollo joins the men. Food is brought in, masked figures come forward from the chorus and perform a wild dance, and a procession of girls carries wine to the men. Among the girls is Leukippos, dressed in Daphne's rejected finery. By his gestures, he invites Daphne to dance with him, and she, not recognizing him but intrigued by what seems to be a mirror-image of herself, joins Leukippos in a slow and solemn dance.

Suddenly the revels are interrupted by an outburst from Apollo who exclaims that Daphne is being deceived and the sacred feast made an empty mockery. The shepherds threaten him, demanding that he give proof of the authority he claims to possess. In answer, Apollo swings his bow through the air, causing immediate thunder. The feast is disrupted, and the gates of the nearby pens burst open, allowing the sheep and rams to run off. A second thunderclap is followed by a third, and all flee except Apollo, Daphne and Leukippos.

Apollo vents his anger upon the young shepherd who had dared to love Daphne, and Leukippos bravely defies him, invoking Dionysus the god of wine, and calling Daphne to his side. She, however, feels she has been betrayed both by Leukippos and by the stranger who presented himself to her as a brother. When Leukippos and Daphne demand that he reveal his true identity, Apollo in one of Strauss's finest rhapsodic outbursts ('*Jeden heiligen Morgen*': Every sacred morning) describes how every morning he rides in his glittering chariot, takes an arrow from his bow and shoots it over the sea, the meadows and the mountains. In short, he is the sun.

Daphne accepts this as truth, though she still rejects Apollo's embraces. Leukippos, however, denounces the god as a liar, and curses him. Apollo quickly raises his bow and shoots. Amid thunder and lightning, Leukippos falls to the ground. Daphne throws herself down by his side, and Leukippos, uttering a final word of love to her, dies in Daphne's arms.

Daphne now sings her version of a *Liebestod* over the body of Leukippos, a beautiful lament in which she accepts responsibility for the death of her beloved companion, offers to place by his side the blossoms she most loved, and promises to remain in silence by his grave until the pitiless gods who brought death to him and demanded love from her should finally take her life away.

Invoking his fellow gods on Olympus, Apollo begs forgiveness of Dionysus for having slain Leukippos, and asks that the young shepherd be carried to Olympus where he may play his flute in homage to Dionysus. He entreats Zeus, father of the gods, to transform Daphne into one of the laurel trees she loves so completely. Wreaths cut from her branches will in future, Apollo declares, be worn by the bravest of mortals.

Apollo disappears. It has grown dark, and Daphne rises, about to hurry away, only to be held immobile as though by magic. She sings a greeting to her brother and sister trees as she feels the earth rise within her, then she too disappears, and a tree stands in her place. From the tree's branches the voice of Daphne is heard, inviting the wind to play through her leaves, and the birds to nest in her branches. Her wordless voice continues for a time to sound from the tree, and then trails into silence. The curtain falls.

This final ecstatic transformation scene, which Strauss completed in Taormina on Christmas Eve, 1937, with the towering presence of Mount Etna to inspire him, brings *Daphne* to a serene yet moving conclusion. Even Pauline Strauss was affected by it at the final rehearsal, leaning forward from her seat in the front row and kissing the conductor, Karl Böhm, though unable to refrain from adding that he wouldn't get another kiss as he was sweating too much. The final pages of *Daphne* almost persuade one that the opera is among the most rewarding of Strauss's later works. It is uneven, it contains very little action, and its melodies lack freshness and inspiration, but it is gloriously scored: this was one skill which never deserted the composer.

Strauss himself had a special fondness for *Daphne*. Perhaps he liked to recall that another *Daphne*, the very first opera ever composed, by Peri in 1957, was a version of the same legend.

FOURTEEN

Die Liebe der Danae

Cheerful Mythology in Three Acts
opus 83

Dramatis personae
Jupiter (baritone)
Mercury (tenor)
Pollux, King of Eos (tenor)
Danae, his Daughter (soprano)
Xanthe, Danae's Servant (soprano)
Midas, King of Lydia (tenor)
Four Kings, Nephews of Pollux (two tenors, two basses)
Semele (soprano) ⎫
Europa (soprano) ⎪
Alcmene (mezzo-soprano) ⎬ their Wives
Leda (contralto) ⎭
Four Watchmen (basses)

LIBRETTO by Joseph Gregor, with the aid of an outline by Hugo von Hofmannsthal

TIME: The mythical past

PLACE: The classical world

FIRST PERFORMED at the Grosses Festspielhaus, Salzburg, 14 August 1952, with Annelies Kupper (Danae), Josef Gostic (Midas), László Szemere (Pollux), and Paul Schoeffler (Jupiter), conducted by Clemens Krauss. (The opera had previously been heard at a private dress rehearsal in Salzburg on 16 August 1944, with Viorica Ursuleac (Danae), Horst Taubmann (Midas), Karl Ostertag (Pollux), and Hans Hotter (Jupiter), conducted by Clemens Krauss).

I

SOME weeks after the première of *Daphne* in October 1938, Strauss returned to Italy to work on his next opera, *Die Liebe der Danae*, which he had begun to compose in June. At this time, Europe was racing towards World War II: Hitler's smoothly accomplished invasion of Austria in March had created remarkably little tension in international relations, but following the German-Czech crisis in September the British Prime Minister, Neville Chamberlain, met Hitler three times before the end of the month. At the third of these conferences, held in Munich and attended also by Mussolini, an agreement giving Hitler virtually everything that he had demanded was signed, and Chamberlain returned to England waving a piece of paper and boasting of having secured 'peace in our time'. On 1 September of the following year, Hitler's forces attacked Poland on land and in the air, and two days later Britain and France declared war on Germany.

On that day, Strauss was away from home, taking the rheumatism cure at the health resort of Baden in Switzerland. He was now an old man. His seventy-fifth birthday, on 11 June 1939, had been widely celebrated in Germany and Austria, and the Nazis, it seemed, had decided not to harass him, although he received no further official commissions after the Berlin Olympic Hymn. He and Pauline lived not too far away from Munich in Garmisch, in the mountains of Bavaria, for most of the time, and Strauss appeared to be unconcerned about the war, mentioning it in correspondence with friends and colleagues only as a background to his complaints about food rationing, restrictions on travel, and the difficulty of getting household help. He continued to undertake conducting engagements in Germany, and to press on with the opera which he was fairly certain would be his last.

II

WHEN Strauss and Joseph Gregor met in a hotel in Berchtesgaden on that July day in 1935, *Friedenstag* and *Daphne* were not the only opera subjects they discussed. One of Gregor's other suggestions was for an opera to be based on the Greek legend of Danae, daughter of King Acrisius of Argos. Because the Delphic oracle predicted that he would suffer death at the hands of his daughter's son, Acrisius built a tower of brass in which he imprisoned his daughter, Danae. However, Jupiter visited her as a shower of gold, as a result of which Danae bore a child, Perseus, to the god. Acrisius locked Danae and her infant son in a wooden ark which he cast into the sea, but the ark drifted towards an island where it was found by a fisherman who broke it open and found both Danae and Perseus still alive.

Gregor's idea was to combine a version of the Danae legend with another Greek myth, that of Midas, the legendary king of Phrygia who requested of the gods that everything he touched be turned to gold. (His request was granted, but since his food turned to gold as soon as he touched it Midas was obliged to ask the gods to withdraw their gift.)

By coincidence, Hugo von Hofmannsthal had many years earlier submitted to Strauss a scenario for an opera combining the same two Greek legends. Strauss had completely forgotten this when Gregor made his suggestion in 1935, but in April 1920, as his response to the composer's request for a political satire set in ancient Greece, Hofmannsthal had sent him a scenario entitled '*Danae oder die Vernunftheirat*' (Danae or The Marriage of Convenience). Strauss had seen and been greatly impressed by Maria Jeritza in *La Belle Hélène*, and wanted to compose for her a German equivalent of Offenbach's operetta. '*Danae* follows exactly the line from *Der Rosenkavalier* through the *Ariadne* Prelude to *Der Bürger als Edelmann*', Hofmannsthal told Strauss. 'It asks for light, nimble-witted music, such as only you can write, and only at this stage in your life. The subject is early mythological antiquity, flippantly treated as a "Milesian Tale" in Lucian's sense.'

However, Strauss and Hofmannsthal did not proceed with *Danae*. The next opera they were to write together was *Die Aegyptische Helena*, based on another Greek legend. By the time Joseph Gregor came up with his idea for an opera about Danae, in 1935, Strauss appears not to have remembered Hofmannsthal's project of fifteen years earlier, even though his ex-collaborator's scenario had been published posthumously in the magazine *Corona* in 1933. In 1936, as Strauss was about to begin the composition of *Daphne*, the Swiss musicologist Willi Schuh reminded the composer of Hofmannsthal's scenario by sending him a copy of the issue of the magazine in which it had appeared, and Strauss then renewed his interest in Gregor's ideas about Danae. Gregor, who of course could have seen Hofmannsthal's scenario in print, always maintained that he did not know of it and that he had arrived quite independently at his Danae project, which differs from Hofmannsthal's in quite important details.

When Strauss decided that he wanted his next opera, after *Daphne*, to be on the subject of Danae, he asked Gregor to produce a libretto on the basis of Hofmannsthal's scenario. Gregor, understandably, preferred his own treatment of the legend; and, although he began to draft a scenario in the early summer of 1936, he found the composer more than usually difficult to satisfy. Strauss was continually attempting to pull Gregor back to Hofmannsthal's conception of the work, whereas Gregor disliked several of Hofmannsthal's ideas which he was determined to replace with his own.

In due course the outcome, not surprisingly, was an extremely confused, confusing and not particularly '*heiter*' libretto (on the title-page of its score, *Die Liebe der Danae*—The Love of Danae—is described as '*heitere Mythologie in drei Akten*'—cheerful mythology in three acts). Strauss rejected the first draft of Gregor's scenario. A second version fared no better. By April 1937, a third attempt had been presented to Strauss, whose comments on it led to Gregor's making a fourth draft which Strauss accepted, asking Gregor now to go ahead and write a complete libretto. Gregor did this very quickly, completing it before the end of August. Unfortunately, Strauss found the second of Gregor's three acts (Hofmannsthal's scenario had been for a two-act opera) extremely boring, and said so. In November, Gregor produced a revised libretto, and visited Strauss in Taormina (where he was finishing the composition of *Daphne*) to discuss it.

Though he still harboured grave reservations concerning not only the form of Gregor's libretto but also the quality of his verse, Strauss began to compose Act I of the opera early in 1938. But 'it's all too much like popular ballads', he complained to the librettist. 'None of it is yet in the style I have in mind! Some of it is too bombastic, like the first draft—and now these poetics in elevated speech tempt one all too readily into hollow phrases, and padding which doesn't say anything, and empty rhyming jingles!' Strauss sought the advice of his friends, the director Lothar Wallerstein, and the conductor Clemens Krauss, but their intervention served merely to complicate matters, although Strauss increasingly involved Krauss in the shaping of the opera. By October, Gregor had become so offended by the harsh tone of Strauss's criticism that he absented himself from the Dresden première of their *Daphne*, and found himself unable to do any further work on *Die Liebe der Danae* for several months.

In December, librettist and composer were on speaking terms again, and came to an agreement concerning the final act during a journey to Salzburg together by car. Strauss composed Act III during February and March, 1939, and then proceeded to the scoring of the opera, which he completed in June of the following year. (In the early part of 1940 he also composed a single-movement orchestral work, *Japanische Festmusik* [Japanese Festival Music] to celebrate the 2600th anniversary of the founding of the Mikado's dynasty.) By this time, World War II had begun, and Strauss decided that he did not want his new opera staged until at least two years after the end of the war. Convinced that he would never live to see Europe at peace again, he had already begun to think of *Die Liebe der Danae* as a work which would be produced posthumously. The première, he told Gregor, 'will take place after my death. So that's how long you will have to possess your soul in patience.'

As soon as Strauss's score was completed, Clemens Krauss persuaded Strauss to allow him to conduct the first performance, whenever that might be. Karl Böhm, in Dresden, was also keen to conduct the première, but Krauss, having been to some extent a collaborator in the venture, clearly had the prior claim. When he was appointed Artistic Director of the Salzburg Festival in 1941, Krauss immediately asked the composer to let his opera be given for the first time at Salzburg. Strauss had recently received from his new publisher Johannes Oertel (who, under the Nazis, had taken over from Strauss's former publisher, the Jewish Adolph Fürstner) a proof copy of the full score of *Die Liebe der Danae*, and therefore found it convenient to let Krauss have a copy and enlist him as a proof-reader. 'Do you really think', he wrote to the conductor,

> that *Danae*, which is so difficult and so demanding, could be at all adequately presented scenically or acoustically in that riding-school barn of a Festspielhaus? The old familiar operas can stand up to even a temporary set-up like that, but a new work whose entire future depends on the manner in which it is presented at its first performance?
>
> You yourself will be the best judge of this when you have had a look at the enclosed score, and provisionally the première of *Danae* can come into your programme as you wish. But as for the date, I would really ask that the previous agreement be allowed to stand: at least two years after the conclusion of an armistice. That is to say, when the other theatres will be half-way to the point when they can guarantee a satisfactory production. For *Die Frau ohne Schatten* still suffers today from having to be staged in German theatres too soon after the last war. . .

Clemens Krauss continued to press Strauss to allow him to set a date to the première of *Die Liebe der Danae*, and in due course, a few days after Krauss had successfully given the first performance of the composer's new opera, *Capriccio*, in October 1942, an opera whose libretto had been written by Krauss, the conductor was able to write to the composer to thank him for having 'during your recent personal visit assigned the première of *Die Liebe der Danae* to me for Salzburg. I shall therefore give the work its first performance at the 1944 Salzburg Festival, as a festive occasion to celebrate your eightieth birthday.' Krauss's intention was to begin the 1944 Festival on 5 August with the first of six performances of *Die Liebe der Danae*.

By 1944, however, things were not going well for Germany. (Austria, of course, no longer existed as an independent nation, its name [Österreich] had disappeared from maps of Europe, and Salzburg was now a German town.) The war in Europe was entering its final phase, many German theatres and opera-houses had been destroyed by the bombing attacks of the Allies, and morale throughout Germany was extremely low. Also, the tactless, selfish and egocentric Strauss was again in trouble with the authorities. The following document, signed by a leading Nazi, Martin Bormann, who was known to be close to the Führer, was circulated to the heads of all official organizations:

Re: Dr. Richard Strauss. Confidential.
The composer Dr. Richard Strauss and his wife inhabit in Garmisch a villa with nineteen rooms. The property includes a lodge which contains, in addition to the porter's dwelling, two rooms with kitchen and bath.

Dr. Richard Strauss has managed to sidestep all demands to give shelter to those who have been injured by bombs, and to evacuees. When we pointed out to him that everyone must make sacrifices and that the soldier at the front is risking his life daily, he replied that this was none of his business, and that he had not asked any soldier to fight for him. He even peremptorily refused the politely voiced plea of the district official to put two of the rooms in the lodge at the disposal of two engineers who were working for the armament industry. The whole question is being widely discussed by the citizens of Garmisch, and is being quite properly criticized.

The Führer, to whom the case has been submitted, has decided immediately to appropriate the entire lodge belonging to the property of Dr. Richard Strauss, and to billet within it evacuees and persons who have suffered from the bombing. In addition, the Führer has directed that all party leaders who have until now had personal intercourse with Dr. Richard Strauss must cease to have any contact with him.

The Nazis considered prohibiting any celebration of Strauss's eightieth birthday, but stopped short of this extreme step probably because of the composer's immense popularity. In the event, the occasion was celebrated most royally in Vienna, with a series of performances of Strauss's operas, culminating in a superb *Ariadne auf Naxos* conducted by Karl Böhm, with Maria Reining as Ariadne, Max Lorenz as Bacchus, and the young Irmgard Seefried as the Composer. (A recording of the performance was circulated widely many years after the war.)

It was also decided at the highest level to allow the production of *Die Liebe der Danae* at Salzburg to proceed, although various set-backs, among them the destruction of the scenery by air-raids on Munich, forced Krauss to announce a postponement of the première from 5 August to 15 August. Late in July, both the discovery of the plot of several German generals to assassinate Hitler and the announcement of a decree by Dr. Goebbels suspending all festivals (with the exception of Bayreuth) threatened the production of the opera. However, it was agreed to allow a severely truncated Salzburg festival to proceed, which would consist solely of *Die Liebe der Danae* and a performance by the Vienna Philharmonic Orchestra under Wilhelm Furtwängler of Bruckner's Eighth Symphony.

While eight German generals were being hanged for their part in the plot against Hitler's life, Strauss's *Die Liebe der Danae* was being rehearsed in the enchanting city of Salzburg which had suffered very little damage throughout the war. Strauss arrived in Salzburg on 9 August to attend the final rehearsals. On the following day, with the war situation deteriorating hourly, the German Seventh Army fighting for its life, and the American forces within a few miles of Paris, Goebbels cancelled the performances of *Die Liebe der Danae*, although the opera was allowed to proceed as far as its dress rehearsal.

At a rehearsal with the orchestra on 11 August, Strauss was deeply affected. He moved to the front of the stalls so that he could see as well as hear the glorious Vienna Philharmonic as they played the interlude preceding the opera's final scene, a piece of which he was especially proud, and at the end of the rehearsal he raised his hands in a gesture of farewell to the orchestra, with the words '*Auf Wiederseh'n in einer besseren Welt.*' (Till we meet again in a better world).

On 14 August the only public event of the 1944 Salzburg Festival took place, the performance of Bruckner's Eighth Symphony by the Vienna Philharmonic. Two days later, at 6 p.m. on 16 August, the 'dress rehearsal' (for a performance which everyone knew would not take place) of *Die Liebe der Danae* was given before an invited audience in the Festspielhaus. (The auditorium is now known as the Altes Festspielhaus, a new and bigger adjacent theatre having been constructed in the post-war years.) Clemens Krauss conducted, his wife Viorica Ursuleac sang the role of Danae, and the other principal singers included Hans Hotter (Jupiter), Horst Taubmann (Midas) and Karl Ostertag (Pollux). The opera was produced by Rudolf Hartman in designs by Emil Preetorius. At the end of the rehearsal, Strauss took several curtain-calls. Afterwards, he was found in his dressing-room, looking over the score. 'When I make my way up there', he said, pointing confidently to the sky, 'I hope they'll forgive me if I bring this along too.'

Strauss had now seen all of his fifteen operas safely onto the stage, and may well have felt that his creative life was drawing to a close, especially after Goebbels finally closed all the German theatres on 1 September.

Immediately after the war, there were plans for simultaneous premières of *Die Liebe der Danae* in 1946 in Stockholm, Zürich and London, but Strauss insisted on adding Vienna with Krauss conducting the 1944 cast, and the project was abandoned. The composer then wrote to Krauss, who was then still awaiting official 'de-nazification', giving it as his view that the time was not yet ripe for the opera to be performed in public. 'The right thing for *Danae*', Strauss told his friend and colleague, 'is therefore to wait patiently, and if I do not live to see the première in five or ten years' time, I can at least close my eyes in peace with the thought that I am leaving the work in the best hands.'

It was three years after Strauss's death that *Die Liebe der Danae* at long last was performed in public, appropriately enough at the Salzburg Festival, when the first of four performances was given on 14 August 1952. Krauss conducted, and the producer and designer were also those of the 1944 aborted première. A new cast was headed by Annelies Kupper (Danae), Paul Schoeffler (Jupiter), László Szemere (Pollux) and Josef Gostic (Midas). The general feeling at the time appeared to be that, although the performance was fine, the work's real première had been that dress rehearsal eight years earlier in the presence of the composer.

After its 1952 Salzburg première, *Die Liebe der Danae* was staged in Vienna, Berlin, Milan and Dresden before the end of the year. A Munich company gave the first London performances at Covent Garden in 1953, when Annelies Kupper and Leonie Rysanek each sang two performances as Danae. The American première (in English) was given by the Opera Department of the University of Southern California, Los Angeles, on 10 April 1964. The producer was Dr. Walter Ducloux, and the performances were the first to be given of the opera without cuts. (Even the Salzburg première omitted a few passages.) Though it is occasionally to be encountered in Vienna and Munich, *Die Liebe der Danae* has not managed to achieve popularity elsewhere.

III

THE brief opening scene of Act I takes place in the throne-room of Pollux, King of the Island of Eos. After a few bustling phrases in the orchestra, the curtain rises to reveal a room which shows a few signs of its former splendour, but which is now for the most part extremely shabby. Only a portion of the King's golden throne remains, most of the gilt having been torn away. A number of creditors who have arrived from such far-off places as Cyprus and Persia are angrily calling for King Pollux, and are being prevented from forcing their way further into the palace by servants and guards. The creditors are angry because they have been unable to obtain re-payment from Pollux of the huge sums he owes them, for wine, horses, pearls, golden ornaments and jewellery supplied to him.

Suddenly King Pollux (tenor) emerges from behind a curtain, and stands in front of his throne as though protecting what remains of it. He attempts to appease his creditors by assuring them that he needs only one more day in order to be able to pay them all. The four Kings of the Islands, married to Pollux's four nieces, Semele, Europa, Alcmene and Leda, are even now travelling abroad, armed with a portrait of Pollux's beautiful daughter Danae, for whom they are seeking a wealthy husband. The creditors are unimpressed for they are aware of Danae's lack of interest in suitors. Even when Pollux informs them that the richest man in the world, King Midas of Lydia for whom everything he touches turns to gold, has expressed an interest in Danae, the sceptical creditors prefer to take what they can lay their hands on immediately. They throw themselves upon the throne, stripping it of what is left of the gold.

The opera has got off to a lively start. An orchestral interlude now anticipates what we are to learn from the second scene, by depicting the shower of gold in which form the god Jupiter has appeared to Danae in a dream. The curtain now rises on Danae's bed-chamber. Danae (soprano) awakens and tells her servant Xanthe (soprano) of the dream she has had, in which she was completely covered by a sensuously caressing shower of gold, which fell on her lips and on her breasts, seeming to embrace her as a lover. As Xanthe comments on what Danae tells her, the two soprano voices blend in duet, each being called upon, a few bars apart, to rise to a high D flat in their delight in the dream.

The sounds of a march are heard in the distance, and Xanthe recognizes it as meaning that Danae's four cousins have returned from their travels with a rich suitor for her. Danae, however, makes it clear to Xanthe that she will not listen to any suitor unless he brings with him as much gold as she has been cavorting with in her dreams. Strauss's music in the first scene had done little more than match the doggerel of Gregor's verse, and here in the second scene it does not rise above the level of a pleasant wander through Strauss's own stock of mannerisms.

The scene now changes to a courtyard in the palace. Deep arcades are visible in the background, allowing a view of the sea through several rows of pillars. King Pollux, his court, and the creditors have filled the courtyard in expectation of the arrival of the four kings and queens and their entourage. Pages enter, carrying a covered object, followed by the four kings and queens who announce that Danae's new suitor is none other than Midas who has sent her a golden garland, the branch of a tree that had turned to gold at his touch. At this, the covering falls from the object being borne aloft by the pages, revealing it to be a slender golden branch.

Pollux's creditors attempt to get their hands on the branch, but Danae snatches it from them. Cries of 'A ship' are heard, and now through the colonnades can be seen the glowing lustre of Midas's golden sails as his ship approaches the harbour. All except Danae rush to the harbour to greet Midas. Danae remains behind, joyously anticipating her suitor and his gold. Suddenly Midas (tenor) appears before her, dressed very simply. He announces himself as Chrysopher, a friend of Midas who has come in advance to prepare Danae for the arrival of Midas himself. Danae, obviously attracted to the handsome man standing before her, cannot conceal her disappointment that he is not Midas. He, in turn, lightly flirts with her, ostensibly wooing her for his friend and master. Strauss has written a splendidly impressive ensemble for the opening of this scene, but the more intimate dialogue between Danae and the disguised Midas fails to get off the ground.

The scene now changes again to the harbour where all have gathered to greet Midas. The man who alights from the ship is actually none other than the god Jupiter (baritone) himself, clad entirely in garments of shining gold. (Gregor apparently preferred the Roman 'Jupiter' to the Greek 'Zeus'.) Jupiter greets Danae in a dignified arioso and, as he approaches her, she manages to return his greeting before, overcome, she sinks unconscious into the arms of her attendants. Jupiter stamps his foot, there is a response of rumbling thunder, and the curtain falls on Act I.

Act II takes place in Danae's bridal chamber. After a brief, cheerful *allegro molto* orchestral introduction, the curtain rises on a magnificent room containing what the libretto describes as 'a marriage bed in the style of Pompei'. The four queens, Semele (soprano), Europa (soprano), Alcmene (mezzo-soprano) and Leda (contralto) are discovered decorating the bed with bouquets of roses, and singing in chorus of their joy in the approaching marriage of Danae to the god. When Jupiter strolls in, still clothed entirely in gold, they greet him, to his annoyance, as 'Jupiter-Midas, Midas-Jupiter'.

Why, Jupiter asks the four queens, did they address him in Lydia as Midas, if they knew his real identity? All four coquettishly remind him that he has been the lover of each of them in turn. To Leda he had appeared as a swan, to Semele as a cloud, to Alcmene as Amphitryon, and to Europa as a bull. They, in turn, are curious to know why he was not content to remain in the guise in which he first presented himself to Danae, as a golden shower. Jupiter is forced to explain that Danae is a special case, being chaste, proud and full of hate for all her suitors. The golden shower was merely a promise. To win Danae's heart completely, it was necessary for the god to assume human form.

Jupiter's explanation greatly offends the four queens who feel themselves betrayed by the god's apparent denigration of his past escapades. Nevertheless, they are intrigued. Who, they now want to know, is the modestly attired young man who has accompanied him to Eos, and why has Jupiter felt it necessary to adopt the personality of Midas? Jupiter tells them that his jealous spouse, the goddess Juno, has a foul temper, and the four queens now recall that their former lover, whether as bull, swan, or cloud, did not remain long with them, and that they were each quickly married off to mortals.

That is no longer sufficient revenge for Juno, Jupiter warns them. Do they not remember what happened to the charming nymph, Calisto? An ugly she-bear is all that is left of her. It is Midas who travels with Jupiter, so that, should Juno find out about the god's latest adventure, Midas can be quickly substituted as the husband of Danae. The four queens are delighted by Jupiter's cunning, and begin to flirt with him, but take their leave with ironic farewells when Midas arrives. Their scene with Jupiter is light and amusing, their more tuneful contributions contrasting effectively with the god's comparatively colourless arioso.

Left alone with Jupiter, Midas comments sarcastically on the scene he has just witnessed of the four royal ladies attempting to woo their mighty, if elderly ex-lover. Jupiter responds irritably not only because he had noticed that Europa's skin was beginning to wrinkle, that Leda's figure was filling out, and so on, but also because he suspects that Danae's preference is for the real Midas. He points out to Midas that he was given the gift of turning everything he touched to gold only on condition that he obey Jupiter's every command. He now threatens the immeasurably wealthy King of Lydia with a return to his former life as a donkey-driver should he attempt to win Danae's love for himself. Jupiter reminds Midas again of the spell: whatever he touches, for whatever reason, shall instantly be turned to gold. The god departs in a state of agitation as Danae is heard approaching.

Danae enters the bridal chamber in her golden wedding gown, accompanied by the four queens as well as a small entourage of maid-servants dressed as golden cupids. The four queens, to the tune of a wedding march whose rhythmic pattern seems to have been deliberately based on the well-known bridal march in Wagner's *Lohenrgin*, boast of having already carnally known the bridegroom. They advise Danae to content herself with the handsome companion of the so-called Midas, who is more likely to bring her joy. When that gentleman, the real Midas, turns angrily upon them, they flee from the room.

Midas, unable to be completely frank with Danae, manages to tell her that, although he is not the suitor who stepped from the ship to greet her, yet he is Midas, and he loves her. Danae, not surprisingly, fails to understand him, but when he transforms first a rose and then the bridal bed into gold, she is delighted. She and Midas embark upon a love duet which, despite its having been prefaced by Strauss with an orchestral

221

reminiscence of the love duet from Wagner's *Tristan und Isolde*, turns out to be a ponderously unmagical piece, in which the two voices blend in unison. At its conclusion, Danae and Midas forget themselves and sink into each other's arms. There is a clap of thunder, and all is plunged into darkness. Midas, aghast, cries out to Danae, and as the room is slowly diffused with a pale light one discovers that Danae has been transformed into a golden statue.

Midas curses his golden touch, and curses, too, the god who had endowed him with it. Jupiter appears, reminding Midas that he, Jupiter, has remained true to his promise. He now claims Danae, but Midas insists that Danae must return to life as his, because she loves him. They address the statue, asking Danae herself to choose between them. Midas can offer only his human love and a life of poverty, while Jupiter promises a golden temple and god-like immortality. From far off, the voice of Danae is heard, choosing Midas. This provokes a violent storm, and in the gleam of the lightning Danae is seen to revive and hurry towards Midas. They both disappear in the darkness, and only Jupiter remains in a circle of light. He sings a lament in which he contrasts the wretched life which Danae will now live, with what could have been hers among the gods on Mount Olympus. Finally Jupiter, too, disappears into the surrounding darkness, and Act II comes to an end in a flurry of orchestral menace.

A brief orchestral introduction precedes Act III, a graceful, flowing piece blandly combining some of the themes associated with Danae, Jupiter and Midas. Its pace slows to a contemplative *lento* in its final bars, and the curtain rises on a dusty road somewhere in the Middle East. Midas and Danae are resting under a half-withered group of palm trees in a desert landscape. As Danae awakens, at first she hardly recognizes Midas, and wonders what has happened to her golden bed-chamber and her rich garments. She asks in some excitement what it is that shines so brightly on the road ahead, and weeps when she is told that it is only a stone glowing in the sunlight.

Midas reminds Danae that she had turned to gold at his kiss. When she asks who he really is, he embarks upon a long narrative in which he tells of his poor beginnings in Syria, his only possession a donkey. One day an old man had approached him, offering him the gift of being able to turn everything he touched to gold. In return, Midas was to change places with him whenever required. The old man was the god Jupiter, who had taken Midas's place on the throne of Lydia when the four kings and queens had come bearing Danae's portrait. Midas was forced to pose as Chrysopher, but as soon as he saw Danae he loved her.

Midas's narrative, '*In Syriens Glut*' (In Syria's heat), is his only solo, a well constructed piece which can be effective in performance. (It was greeted with enthusiastic applause at the 1952 Salzburg première when it was sturdily delivered by Josef Gostic.) Danae is sufficiently moved by it to forget her obsession with gold, and to remember that it was Midas whom she had chosen when given the chance to accept riches with Jupiter or love and penury with his friend. Midas now lifts her gently on to the donkey, and they make their way along the road, singing in unison a duet of contentment with their lot. The duet has in it something of the feeling of the music which Tamino and Pamina sing when they are facing the trials in *Die Zauberflöte*, which one cannot help thinking must have been in Strauss's mind when he composed this scene.

The second scene of Act III takes place in a forest landscape in the mountains. Jupiter appears, lost in deep thought, and Mercury (tenor) suddenly comes flying down from the sky. We are now to experience Strauss in his *Rheingold* vein, with Jupiter as Wotan, Mercury as Loge, the four queens as Rhinemaidens and, later, Pollux and his creditors as Fasolt and Fafner. Mercury reports to Jupiter that everyone on Olympus, even Juno, is laughing over Jupiter's failure to seduce Danae, and that on the island of Eos Pollux's palace is destroyed and Danae has disappeared.

A disheartened Jupiter is prepared to return to Olympus, but is prevented by the arrival of the four queens who had been informed by Mercury of Jupiter's whereabouts. For the sake of old times they have come, they claim, to comfort him, and this they do by pretending to believe that the Danae episode was a trick of Jupiter to distract Juno so that he could cavort again with them, the four loves of his youth. Jupiter is flattered by their attentions, but after they have all reminisced happily, he bids farewell to all four, and to the earth whose delights he had enjoyed in so many guises, but most of all as a shower of gold.

Again Jupiter is about to depart when Pollux, accompanied by his creditors and also his nephews, the husbands of the four queens, arrives upon the scene. The creditors want their money, Pollux wants restitution for his destroyed palace, and the nephews are furious with Midas, or whoever he may be, for apparently having seduced their wives. At the helpful suggestion of Mercury, Jupiter causes a shower of gold to fall upon the crowd. As they all rush to pick up the gold, the shower moves off into the background, and they all follow, brawling amongst themselves as they fight for the gold. Mercury now recommends to Jupiter that he should not give up his pursuit of Danae. As the daughter of a king, she may have preferred love to wealth, but now, as the wife of a poor donkey-driver, she will probably feel differently.

Jupiter thanks Mercury with an affectionate handshake and a smile, the curtain falls, and the orchestra now begins the final interlude which so moved the composer when he first heard it played by the Vienna Philharmonic at the 1944 dress rehearsal. It is a fine piece in Strauss's golden autumnal vein, full of mellowness and resignation. The god, it would seem, does not really expect to win Danae. His farewell to the four queens and to all earthly delights was seriously intended. Strauss himself referred to this interlude as 'Jupiter's Renunciation'.

The curtain rises on the opera's final scene, Midas's poorly furnished hut, through whose open window bright sunlight can be seen. Danae sings a lyrical aria expressing the peace and contentment she has found in her life with Midas. (The aria was requested by Clemens Krauss on behalf of his wife Viorica Ursuleac, the Danae of the 1944 rehearsal.) Jupiter now enters, dressed in the simple burnous which he had worn when he first encountered Midas, and it does not take Danae long to recognize him as the old man described to her by Midas. She says as much to Jupiter who, affronted at being described as an old man, exclaims 'Das Ende!' (The end), Wotan's phrase of solemn anticipation from *Die Walküre* and probably inserted jocularly by Strauss rather than by Gregor. There is something of *Die Meistersinger*'s Hans Sachs and Eva, as well, in this Jupiter-Danae scene.

Jupiter attempts to make Danae feel discontented with her present situation, reminding her of the night when he came to her as the dream of a golden shower, but Danae, after a moment's confused indecision, addresses him calmly, secure now in her love for Midas. Moved by her devotion to the no longer rich mortal, Jupiter tells her the story of Maia whom he once loved, and who was transformed into eternal spring. Danae points out that Maia is renewed each year with the return of spring, but that what the god offered her was merely lifeless gold.

Defeated, Jupiter turns to go, but Danae first presses upon him a gift of gold, a clasp which she has been hiding. She asks Jupiter to accept it in remembrance of the happy couple, and especially of Danae who will praise the gods for having brought love to her. Jupiter, deeply affected by the strength of Danae's human love, bids her a tender farewell, and departs. Danae looks after him for a long time, but then, as Midas's theme is heard in the orchestra, heralding his approach, she calls out joyfully to her husband, and rushes out to meet him as the curtain falls.

Die Liebe der Danae is an unsatisfactory work, in that dramatically it could easily end after the second of its two acts, while musically it only really rises to heights of intermittent inspiration in Act III. It is, perhaps, a more moving work to contemplate than actually to experience in the theatre, for it is not difficult to identify the aged Strauss, turning in upon himself in a country totally dedicated to war, with the god, Jupiter, renouncing earthly delights. Hofmannsthal, in 1920, had thought that

Danae was a project exactly suited to Strauss. But he had added that it called for 'light, nimble-witted music, such as only you can write, and *only at this stage in your life.*' (My italics.) In 1920, no doubt Strauss could have written a lighter, more swiftly moving opera on the subject of Danae (although *Die Frau ohne Schatten*, premièred the previous year, was not exactly light opera). Twenty years later, in his mid-seventies, *Die Liebe der Danae* was probably not an appropriate subject for Strauss to have tackled, though there are pages in Act III which seem to usher in his last, late flowering, the period in which he was to produce the nostalgic, beautiful pieces of his final years such as the *Vier letzte Lieder* ('Four Last Songs') and *Metamorphosen*.

Critical opinion will no doubt continue to differ about *Die Liebe der Danae*, some writers on Strauss finding it a delightful work, while others assign it a fairly low place in the composer's total *oeuvre*. I incline to the latter view. Strauss himself realized that he had composed an uneven work which would greatly depend upon skilful and imaginative production for its effect, though he also thought that the third act contained some of the finest music he had written. It is a not unfair judgment.

FIFTEEN

Capriccio

Conversation Piece for Music in One Act
opus 85

Dramatis personae
The Countess   (soprano)
The Count, her Brother   (baritone)
Flamand, a Musician   (tenor)
Olivier, a Poet   (baritone)
La Roche, the Theatre Director   (bass)
Clairon, an Actress   (contralto)
Monsieur Taupe   (tenor)
An Italian Singer   (soprano)
An Italian Singer   (tenor)
The Major-Domo   (bass)
Eight Servants   (four tenors, four basses)

LIBRETTO by Clemens Krauss

TIME: About 1775, at the time when Gluck was engaged on his reform of opera.

PLACE: A château near Paris.

FIRST PERFORMED at the Bayerische Staatsoper, Munich, 28 October 1942, with Viorica Ursuleac (The Countess), Walter Hofermeyer (The Count), Horst Taubmann (Flamand), Hans Hotter (Olivier), Georg Hann (La Roche) and Hildegard Ranczak (Clairon), conducted by Clemens Krauss.

I

A note at the end of the score of *Die Liebe der Danae* tells us that the composer completed it at Garmisch on 28 June 1940. Having decided not to allow *Danae* to be staged until after the war had ended, Strauss began in the following month to compose his next opera, *Capriccio*, which was to be his last. The idea for an opera which in due course turned itself into *Capriccio* had first occurred to Strauss several years earlier when, at the beginning of 1934, he had finished writing *Die schweigsame Frau*, and was urging the librettist of that work, Stefan Zweig, to come up with an idea for the next one. At the end of January 1934, Zweig wrote from his home in Salzburg to say that he would be in London in the following month, and planned to examine at the British Museum 'all the libretti that the Abbate Casti wrote for Pergolesi who, second-class musician that he was, could not do justice to the great charm and the perfect comedy style of these texts.'

Giambattista Casti (1724–1803) was an Italian poet and librettist who, during the years he spent in Vienna, was Lorenzo da Ponte's great rival. His libretti were set by Paisiello and by Salieri (who is presumably the composer Zweig meant to describe as a 'second-class musician') but never by Pergolesi. In August 1934, Zweig mentioned specifically a libretto by Casti entitled *Prima la musica e poi le parole* (First the music, and then the words) which he was then studying. He did not think the piece itself would be suitable for Strauss as it stood, but considered that it would lend itself to adaptation. He had in mind a light comedy, based on Casti's plot.

'What's happening about Casti?' Strauss asked in October, having by this time completed the full score of *Die schweigsame Frau*. The following April, he was still awaiting news of *Prima la musica e poi le parole* as well as two other subjects he and Zweig were considering (one of which was to come to fruition as *Feuersnot*.) But further references in the Strauss-Zweig correspondence to the Casti libretto are fleeting, and before long the political situation in Germany put an end to their collaboration. Zweig, however, discussed his idea for an opera based on Casti with Joseph Gregor, the librettist he was urging upon Strauss, and in June 1935, Gregor sent a scenario on Casti's theme to Strauss who realized that it was largely the work of Zweig, to whom he wrote (in that famous letter intercepted by the Gestapo: see p. 177): 'The comedy you sent me is charming, and I don't doubt for one moment that it is your idea exclusively. I won't accept it under an assumed name any more than *1648* [Friedenstag].' But, of course, he did accept *Friedenstag* under Gregor's name, and for the time being *Prima la musica e poi le parole* was put aside.

Casti's libretto had been written for Antonio Salieri who was one of two composers (the other was Mozart) commissioned to write one-act pieces for a special occasion at the court of the Austrian Emperor Joseph II at the palace of Schönbrunn in 1786. The Governor-General of the Austrian Netherlands and his wife, a sister of the Emperor, were visiting Vienna, as was also Prince Stanislas Poniatowski, nephew of the King of Poland. Joseph II gave a reception for his distinguished guests in the long Orangery at Schönbrunn on 7 February 1786. A banquet was followed by the performance, on a stage specially erected at one end of the Orangery, of one of the two new works, *Der Schauspieldirektor*, whose music was by Mozart. At its conclusion, the other work, an opera buffa by Salieri entitled *Prima la musica e poi le parole*, was performed on another stage erected at the opposite end of the Orangery.

Casti's libretto is about a poet and a composer who have been commissioned to write an opera. Zweig appears to have taken from this nothing but the characters of poet and composer. On a lakeside holiday near Zürich in June 1935, he and Joseph Gregor worked on a scenario. As Gregor wrote later,

> Strauss had expressed the desire for a kind of discourse in dialogue in the style of Plato, on the old argument: which is more important in opera, the music or the words? Zweig came along with his head full of history, with Casti's little comedy, *Prima le parole, dopo la musica* [*sic*], but neither of us knew what to do with it. A few glorious summer days changed our mood to one of wild dionysiac poetry. We became obsessed with an idea: a troupe of strolling players arrives at a castle, where they find themselves in the middle of a delicate situation: a poet and a composer are both in love with the lady of the castle, who does not know which of them to choose.

Zweig and Gregor intended the director of the theatrical troupe to be a caricature of the grandiloquent figure of Max Reinhardt. This was the scenario which Strauss at that time refused to accept from Gregor, hoping to be able to develop it with Zweig alone.

However, in March 1939, Zweig having by then fled to England, Strauss, who was at work on *Die Liebe der Danae* but already beginning to think about its successor, mentioned the subject of *Prima la musica e poi le parole* again to Gregor. They referred to it now as *Erst die Worte, dann die Musik* (First the words, then the music), the precise opposite of Casti's title, but then neither Zweig nor Gregor nor Strauss ever seemed to get the details of this project exactly correct, confusing Salieri or Paisiello with Pergolesi, misspelling the Italian title, when they were not getting it the wrong way round, and giving Casti's name the unwanted prefix 'de'.

Gregor now discarded the 1935 scenario and produced a new draft which he sent to Strauss in May 1939, but this proved not to be the kind of thing Strauss had in mind. The difficulty was that Strauss really did not know what he wanted, except that he had become intrigued, not by the plot, but by the title of Casti's libretto. Without being able to explain precisely what he envisaged, he tried to convey his requirements to an uncomprehending Gregor:

Your de Casti draft was a disappointment . . . nothing like what I had in mind—an ingenious dramatic paraphrase on the subject of
First the words, then the music (Wagner)
or First the music, then the words (Verdi)
or Words alone, no music (Goethe)
or Music alone, no words (Mozart)
to jot down only a few headings.
In between, there are of course many half-tones and ways of doing it, all of them presented in various light-hearted figures, which overlap and are projected into light-hearted comedy figures—that's what I have in mind. . . . Take, for example, the love duet in Act II of *Tristan*: the beginning, '*O sink hernieder, Nacht der Liebe*', doesn't require any words. The music says all there is to express here, and so too does the B major finale. . . .

Gregor clearly found Strauss's vaguely expressed requirements extremely daunting. Although he continued to tinker with his scenario, none of his ideas seemed to please the composer. Strauss was in the habit of passing Gregor's ideas on to the conductor Clemens Krauss for comment, and Krauss's comments were scathing. 'I really don't want to compose any more operas, but with the de Casti I would like to write something exceptional, a dramatic treatment, a theatrical fugue', Strauss explained to Krauss. To Gregor, he sent at last, on 7 October 1939, some detailed suggestions, in fact a scenario which is close to the plot of the opera as we know it. Five days later, Strauss, Krauss and the producer Rudolf Hartman met in Garmisch to discuss Strauss's ideas. As a result of this meeting, Krauss produced a scenario of his own, based on Strauss's ideas, and suggested that the composer write the libretto himself, since he had already proved his competence as a librettist with *Intermezzo*.

At one stage, all three people involved, Strauss, Krauss and Gregor, seem to have been busy producing their own versions of the libretto, but the two musicians soon came to the conclusion that too many cooks were concerned in the preparation of this particular broth, and on 28 October Strauss instructed Gregor to abandon work on the project. Krauss continued to advise the composer who worked on his own libretto for a few more days, but by early November, perhaps because Strauss was not well, Krauss had taken over the actual writing.

Over the following months, the libretto slowly assumed its final shape. By July 1940, enough of it had been written for Strauss to be able to begin composing the opera which, by the end of the year, he and Krauss had decided to call *Capriccio*, having rejected *Wort oder Ton* (Word or Note) and several other possible titles. The libretto was finally completed by Krauss on 18 January, 1941, and by the end of the following month Strauss had completed his vocal score. He spent the next few months working on the orchestration of the opera, finishing the task on 3 August.

Strauss would have preferred the première of *Capriccio* to be given at the 1942 Salzburg Festival, but Krauss wanted to stage it in Munich in June, some weeks before the Salzburg Festival. Eventually, the major Strauss festival which Krauss was planning in Munich had to be postponed until after Salzburg because of shortage of transport due to military movements, and also because the baritone Hans Hotter whom both Strauss and Krauss wanted for the role of Olivier, the poet, was known to suffer from hay fever every June. *Capriccio*, therefore, was given its première by the Bavarian State Opera in Munich, on 28 October 1942. (On 23 February 1942, Stefan Zweig, who had first brought the Casti libretto to Strauss's attention, killed himself in Brazil. He ended a farewell message with the words, 'I salute all my friends! May it be granted them yet to see the dawn after the long night! I, all too impatient, go on before.' Zweig's wife Elisabeth chose to die with him.)

Capriccio was a great success at its première, and was given a number of performances in Munich until, in October of the following year, the opera house was destroyed in an air-raid. The first Viennese performance of the opera was given on 1 March 1944, and in June Karl Böhm conducted it in Zürich. *Capriccio* reached Salzburg in 1950, when Karl Böhm was again the conductor, and the lovely Lisa della Casa undertook the role of the Countess. London first heard the opera when the Bavarian State Opera visited Covent Garden in 1953. Robert Heger conducted the first of two performances on 22 September, and Maud Cunitz was the Countess. A new production in Vienna in 1960, graced by the Countess of Elisabeth Schwarzkopf, was conducted by Böhm, who by this time had established himself as the pre-eminent Strauss conductor of the day. The first fully professional performance of the opera in the United States of America was given at Santa Fé, New Mexico, on 1 August 1958, conducted by John Crosby, with Maria Ferriero as the Countess. (There had been a production at the Juilliard School of Music in New York in April 1954, conducted by Frederick Waldman, with Gloria Davy as the Countess.) Though not amongst Strauss's two or three most often performed operas, *Capriccio* is quite frequently to be encountered, especially in the opera houses of German-speaking countries. It has also proved popular at the

Glyndebourne Festival, in a production first seen in 1963 when the Countess was Elisabeth Söderström.

II

STRAUSS wrote a preface to the published orchestral score of *Capriccio*, dated 'Vienna, 7 April 1942'. It is a somewhat rambling piece, but contains the following advice for producers and conductors of the opera:

In view of the great diligence with which conductors, solo repetiteurs and singers on all operatic stages devote themselves to musical studies, and considering the importance given to the spoken word in this particular work, it would not seem inopportune to suggest that, before study of the score begins, the producer should arrange a few complete reading rehearsals, solely based on the text, with special emphasis on the clearest possible pronunciation of consonants: e.g. of the letters of the beginning and the end of words—readings which should moreover be repeated without any music before the last stage rehearsals (two or three days before the dress rehearsal).

As far as the orchestral score is concerned, I need hardly mention today that there must be a number of thorough rehearsals for strings, woodwind and brass alone. But it is particularly profitable to carry out rehearsals for the whole orchestra so thoroughly that detailed adjustments in the playing of individual groups and of individual instruments in the orchestra are no longer necessary when the singers join the rehearsal. At this point I would suggest that, after a few stage rehearsals, the conductor should entrust his baton to a colleague who is also familiar with the work, and should himself spend several rehearsals listening from different positions in the house to the whole body of sound of which, no matter how great his ability and how good his ear, he will never be able to gain an entirely accurate impression from his rostrum.

III

THE opera that Strauss wrote is in one act, playing for well over two hours. Some years after the composer's death, Rudolf Hartmann, who had been the producer of the Munich première in 1942, divided the work into two parts for its first Hamburg performances in 1957, making it a two-act opera with an interval. This does no damage to the work, and it is in two acts that *Capriccio* is now quite frequently given: at Glyndebourne, of course, where the long interval is considered an integral part of the total experience, but also in German and Austrian opera houses.

It is not easy to give the plot of *Capriccio* in synopsis, for there is not a great deal of plot to give. There is, instead, a situation, which one may or may not think is satisfactorily resolved at the end of the work, and there is also a great deal of conversation about theatre and opera. The essence of *Capriccio* lies in this conversation and the music to which it is set; consequently, more so than with any other Strauss opera, a knowledge of the complete libretto is highly advisable. Strauss took care to set the work in such a manner that the words sung are audible for most of the time. One's enjoyment of the work will nevertheless be enhanced by a reading of the libretto, whether in the original German or in translation, before listening to a performance, unless one is attending a performance accompanied by sur-titles. As for the plot, it could be summarized thus:

In a château near Paris, in the eighteenth century at the time of Gluck's operatic reforms, a young widowed Countess and her guests discuss whether the words or the music are more important in opera. During the course of the evening the Countess is also called upon to decide which of two suitors she prefers, the poet Olivier or the composer Flamand. The opera ends with a solo scene for the Countess in which she addresses the question, without arriving at a definite answer.

Unlike most of Strauss's other operas, *Capriccio* has an orchestral prelude which can stand alone to be performed away from the context of the opera, an elegant, and at moments ardent string sextet which is intended to evoke the century in which the events of the opera take place. As it comes to a close, the curtain rises on the elegantly furnished garden room of a rococo château outside Paris which is the home of the Countess (whose name, we discover later, is Madeleine) and her brother, the Count. At the rise of the curtain, the sextet is still being played, in an adjacent room, and its composer, Flamand (tenor), and his colleagues Olivier (baritone), a poet, stand by the door to listen to it and to watch the reactions of the Countess (soprano) for whom it is being played. Nearer the centre of the room, the Theatre Director, La Roche (bass), sits in an armchair, sleeping.

As an example of the informal, conversational style of the dialogue of *Capriccio*, set by Strauss in a recitative broadening, when required, to arioso, here are the words of the opera's first few minutes:

Flamand: She is enchanting again today.
Olivier: You too?
Flamand: With closed eyes she listens, deeply stirred—
Olivier (*indicating the sleeping Director*):   This one, too?
Flamand: Be quiet, mocker!
Olivier: When she's listening to my verse, I prefer those shining eyes of hers to be open.
Flamand: You too?
Olivier: I don't deny it.

Flamand: And so we are—
Olivier: Loving enemies—
Flamand: Friendly rivals—
Olivier: Words or music?
Flamand: She will decide it.
Olivier: Prima le parole—dopo la musica!
Flamand: Prima la musica—dopo le parole!
Olivier: Music and words—
Flamand: —are brother and sister.
Olivier: A daring comparison!
(*The sextet off-stage finishes. The Theatre Director now awakens.*)
Director: Soft music is best for making one sleep.
Olivier (*pointing to the Director*):   Our fate lies in hands such as those!
Director: What do you mean? Without me, your works are—lifeless
   paper.
Flamand: *With* you their authors are slaves in fetters!
Director: My beautiful scenery?
Flamand: Empty back-drops!
Director: My artist paints for the Royal Opera.
Flamand: Then I can only sympathize with Chevalier Gluck.
Director: Who overwhelms our classical *Iphigénie* with his learned
   music.
Flamand: The prophetic successor of the great Corneille!
Director: One can't remember a single melody, or understand a word
   above the tumult of the orchestra!
Flamand: His music is gripping—
Olivier: —and his timing so dramatic—
Director: Endless rehearsals, going on for months, and then the
   'heroic drama' that follows is a flop.
Flamand: The public is divided into hostile camps—
Olivier: One's feelings are agitated—
Director: Problems—reforms. I hear enough of them!
Flamand: The theatre is packed to overflowing—
Olivier: For weeks on end, the house is sold out—
Director: That's all nothing but fashion! High society sits in the
   boxes, yawns with boredom, and chatters. They notice only the
   splendid scenery, and wait impatiently for their favourite tenor's top
   notes. Everything remains just as it was with the operas of Lully and
   Rameau. There is nothing to surpass *Italian* opera!

Olivier and Flamand continue to argue with him, the orchestra helpfully quoting the overture to Gluck's *Iphigénie en Aulide* at the mention of

that composer and, a little later, two themes by Piccini, Gluck's major rival in Paris. When La Roche talks of the beauty of his leading actresses, Flamand mentions one of them, the famous Clairon, with whom Olivier had once been romantically involved, and who is expected to arrive soon at the château to rehearse Olivier's play in which the Count also proposes to appear. Still talking, the three men go off into the adjacent theatre as the Count (baritone) and the Countess (soprano) enter from the music room on the opposite side.

Brother and sister engage in arch teasing of each other. The Countess is aware of her brother's amorous interest in the actress, Clairon, and he in turn tries to discover whether his sister's preference is for, as he thinks, the composer Flamand, or for the poet Olivier. The Countess avoids a direct answer, speaking instead of her love for the music of Couperin, and singing three bars of a little-known Italian air by Rameau ('*Fra le pupille di vaghe belle*'), a composer whom she considers a genius but whose uncouth behaviour displeases her. (How old is this 'young' Countess? Rameau had died at the age of 81, in 1764, a good ten years before this conversation. He had been considered by his contemporaries to be ungenial and argumentative.)

La Roche, Flamand and Olivier re-enter from the theatre, and the entertainment which is being arranged in celebration of the Countess's birthday is discussed. The programme is to begin with a symphony by Flamand, which will be followed by a drama by Olivier in which the Count is to play the lover. This calls forth a pleasantry from the Countess, but the closing item, a grandiose *azione teatrale* which La Roche announces will be performed by artists from his studio, attracts derisive comment from both Flamand and Olivier. While La Roche is promising the Countess sublime scenery, delightful ballet and virtuoso singers 'from the Italian Opera', a clarinet flourish suddenly emerging from the string-dominated sound of the orchestra announces the arrival of Clairon's coach, and the Count rushes out to greet the famous actress.

Mlle Clairon (Krauss took her name from that of a well-known French actress of the period) now enters with the Count, and is presented to the Countess. After an exchange of compliments, Clairon (contralto) asks if Olivier has yet finished his play which at present is lacking its love scene. Olivier, with a significant glance at the Countess, tells the actress that he was, that morning, inspired to write a beautiful sonnet as a climax to the love scene. The Count produces the manuscript, from which he and Clairon proceed to read the scene, ending with the Count's ardent declamation of Olivier's sonnet (which is actually a German translation by Hans Swarowsky of a sonnet by the sixteenth-century French poet, Ronsard.)

La Roche bears Clairon and the Count off to rehearse, forbidding the author to follow them. (La Roche's behaviour, though anachronistic, is probably *echt* Reinhardt.) Olivier is content to be left behind, for this gives him an opportunity to address the sonnet himself to the Countess as a personal utterance. While he does so, Flamand goes to the harpsichord and begins to improvise a melody. The Countess remarks that Olivier's sonnet is indeed beautiful but that she can hardly be expected to believe it as a declaration of love when Olivier has already allowed it to be heard by other ears.

Flamand agrees that the poem is certainly beautiful, adding that he can already hear it as music. He hurries off to the music room with Olivier's manuscript. Fearful that he is about to be set to music, Olivier attempts to hurry after him, but is prevented by the Countess who asks him to forget his poem for a moment. Has he nothing to say to her in prose? Indeed he has, and he proceeds to say it, but the rather coquettish Madeleine will not commit herself. She cherishes the words the poet has written, but they do not express everything. Through the open door she observes the composer at work, competing with his rival. This little scene in which Olivier, challenged to declare his love in prose, actually does so in music, allows Strauss to expand somewhat in an ardent (at least on Olivier's part) duet.

Flamand runs in with a sheet of music in his hand. It is his setting of Olivier's sonnet which the composer now sings to his own harpsichord accompaniment, with the orchestral strings also joining in discreetly (Ex. 19). A tender, though somewhat restrained love song, it was in fact

Ex.19

Kein An-   dres dass mir so im   Her – zen loht –

composed by Strauss in advance of the rest of the opera, when Hans Swarowsky first presented him with his Ronsard translation. Strauss immediately set it to music, with a piano accompaniment, and dedicated the song to Swarowsky. (It does, in fact, make a graceful *Lied* for the tenor voice, and has also been appropriated by sopranos.)

At the conclusion of Flamand's performance of the sonnet, a trio develops. The Countess ponders on the mysterious relationship of words and music. Did Olivier's words already imply the melody, she wonders, or was Flamand's melody waiting to enfold the words so lovingly? Olivier meanwhile grumbles at the destruction of his verbal symmetry by the composer's phrasing, while Flamand remains seated at the harpsichord, correcting his manuscript and occasionally singing parts of the sonnet aloud. When poet and composer quarrel over the intellectual ownership of the work, the Countess temporarily solves that particular problem by taking the manuscript from Flamand's hands and claiming it as a birthday gift from them both. La Roche now enters, having need of the poet to authorize a creative cut in his play. He drags Olivier off to the theatre, thus giving Flamand a chance to make his declaration of love to the Countess.

Flamand makes his declaration more passionately than Olivier. He tells Madeleine that his love for her was awakened when he watched her reading in the château's library. After she had gone, he took up her book and read 'In love, silence is better than speech. . . .' A footnote in the score helpfully informs us that the Countess had been reading Pascal. Flamand now asks her to give him an answer, and she agrees to do so, but not now. She will meet him the next morning at eleven, she promises, in the library where he had fallen in love with her. Flamand impetuously presses a kiss on her arm and rushes out. For a long time, the Countess remains alone, visibly moved, while Strauss's orchestra reflects the turmoil in her mind. Sounds of the rehearsal next door arouse her from her thoughts, and she rings a bell to summon her Major-Domo (bass). 'We shall take chocolate here in the Salon', she tells him. Her words are spoken.

It is at this point that an interval is sometimes inserted into *Capriccio*. When this happens, the Countess usually changes her instructions to 'We shall take chocolate in the garden' (*Wir werden die Schokolade im Garten einnehmen*), and walks through the french windows into the garden as the curtain descends to a few bars of music associated with Flamand and his sonnet. When it rises on Act II, to the same few bars, we are to assume that the Countess and her guests have partaken of their chocolate during the interval. The Countess is discovered alone in the salon, but is joined immediately by the Count.

If the opera is given without interval as Strauss intended, the Count enters quickly from the theatre as soon as the Countess has given her order to the Major-Domo. The Count sings the praises of Clairon, who it seems has been praising his dramatic prowess, but his sister is more concerned to tell him of her problem with two suitors pressing her for an answer. She explains how she was more affected by the sonnet after it had been set to music. 'What will come of it?' asks the Count. 'Perhaps an opera', replies his sister. The Count makes it clear that, between words and music, his preference is for words. 'Good luck with Clairon', is the Countess's comment.

Their rehearsal now over, La Roche returns from the theatre with Clairon and Olivier. Clairon has to return to Paris that evening, to finish learning her part in Voltaire's *Tancred* in which she is performing the following day. But she will stay long enough to take chocolate with the others. To accompany the refreshments, La Roche has arranged for the company to be entertained first by a young dancer, a girl whom he had discovered in the establishment of a certain Viscount, and then by two Italian singers. To the on-stage accompaniment of violin, cello and harpsichord, the dancer performs three items, Strauss providing for all three dances graceful imitations of Couperin. During the passepied, La Roche whispers incessantly about the dancer to the Count. Throughout the gigue Olivier makes a half-hearted attempt to resume his liaison with Clairon who energetically rejects him. La Roche, who has overheard, remarks that Olivier is not likely to play a large part in the actress's memoirs.

Only the gavotte is enjoyed in silence. At its conclusion, the Count compliments the dancer and asks Flamand to admit that, in the art of dance, music plays only a subsidiary role. Flamand will not accept this. 'Without music', he asserts, 'it would never occur to anyone to lift a leg.' A fugal discussion on the theme 'Words or Music' is immediately embarked upon by the entire company, each person vigorously putting forward his or her own view. The discussion narrows down to an argument about the merits and demerits of opera. When La Roche gloomily prophesies the death of *bel canto*, the Countess suggests that, before it dies, he should let them hear the singers he had promised.

Two Italian singers, a soprano and a tenor, now enter, and La Roche announces that they are to sing a duet whose words are by Metastasio. Strauss has composed on the Italian poet's words of farewell a rather cheerful, florid *andante* followed by a distinctly ebullient cabaletta, which the two Italians render with great enthusiasm. At the conclusion of the duet, the Count continues his flirtation with Clairon and arranges to accompany her back to Paris later that evening. Meanwhile, La Roche is prevailed upon to describe the entertainment he is arranging for the Countess's birthday. When he begins to recount the plot of his stupendous *azione teatrale* in two parts, the first of which is called 'The Birth of Pallas Athene', he is constantly interrupted by the others with ribald comments.

La Roche attempts to continue his description of the birth of the goddess out of the head of Zeus, but the company is in no mood for Greek myths. After a few sarcastic interjections, they launch gleefully into an octet, the first part of which is entitled *Lachensemble* (Laughing ensemble) in Strauss's score. They recover themselves sufficiently for the Countess to ask the subject of the second part of La Roche's spectacle. This turns out to be 'The Fall of Carthage', the director's description of which infuriates Olivier and Flamand and leads to the second part of the octet, a *Streitensemble* (Dispute Ensemble). This two-part ensemble is an octet because, although the main contributors to the argument are the

Count and Countess and their four guests, the two Italian singers also join in as they help themselves to the food and drink provided (which apparently includes something more potent than chocolate), become somewhat tipsy, and revert to a lachrymose rendition of their duet of farewell.

Finally, La Roche manages to quieten the assembled company whom he then treats to a lengthy monologue delivered in Strauss's best arioso style, a kind of *apologia pro vita sua* in which the impresario boasts of his achievements, pours scorn on the modernists and reformers, and describes himself as a great man of the theatre now at the peak of his career. 'My goals are sound, and my merits will endure for ever—I strive for the beauty and the noble dignity of the theatre', he insists. When he at last brings his harangue to an end, he quotes the inscription he confidently expects will be engraved on his tombstone: 'Here lies La Roche, the unforgettable, the immortal theatre director. The friend of the cheerful muse, the patron of serious art, a father to the stage, a guardian angel to artists. The gods loved him and mankind admired him.' 'Amen', he adds solemnly, as his egocentric tirade is greeted with enthusiastic, if slightly satirical applause by all. The Italian soprano, now thoroughly inebriated, sobs loudly, and is led off into the theatre by the tenor who murmurs to her in Italian, 'What's the matter? He's not dead yet!'

The Countess now takes the stage. In a more lyrical arioso than Strauss had allotted to La Roche, she suggests that the two friendly rivals, Flamand and Olivier, should collaborate in writing an opera for La Roche to direct. Although her unmusical brother, the Count, is horrified at the thought of being involved in opera, it is he who, after giving in gracefully to his sister's whim, actually chooses the subject of the opera. *Ariadne auf Naxos* ('Already composed too often', says Flamand) and *Daphne* ('Difficult to stage', says Olivier) having been rejected, the Count proposes what he describes as a particularly captivating theme. 'Write an opera', he suggests, 'about all of us, about the events of today. Let us be the characters of your opera.'

In a lively ensemble, the idea is taken up and explored, and amid a flurry of nervous jokes, with La Roche fearful of ending up as a comic bass, Olivier and Flamand agree to write the opera and La Roche to stage it. The company now disperses, the Count accompanying Mlle Clairon to Paris, the Countess making an exit to the adjacent music-room, and La Roche, Olivier and Flamand still discussing the proposed opera as they take their leave, the two younger men each convinced of having won the Countess's love.

A group of eight servants now enters to tidy the salon. In a light-hearted ensemble in which they each have solo opportunities, they discuss the quarrel they have overheard, the guests, the world of the theatre, and the romantic attachments of both their employers. They are planning an entertainment of their own in honour of the Countess's birthday when the Major-Domo enters to tell them they may have the evening off after they have prepared supper for the Countess. The servants express their delight as they leave, continuing to discuss the Count and the Countess.

It has now become quite dark. The Major-Domo is about to leave when a voice is heard, crying 'Herr Direktor!', and a small, insignificant-looking man with a large book under his arm enters from the theatre. He is Monsieur Taupe (or 'Mr. Mole'), the prompter (tenor), who had fallen asleep and been left behind. His quaint scene with the Major-Domo is accompanied by shadowy, shifting harmonies as he tells of his life in the prompter's box, from which he very rarely emerges into the real world. But he is an important personage. If he falls asleep in his box, the actors cease to speak their lines, and the public awakens! The Major-Domo treats Monsieur Taupe with respect, promises him a coach to take him back to Paris, and leads him off to the pantry for a meal.

By now it is completely dark. As Monsieur Taupe's harmonies die away the orchestra's first horn introduces a romantic theme (Ex. 20) which has

Ex.20

already been heard very briefly during the fugal discussion on words and music. Strauss borrowed it from his satirical song cycle, *Krämerspiegel* ('Tradesman's Mirror'), composed during World War I, putting it to different use here to introduce the Countess's solo scene which brings *Capriccio* to an end. The Countess now enters, elegantly dressed for supper, and goes out onto the terrace where she stands deep in thought, bathed in the glow of the moonlight. The Major-Domo and two servants enter to light all the candles in the salon, and when the Countess comes in from the terrace, asking for her brother, the Major-Domo replies that he has accompanied Mlle Clairon to Paris and has begged to be excused for the evening.

The Countess asks that supper be prepared for her alone. Before he leaves, the Major-Domo has another message for her. Monsieur Olivier will call on the Countess tomorrow to learn how the opera should end. He will be in the library at eleven. The Major-Domo bows and leaves, and the Countess is amused at the thought that Olivier will encounter not her but Flamand in the library at that hour. She muses on the opera, and how it should end. Is she more strongly moved by words or by music? Does she love Olivier or Flamand? She begins to sing Flamand's setting of Olivier's sonnet, accompanying herself on the harp, and then questions her reflection in the mirror. Can her mirrored image help her to decide whom she loves, and thus how the opera should end? Can there be, she wonders, an ending that is not trivial?

The Major-Domo returns to announce that supper is served. The Countess waves cheerfully to her reflection in the mirror, curtseys to it, and then, in high spirits and humming the melody of the sonnet, she slowly exits. The puzzled Major-Domo watches her, then looks back into the mirror as the horn sounds twice and the curtain falls.

'We must end with a question mark', Strauss had said. But is there not, perhaps, a clue in the fact that Madeleine leaves humming the wordless melody of the sonnet? Is it not likely that, as her brother has chosen Clairon and words, she will choose Flamand and music? One cannot be certain. What is certain is that Strauss has ended his final opera with one of the most magical and affecting of his bitter-sweet outpourings for the soprano voice.

The enchanting *Capriccio* makes a fitting end to Strauss's operatic *oeuvre*. Though it is never likely to achieve the popularity of *Der Rosenkavalier* or *Salome*, it is considerably more attractive an opera than any he had written since *Arabella*, and it is the major work of his last years, years in which he appears to recover the confidence of his youth, allied now to an autumnal mood of farewell. In his late seventies, the composer's early genius, which seemed to have deserted him for long stretches in his middle years, returned in a glorious final flowering. Strauss himself was completely satisfied with *Capriccio*, and was content that his theatrical career should end with it. Though Joseph Gregor attempted to interest him in future operatic projects, Strauss never seriously considered writing another opera.

IV

LIFE in Garmisch was becoming increasingly difficult for the Strauss family, largely because Strauss and, more particularly, Pauline did not trouble to disguise their contempt for Nazi officialdom. The local Nazis retaliated by ensuring that Strauss's Jewish daughter-in-law was publicly ostracized, and that his grandsons Richard and Christian were given a rough time at school. Late in 1941, therefore, Strauss and his family moved to Vienna where the composer made a deal with the Nazi controller, Baldur von Schirach, whose hope it was to restore Vienna to its former position as a major European cultural centre. Strauss would play a public role in the musical life of the city, and he and his wife would refrain from making anti-Nazi statements, in return for which they and their family would be allowed to live in Vienna unmolested. In gratitude for this, Strauss allowed the String Sextet which serves as the prelude to *Capriccio* to be given its first performance at a reception in Schirach's house in Vienna, six months before the opera's première in Munich. (These amicable arrangements apparently did not prevent Pauline from telling Schirach that, when the war was over, he would be welcome at their villa in Garmisch, but not 'the rest of that gang'.)

Strauss had hoped to compose a symphonic poem about the Danube for the Vienna Philharmonic Orchestra's centenary in February 1942, but found himself unable to complete the work. (In 1949, in response to the orchestra's congratulations on his eighty-fifth birthday, he sent a page of the manuscript, inscribed 'A few drops from the dried-up source of the Danube'.) He did, however, complete a Horn Concerto (his second) in 1942. In October 1943, the Munich National Theatre, where his father had played in the orchestra for so many years, was destroyed in an air-raid, and Strauss wrote that it was the greatest catastrophe of his life. Fifteen months later the opera house in Dresden, where several of his operas had received their first performances, also lay in ruins, and some weeks after that the Vienna State Opera, too, was destroyed. 'I am in despair', Strauss wrote to Gregor. But from his despair there arose *Metamorphosen*, which he composed for string orchestra, a threnody for the lost German culture of his youth.

When the war ended, the Strausses returned to Garmisch. 'I am Richard Strauss, the composer of *Der Rosenkavalier*', Strauss said to the American officer who approached the door of the villa, looking for somewhere to billet a few of his men. Some months later, he and Pauline were given permission to go to Switzerland, where he completed an Oboe Concerto which one of the American soldiers, John de Lancy, principal oboist of the Philadelphia Orchestra, had asked him to write. In 1947, taking to the air for the first time at the age of eighty-three, he visited London where, at the instigation of Sir Thomas Beecham, a Strauss Festival was being held. Strauss conducted two of the concerts himself, and it was at a rehearsal that he uttered a piece of acute self-analysis: correcting the orchestra's playing of a passage, he added, 'I may not be a first-rate composer, but I *am* a first-class second-rate composer.'

In Switzerland, Pauline complained so vigorously about the hotels in which they stayed that they were forced to move several times as hotel after hotel requested them to leave. In 1948 they settled at the Palace Hotel in Montreux, where Strauss wrote his final songs for the voice and orchestra, those known and performed together as *Vier letzte Lieder*. There are actually five of these songs, a fifth having come to light in recent years. The composer had given its manuscript to the soprano Maria Jeritza.

Cleared by the Denazification Board in 1948, Strauss returned with Pauline the following year to Garmisch where, on 11 June, he celebrated his eighty-fifth birthday. During August 1949, he suffered several minor heart attacks. 'Dying is just as I composed it in *Tod und Verklärung*', he told his daughter-in-law Alice. On 8 September 1949, he died in his sleep. At his cremation in Munich three days later the *Rosenkavalier* Act III Trio was sung. On 13 May of the following year, Pauline Strauss died, a few days before the soprano Kirsten Flagstad and the conductor Wilhelm Furtwängler gave, in London, the first performance of the 'Four Last Songs'.

DETAILS OF MUSIC EXAMPLES

Short bibliography

N. Del Mar: *Richard Strauss: a Critical Commentary on his Life and Works* (London, 1962–72)

A. Jefferson: *The Operas of Richard Strauss in Britain 1910–1963* (London, 1963)

A. Jefferson: *Richard Strauss* (London, 1975)

M. Kennedy: *Richard Strauss* (London, 1976)

E. Krause: *Richard Strauss: Gestalt und Werk* (Leipzig, 1955; Eng. trans. 1964)

L. Lehmann: *Singing with Richard Strauss* (London, 1964)

W. Mann: *Richard Strauss: a Critical Study of the Operas* (London, 1964)

G.R. Marek: *Richard Strauss: the Life of a Non-Hero* (New York, 1967)

R. Myers, ed: *Richard Strauss and Romain Rolland: Correspondence* (London, 1968)

W. Schuh, ed: *Richard Strauss und Hugo von Hofmannsthal; Briefwechsel* (Zurich, 1952; Eng. trans. 1961)

W. Schuh, ed: *Richard Strauss, Stefan Zweig: Briefwechsel* (Frankfurt am Main, 1957; Eng. trans., 1977)

R. Specht: *Richard Strauss und sein Werk* (Leipzig, 1921)

R. Strauss: *Recollections und Reflections* (London, 1953)

ILLUSTRATION CREDITS

Index